LETTERS

TO HIS CHILDREN FROM AN UNCOMMON ATTORNEY

a Memoir

DAVID ROBERTS Q.C.

Produced by:

FriesenPress
Suite 300 – 990 Fort Street
Victoria, BC, Canada V8V 3K2

www.friesenpress.com

Distributed to the trade by The Ingram Book Company

To my dear children to whom these letters were written:
Peter, Kiffa, Hewitt and Kate.

TABLE OF CONTENTS

LETTER TO THE READER

Letters have fallen into disuse—overtaken first by the telegraph, then the telephone, followed by the teletype and the fax (itself now dwindling in use), as well as such magic as email, and an array of digital contrivances that now pass for appropriate means of communication.

Few mourn the passing of the letter, except for the post office, because its main source of revenue has wilted in the face of competition from more ethereal forms of communication, which are less expensive, faster, and more certain of delivery. (Some twenty years ago, the Canadian National Railway Company stumbled upon a forgotten rail car full of mail that had been posted at Christmas 1917.)

There was a time when the literati penned letters with a diligence unimaginable today. Thomas Hardy was an indefatigable letter writer. No less than five volumes of his correspondence have been published in recent years. He wrote letters so frequently that the post office was persuaded to install a letterbox in the brick wall of his garden.

Historians can derive an amazing array of information from the correspondence of those whose biographies they write. One wonders how people like Abraham Lincoln, Neville Chamberlain, Queen Victoria, George Orwell, and other souls engaged in serious, time-consuming work, ever had time to write so many letters. Not just business letters that a secretary would produce either, but missives penned personally to friends and relations, discussing the events of the day and revealing thoughts and opinions they preferred to keep confidential. It is a matter of no little sorrow that the art of letter writing has thinned away into insignificance and oblivion.

Now, Dear Reader, know that not all the stories that follow originated as actual letters. Some did. In particular, the letter that ends the book, written to my youngest grandchild, explaining how it was that, despite her parents' fond belief to the contrary, she was not the first person in the family to be named Lily. And, Dear Reader, some of the letters are written to you.

The collection of stories that follows came about because I once told my daughter, Kate, about the incident of the Polish airmen. Kate said,

"Dad, you must write down all these stories so your grandchildren will be able to know about them. And you must get on with it ... before you die."

Stung by such an exhortation, I embarked on the project. "A Child's History of the Battle of Britain" was followed by "Paris". Many of the stories that followed were written for a writing group I belong to. Those I deemed worthy, I would email to my children. I occasionally wrote letters to my grandchildren, incorporating a story in each letter. All the tales in this book are true, except for the occasional flight of literary descriptiveness, which I suppose to be the creative part of creative non-fiction.

It had crossed my mind, however briefly, to write an autobiography. I dismissed this thought out of hand. Autobiographies, to be of any interest, should be written by those who have led public lives that in themselves are worth reading about, or by a truly talented scribe, so that an otherwise ordinary, humdrum existence springs to life as the ink drips from the nib onto the page. That takes real talent.

So, an autobiography was out. Mine would not qualify on any count. Memoirs are a different matter. Memoirists can cheerfully and legitimately exclude events, disasters, and mistakes the author prefers to keep confidential. They are free to recount only incidents that will interest the reader, because those incidents are interesting in themselves—or so the memoirist will piously hope.

This memoir was inspired by Kate's relentless prompting. The stories do not need to be read in order. It is, I hope, the kind of book you keep by your bedside—the stories to be picked at random and read one at a time. I suspect it may well lull some insomniac readers to an immediate and dreamless sleep.

I wish to tell you, Dear Reader, that the front cover is a caricature of me created by the late Bob Banks while I was the editor of the Advocate (the magazine of the legal profession in BC). Banks was a commercial artist of great talent who painted a hundred and twenty-six caricatures, over twenty-one years, for the front covers of the Advocate. He did this one of me for fun—both his and mine.

I thank my dear wife, Gillian, for her frequent and judicious use of her editorial blue pencil, which eliminated a host of spelling and syntactical errors and generated much needful rewriting.

Most of the characters in these stories walk onto the page bearing their own names, but some names have been changed to avoid embarrassing the people I talk about. In particular, I have been careful not to transgress the obligation of confidentiality I owe to clients whose stories I tell. I needed to preserve the sensitivities of those who reposed confidence and trust in me while I was acting for them.

THE
YEARS OF MINORITY

A CHILD'S HISTORY OF THE
BATTLE OF BRITAIN

I t was a damned close run thing," said the Duke of Wellington, of the Battle of Waterloo. He would have surely said the same about the Battle of Britain. Over the centuries, some weapons, devised by mankind to subdue his enemies, have become legendary: the English yeoman's longbow, HMS Victory—Nelson's flagship, now in dry dock in Portsmouth—and the French 75, the field gun, about which Captain Alfred Dreyfus was falsely accused of selling secrets to the Germans.

In the Second World War, at least to the British, the Spitfire became the legendary weapon that won the Battle of Britain. It had been designed in the 1930s by a team of aeronautical engineers, led by Reginald Mitchell, at the Supermarine aircraft factory on the Solent, just south of Southampton. Supermarine was in the business of manufacturing flying boats. In the 1920s though, the company became involved in building high-speed seaplanes to compete for the Schneider Trophy, an annual seaplane race. It won the race three times with the S.6B aircraft, powered by a Rolls Royce Kestrel aero engine. This seaplane was the immediate predecessor of the Spitfire. By 1931, the industrial giant Vickers had taken over Supermarine and embarked on the design of fighter aircraft. Mitchell designed it to be powered by the improved Rolls Royce Merlin engine, which was also used in the Hurricanes. Both these aircraft owed much of their success to this beautifully designed engine and to their armament: the light, small, reliable Browning machine guns. Later designs of Spitfires carried cannon as well. The first Spitfire was flown in 1936. By the time of the Battle of Britain, the Spitfire Mark 2 was in production. With a three-blade propeller, it could operate 7000 feet higher than the Mark 1 and had an improved rate of climb. It also had a rear-view mirror, the absence of which had been a serious oversight in the Mark 1 and the early Hurricanes. Prior to that, pilots had been in the habit of buying rear-view mirrors from local garages and fitting them in their aircraft. Modifications continued throughout the war, and by the time it ended, the Spitfire Mark 21 was in production. But it was the Marks 1 and 2 that fought in the battle of Britain. It was a surprisingly small aircraft, with a wing-span of only thirty-six feet ten inches, and a small cramped cockpit. It was designed to carry only its pilot, its fuel, and its guns and ammunition. In its time, it was the fastest, and given its speed, the most manoeuvrable aircraft in service. By March of 1940, Fighter Command was beginning to convert Merlin equipped Spitfires and Hurricanes to be able to use 100-octane fuel. The German Messerschmitt pilots were puzzled by the startling improvement in the performance of their opponents. Then, late in October, the fuel from a crashed R.A.F. fighter was analyzed and the Germans discovered that the British fighters were no longer using 87-octane fuel.

There were more Hurricanes engaged in the battle than Spitfires, and consequently, brought down fifty per cent more enemy aircraft than did the Spitfires. However, in proportion, the Spitfires destroyed about 6 per cent more than did the Hurricanes.

Legend has it that at some point in the summer of 1940, when it was obvious to the Luftwaffe that it was failing to destroy the R.A.F., Reichsmarschall Hermann Goering visited a Jagdgeschwader of Messerschmitts in Northern France. It was commanded by Adolf Galland, who had fought with the Legion Kondor during the Spanish civil war. It was that legion that had been responsible for the bombing of the Basque Village of Guernica, a war crime immortalized by Picasso in his famous painting, now in the Museo Reina Sofia in Madrid. Goering asked Galland what he needed in order to beat the British. Galland's instant response was, "a squadron of Spitfires, Reischmarschall, if you please". Goering was not amused, and left for Berlin in a bad mood.

In 1940, my parents lived in a house on the Purley Downs on the southeast edge of London, and in the direct flight path of German bombers bent on destroying the city. It was quite high up, and looked out over a long valley full of houses that formed the southern boundary of the downs—a large, rolling, partly wooded stretch of country that provided a huge playground for my friends and me. We were familiar with every inch of it, exploring its extent on our bicycles and building secret encampments and tree houses. The downs were a small boy's paradise. After every air raid, we would rush out, and against fiercely expressed injunctions from the authorities and strict warnings from our parents not to do so, we would collect souvenirs from the raids, scattered about the neighbourhood. These consisted mostly of shrapnel from anti-aircraft shells, but occasionally we retrieved more deadly devices. My prize was a set of tail fins from a German incendiary bomb.

We children learned to recognize every aircraft, both British and German, that flew in the skies above our homes. There were the yellow Harvard trainers, big lumbering, yellow two-seaters, with a cockpit covering that looked like an ill-constructed greenhouse, and a raucous engine that constantly sounded in need of tuning. Messerschmitts had a distinctive profile that was easy to identify. Heinkels, Dorniers, and even (early on) Stukas, were in constant action above us. The Stukas did not last long. Though effective and frightening as dive-bombers, they were slow, cumbersome, and badly armed. Few survived an encounter with any British fighter. The Defiant was a British fighter, designed with a gun turret immediately behind the pilot to protect it from attack from the rear. This made it slow and awkward and no match for the Messerschmitts.

One day early in the war, my parents took me to stay at a hotel in the Cotswolds. It was close to an R.A.F. airfield. Also staying at the hotel was a senior R.A.F. officer who struck up a conversation with my parents, and as a result of which, took me on a tour of the airfield. There were Hurricanes, Spitfires, and the two-engined Blenheim fighter-bombers parked beside the grass runways. These aircraft were not smartly lined up, as was the German routine, but scattered about so that they were less susceptible to attack from low-flying enemy aircraft. There was also one Defiant, and my friendly officer lifted me up to sit in the pilot's cockpit, and explained the use of all the controls. He then took me back to the officers' mess and bought me two chocolate bars. This was an even more exciting event than the encounter with the Defiant. Rationing was very strict in Britain at that time, and chocolate was an exceedingly scarce commodity. When I got back to the hotel, I secretly wolfed down both bars for fear that my parents would confiscate them and feed them to me bit by bit over several weeks.

My friends and I could recognize the distinctive sound of the Rolls Royce Merlin engine with instant and unfailing certainty. It was as distinctive as the deadly drone of a squadron of Heinkels, a sound that I remember to this day. My wife and I once went to see *The Battle of Britain*, some thirty years after the end of the war. The movie's producers had gone to no little trouble to make the movie authentic, with real Player's Navy Cut cigarette packages from the time, and genuine old aircraft collected for the occasion. At one point in the movie, the soundtrack of a documentary film was used to produce the sound of a squadron of Heinkels. It was an eerie moment for both of us as we heard a sound that had, until then, been buried in the dusty recesses of our childhood memories: the deadly drone of enemy bombers in the darkness of night, trying to kill us frightened children.

Sometime in the early 1970s, Gill and I took our four children to the Abbotsford Air Show, in the Fraser Valley east of Vancouver. It was a mistake, as Kate, then aged four, was terrified by the noise and spent much of the show in tears. We decided to leave early, but not before we saw an old Spitfire flying around the airfield. I watched it with keen interest. Then I noticed that there was something wrong. It was the sound. This aircraft was not making the noise I remembered hearing when I was nine years old. It landed, and curious about this old fighter, I went over to where its pilot was climbing out of the cockpit. He was immediately surrounded by a small knot of officious old veterans engaging him in conversation, like a whole troop of ancient mariners. He was obviously enjoying this, and held forth at length about his Spitfire to this group of self-important know-it-alls. I slowly edged my way through this crowd, and with difficulty, attracted the pilot's attention. He was an American. I introduced myself and he greeted me cheerfully. His handshake nearly dislocated my wrist. He beamed with good humour. I broached the subject of the Spitfire's engine and noticed that his smile waned a little. I explained that, as a little boy, I had listened to the sound of the Rolls Royce Merlin engine day after day during the Battle of Britain. I wanted to know why his aircraft sounded different. His smile vanished. His shoulders seemed to sag and his hands, which hitherto had been gesticulating wildly dropped to his side. "Well you see," he said, "it's a Ford. The old engine wore out and I had to replace it."

German aircraft outnumbered the British by a significant margin. In all, apart from reconnaissance aircraft, the Luftwaffe had, at the beginning of July 1940, 1260 bombers, 316 dive-bombers, and 1089 single and twin-engined fighters. The R.A.F. had 800 fighters, but 100 of these were the slow, twin-engined Blenheim fighter-bombers, which were unable to hold up against single-engined fighters, and were accordingly increasingly used for night fighting. The R.A.F. did have some advantages, however. Hitler was building up a force to invade England, but invasion was impossible without subduing the Royal Navy. To do this, he needed to destroy the R.A.F. and gain air superiority over southern England and the Channel. The Luftwaffe began its offensive by bombing the fighter airfields. The bombers were vulnerable to the British fighters and so had to be escorted by their own fighters. Flying from airfields in Northern France, the Germans had farther to go than the British, and consequently ran out of fuel earlier. The fighters would have to turn and head for home after ten or fifteen minutes of combat.

By the outbreak of war, twenty radar stations stretched in a chain from the Thames estuary down to the west country. These were the CH (Chain Home) stations, which could detect an enemy aircraft 100 miles away. They gave Fighter Command advance warning of the approach of enemy aircraft, and thus permitted the British fighter pilots to take off and gain altitude above the oncoming enemy—a tremendous tactical advantage.

The original radar could not detect aircraft flying under 3000 feet, so the CHL (Chain Home Low) stations were developed. British aircraft were equipped with a transmitting device that permitted the radar stations to distinguish British from enemy aircraft.

The final advantage the British had was that, if a fighter was shot down and its pilot survived, he would parachute onto British soil and promptly be returned to action. German pilots who survived after bailing out were either taken prisoner or drowned in the English Channel. There was, therefore, a higher attrition rate of German pilots. What finally turned the tide in favour of the British were two tactical mistakes made by Reischmarshall Goering. Because the radar stations were difficult to destroy, he gave up attacking them. Their lattice-work towers were almost immune to high explosives, unless destroyed by a direct hit, which was rare. Then, influenced by the Fuehrer, who yearned to exact revenge for the bombing of Berlin, Goering switched his attacks from the R.A.F. airfields and began to bomb London. This gave Fighter Command a sorely needed respite and permitted its squadrons unimpeded use of their own airfields. By October, the battle was over. The Luftwaffe had failed to gain the air superiority the Fuehrer needed, so he gave up his invasion plans for good.

In the summer of 1940, it was common to see aircraft fighting in the skies above us. These encounters were known as dogfights. I once saw an aircraft shot down. That particular dogfight was taking place so high up that some aircraft were leaving vapour trails. About ten or twelve aircraft were involved but the activity was occurring at too great an altitude for the individual fighters to be identifiable, though we could still hear faintly the sound of intermittent bursts of machine-gun fire. Suddenly, I saw one aircraft plunge straight downwards. It caught fire as it hurtled to earth and began trailing smoke. The pilot did not bail out and he must have been killed when it struck the ground several miles away. I could not tell if it was one of ours.

Our house was located between three airfields. Before the war, Croydon Aerodrome had been the base for Imperial Airways, flying old four-engined passenger aircraft, known as Hannibals, to destinations in Europe and the near east. After the war, Imperial Airways became British Overseas Airways Corporation and then British Airways. The R.A.F. had taken over Croydon on the declaration of hostilities and one squadron each of Hurricanes and Spitfires was stationed there. The other two airfields were Biggen Hill and Kenley, at both of which squadrons of Spitfires and Hurricanes were stationed. There was a constant stream of fighter aircraft flying to and from these three airfields. When the wind was in the right direction, the fighters from Croyden would take off and fly at house-top height up the valley at the foot of our back garden—always from right to left, gaining height as they approached the Purley Downs to our left.

One clear, sunny summer day, I was standing in our back garden. In the distance, I heard faintly the unmistakable sound of a Spitfire engine, way over to my right. I peered over to where I could hear the sound of the Merlin engine—a powerful, friendly, protective sound. Sure enough, in the distance up through the valley came the sleek and powerful Spitfire, slowly gaining altitude, and since it had just taken off, not flying at its full speed of three hundred and fifty-five miles per hour. I noticed that the pilot had his hood back, and as the aircraft approached, I could quite distinctly see him, his goggles pushed up on the forehead of his leather helmet. As he came abreast of the garden, I started jumping up and down and waving my arms at him in greeting. I saw that he looked over in my direction just as he turned the aircraft gently towards our house to go over the Downs. As he looked directly over at me, he thrust his left hand up and forward with his thumb up. I know now that it was not possible, but I was sure then that I saw him grin.

It was the height of my career as a small boy during the war.

THE POLISH AIRMEN

It was in the summer immediately following the evacuation of the British Army from Dunkirk. I was nine years old. My mother and I were walking along a quiet residential street in Torquay, overhung with large elm trees.

As we made our way along the wide sidewalk between the granite garden walls and the elms, I noticed two figures ahead of us. We were gaining on them, as they were sauntering along, apparently indifferent to what was happening around them. One was an officer dressed in the unmistakable light-blue uniform of the Polish Free Air Force, with a high-peaked cap with a black visor, resting at an unsteady angle on his head. The other, whose waist was firmly encircled by the officer's arm, was a young girl in a light summer dress. It is odd how insignificant details of long-remembered scenes lurk in one's memory. This girl wore a pair of silk stockings with seams. All stockings had seams back then. This girl's seams were twisted, and wobbled up her legs to disappear beneath her skirt, each at a different angle. My mother used to fuss about that sort of thing, so I had learned from an early age that twisted stocking seams were not what one expected of a properly dressed lady. Twisted stockings, my mother maintained, were bad etiquette. A lady with twisted stockings was not well turned out. It was what you would expect of a scullery maid. That was all there was to it. My mother said so and she had unshakeable views on that sort of thing.

Now my mother was a woman of firm views. Looking back on her frequently expressed opinions, I realize that I would now disagree with many of her most cherished concepts. But I was then only a small boy and had hardly reached the stage of questioning anything my parents said. My mother not only held firm opinions but she was also not averse to express-ing them, often at inappropriate moments. Tact and finesse were not her strong suits. Political correctness had not yet gained any of its current popularity and the English, and my mother in particular, cheerfully and frequently unburdened themselves of opinions about foreigners, racial inequality, religion, and what she chose to refer to as 'the lower classes' in ways that would now attract instant criticism.

My mother chose this moment to express her views about central European servicemen. "The trouble with this war," she announced, "is that it has filled this country up with foreigners." Both my mother's parents had been on the stage, and consequently she had picked up the actor's ability to project her voice. Without apparently raising it, she was capable of making herself heard at surprisingly long distances. Thus I knew that the Polish airman could undoubtedly hear what she was saying. I prayed that he understood no English. "This place is just filling up with riffraff. Look at that fellow in front. Dressed in that awful uniform. Something you would see outside a circus. Or a bus conductor. Dreadful colour. So undignified. And look at his hat. Black peak and sky blue cloth. Have these people no taste?" "But Mother," I said, "I think he is an officer." "Well," she retorted, "then he ought to know better." "But Mother," I said, "isn't it given to him by his air force? I mean, I think he has to wear it."

By this time we had gained on the airman and his girlfriend and were only a few paces behind them. So far they gave no indication of having noticed my mother's strident monologue. "And look at our silly girls,"' she continued unabated, "going out with any foreigner. What's the matter with our own soldiers? Why do they have to waste their time on people like that?"

I was, by this time, acutely embarrassed, as I realized that it would only be a matter of a short time before one or other of the pair would realize what my mother was saying. I think I also understood that my mother intended that they should, as she seemed determined to make a point, strike a blow for English womanhood, and right a social wrong. But they did not, and the reason they did not slowly became apparent. Walking towards us, on the other side of the road, not forty yards away, was a Polish Free Air Force officer, dressed in an identical uniform to that of the man ahead of us. He was also accompanied by a young woman. They were ambling along arm in arm. The couples drew closer, and suddenly each officer dropped the girl on his arm and stopped, staring across the road at one another. The one in front of us flung his arms outwards and yelled a name I did not catch. The other shouted back a different name and then each ran to the middle of the road where they flung their arms around each other in a great hug. Their circus hats were rolling in the road as each held the other at arm's length, both talking at the same time in an incomprehensible language, alternately hugging and dancing in a circle, sheer joy written on their faces as they shouted at each other. I was not sure if either was listening to the other.

The girl in front of us, she with the crooked seams, was looking across at the other officer's companion. She drew her shoulders up close to her ears and spread her hands out, palms upwards. The other girl had put her head on one side with the palm of her hand against her cheek. She looked as if she was about to cry.

Now, although I was only nine, I knew about the occupation of Poland. I had listened, with my parents, to Neville Chamberlain's speech on the radio, announcing the outbreak of war. I wondered if these officers were brothers. Or just fellow airmen who had made their separate ways to England after the fall of Poland. Did they leave their families behind? Even to a small boy what was clear was that each must have thought that the other was dead or had been imprisoned.

These thoughts encouraged me to ask my mother some questions, and I turned and began speaking to her. But she was not listening. My mother was in tears.

The 1952 Pea-Souper

In the early 1950s, my father owned a four-cylinder Wolseley. This was viewed by those who care about such things as an upmarket car, though in truth it was nothing more than a tarted up Morris Oxford, selling at an inflated price as an appeal to those who fancied themselves driving a saloon of superior dignity. It was painted hearse black, which added to its meretricious popularity.

December 1952 is remembered, by those who dwelt in London at the time, as the occasion when the great city experienced the worst fog in its recorded history. It became known as The Great Smog. On the fifth of December, a cold fog enveloped the city, which caused its inhabitants to burn more coal than usual in order to keep warm. The increased air pollution became trapped by the inversion layer formed by the dense mass of cold air. This resulted in a build up in the concentration of pollutants—especially coal smoke. All this was before the run of clean air statutes that the government was galvanized to enact as a direct result of this smog, which was estimated to have killed some four thousand people and one bull: an Aberdeen Angus of some considerable value to its Highland owner. The smog lasted four days. Unfortunately, it coincided with the Smithfield Fair, the annual agricultural show that was scheduled to take place at Earl's Court. The Scottish farmers who had brought their cattle to the show managed to preserve the lives of most of them by the ingenious device of soaking cloths in Scotch whisky and draping them over the noses of any cattle exhibiting respiratory problems.

In those days, the majority of homes had no central heating. Houses were warmed by coal fires. The coal was delivered by lorries, manned by men who habitually wore a coal sack, folded in on itself, draped over their heads, and left to cascade down their backs. They would heave the sacks of coal off the lorries and carry them on their backs to the manholes, where they would be emptied. These manholes had chutes to convey the coal down into the coal cellars, situated in everyone's basements. The coal was then shovelled into coal-scuttles and brought up to feed the fires that kept us all warm in winter. The result was a permanently soot-blackened city, with grimy buildings and surfaces that left black marks on your hands when you touched them.

The Great Smog caused chaos to London's transportation system. The buses ceased running. Icy roads caused an increase in the rate of motor vehicle accidents and the ambulance attendants and firemen who went to the aid of accident victims were forced to walk in front of their vehicles, in order to guide them through the smog. Visibility was down to a few yards. A BBC announcer, keen to use language his audience would understand, was heard to warn his listeners that you couldn't see more than "half a cricket pitch" ahead. Of course, as everybody knew, that was eleven yards, precisely. Breathing became difficult. The smog seeped into buildings. There was nowhere one could flee—except the countryside, which was difficult because of the chaotic condition of the roads. London Airport shut down. Cross Channel ferry traffic was disrupted. Theatrical performances ceased. Soccer and Rugby matches were cancelled. Only the London Underground remained in service and it became seriously congested by those who would normally have taken the bus or driven their cars.

My father, against my mother's strident advice not to go out in this foul weather, was driving me to a destination downtown. We had got as far as Baker Street. Progress had been at the speed of a donkey cart. Where there sprung up a light breeze, we could trundle along at a smart walking pace. At other times (and that was most of the time), we would have made better progress if we had walked to where we were going. Father drew up behind a stationary vehicle. He waited for it to move. It was a London taxi. "Probably waiting for a fare," Dad remarked. As it remained motion-less, Dad blew his horn. Nothing happened. Not the most patient man, he sounded it again at some length. Still no response. Cars were parked on his left and traffic was creeping by in the opposite direction to the right. So it was difficult to swing around the taxi. I got out to investigate. The taxi driver had simply parked his vehicle and left it in the middle of the road. Everyone had their lights on, so it was not difficult to see traffic a few yards away. I managed to stop traffic for a brief moment, long enough so that Dad could manoeuvre his old Wolseley around the abandoned taxi. I climbed back on board and we trundled along for another half hour. I don't believe he ever got the car out of first gear.

It was becoming obvious to us that we were not going to reach our destination on time, or for that matter, at all. A short consultation led us to decide to abandon the expedition. Dad cautiously edged his car over to the curb. We got out. He locked it. Twenty minutes back we had passed an underground station, so we walked back the way we had come until we reached it. We entered the station and Dad bought two tickets from the man at the sales counter. "Two tickets to Hampstead please." He proffered the cash and received two of the familiar, bile-green cardboard tickets that the London Passenger Transport Board had designed for its passengers.

We descended to the appropriate platform and waited for the train, which would convey us home to Hampstead.

When we arrived home, Dad had to admit, under close cross-examination from my mother, that we had been forced to terminate our venture, leave the Wolseley, and return home by tube. Mother, who could never resist any gesture of self-vindication, bestowed a look of scornful reproach upon my father.

The smog slowly dissipated, so that by the ninth of December, traffic was able to resume its normal state of orderly confusion. The whole town was covered in a damp sooty slime. It took several episodes of rain to return it to a state of relative cleanliness. Questions were asked in the House of Commons. Four years later, the Clean Air Act of 1956 was passed, which restricted the burning of domestic fuels in urban areas. Eventually coal ceased to be used at all as a domestic fuel, and London began to clean its buildings, so that they changed from grimy black blocks to pretty stone edifices.

On the tenth of December, my father decided to go and fetch his car."David, what tube station did we come home by?"

"Well I don't know. I didn't look. It was past Baker Street but I don't know how far."

I was favoured with the look that I had grown used to since early childhood—the one that said: "You thoughtless boy, why don't you learn to concentrate? Daydreaming again." But he instantly realized that he had also neglected to look for the name of the station we had retreated to on our journey home. The smog had been so dense that we could not have seen it unless we'd actually taken the trouble to look for the well-known roundel, with the name of the station inscribed on it, and neither of us had bothered to look at the tickets either, which of course, we had surrendered upon arrival at Hampstead.

Dad set off, by tube, to seek his car. He returned home that night: By tube. No car. It actually took him three days to find it, parked in a side road just off Leicester Square. My mother estimated that Dad had walked farther in those three days than he had in all of the previous year.

Doodlebugs and Other Inconveniences

The outbreak of World War II caused no little disruption to my early education. I was eight years old when I listened, on my parents' old Marconi radio, to Neville Chamberlain's radio broadcast, during which a deeply depressed man gloomily announced, "This nation is, therefore, now at war." His voice carried an undertone of embarrassment. After all, he had promised us "peace in our time," and he seemed somehow surprised at this new development, which was unexpected ... at least by him. He appeared to have no plans for what to do next.

My first school was a convent kindergarten in Hampstead, run by a group of dedicated, earnest nuns. Some unspecified ailment kept me out of school for a year and then, two schools later, I was enrolled at the Junior Branch of University College School, always referred to as Holly Hill, after the little street that gave access to it. In spite of being one of its least accomplished students, I retain fond memories of Holly Hill. The headmaster, Dr. Lake, was always known as Bunny Lake. No one knew why. It must have been a nickname bestowed by some now long-forgotten pupil. Bunny was a strict, authoritarian little man, always dressed in a brown tweed suit. His martinet-like qualities were ascribed by all of us to the fact that he had studied in Berlin, presumably for his PhD. It was universally held as a fact that this was where he'd picked up his stern demeanour. Bunny taught us Latin and Greek. He presided over assembly each morning. When the whole school was gathered, Bunny would read a prayer, and make any announcements, but before all this he would cry out "Noses!" and everyone was required to pull out their handkerchiefs and blow their noses, presumably to clear our heads for the day's studies.

On June 6, 1944, classes were interrupted and we were all ordered out into the playground. Puzzled, we assembled. Bunny Lake stood at the top of the long flight of stairs leading to the school's front door, waiting for us to settle down. When we were quiet enough, he announced that British, American, and Commonwealth troops had landed on the beaches of Normandy. We all cheered wildly.

Then I was translated to the senior school. The headmaster was C.S. Walton, who was just as stern and authoritarian as Bunny, but much less belligerent. He was known as "Fruity". I hasten to explain that the reason for this nickname was not what one would now assume. There existed, somewhere in Hampstead, a shop. It had a small fleet of vans. Inscribed in large gold and green letters on the side of each van was the name "T. WALTON: FRUITERERS". The nickname was inevitable.

Like the junior school, the senior branch conducted a daily assembly. Instead of a prayer, we sang a hymn, with no little gusto, accompanied by Mr. Flook on the grand piano, which stood in the beautiful panelled hall, around which the classrooms were clustered. Mr Flook taught general science, with the assistance of a three volume book by J. M. Harrison, called (appropriately) *Elementary General Science*. I still have my copy, and out of date though it now is, I refer to it when in need of elementary scientific information. Whenever somebody asked Mr. Flook a question, he would give the answer, always ending it by saying, "It's all in Harrison." This became a standard response in the school for any question to anyone, regardless of the subject under discussion. "It's all in Harrison" found its way into the school lexicon.

Assembly was attended by all pupils and masters, except Mr. Meek, who taught us Latin. He was a dear, gentle, cultured Jew and chose not to attend what was, in effect, a Christian Protestant service. Looking back, I now realize that about twenty percent of the pupils must have been Jewish. None of us gave it a thought; we were all just boys and we all attended assembly. I do remember that on the day Mr. Meek retired, he showed up at assembly. It was the only time he ever did. That day my class gave him a book as a retirement present. David Pocock presented it to him on our behalf, and I detected a tear in Mr. Meek's eye as he accepted it.

Some time in the summer of 1944, I hustled down to the school, late for assembly (as I too often was), and slid into my place in the hall, just in time. There had been an air raid warning. It was the summer of the V-1 flying bombs known as doodlebugs or buzz bombs to us, and as Vergeltungswaffe to the Germans, which translated literally as "vengeance weapon". That summer, they flew over London with such frequency that there was almost a permanent air raid warning in effect. Eventually people began to pay little attention to the air raid warnings, at least until the sound of the aircraft's engine became evident—a loud, raucous rattle that sounded like a badly calibrated lawnmower.

Doodlebugs were pulse-jet powered, unmanned aircraft—the world's first cruise missile. They were 27 feet long, with a wing span of 18 feet, and weighed 4,900 pounds. They carried a warhead of about 2000 pounds of high explosives. Later models were equipped with a heavier payload. They had a range of a maximum of 200 miles and were slow (by 1944 standards), inaccurate, and could easily be intercepted and shot down. A total of 4083 were destroyed—1979 by R.A.F. fighters, 1860 by anti-aircraft fire,

232 by barrage balloons. The Royal Navy shot down 12. They usually flew at an altitude of 1500 to 2000 feet. The specification of the V-1 provided that, after a designated distance flown, governed by a small windmill in the nose, the flaps were pushed down and the machine would go into a power dive. The designer miscalculated though, because when the device began its descent, the remaining fuel would slosh to the front of the fuel tank, which caused the engine to cut out due to fuel starvation. Because of this flaw, those on the ground knew that, once the engine stalled, they had about fifteen seconds to take cover.

The blast would carry a distance of up to 400 yards in all directions. The V-1s drove many people to evacuate London, and the effect on morale was not good. People resorted to sleeping in the London tube stations again, in Anderson shelters in their gardens, and in Morrison shelters, which resembled a large table with a steel top. The onslaught of V-1s and V-2s killed 8,938 people, and countless more were injured. The first flying bomb fell on London on June 13, 1944. A total of 4419 fell on London, eight of which fell in the borough of Hampstead.

On this particular morning, I had only just settled, breathless, into my place in assembly when the unmistakable sound of a doodlebug became audible, at first faint and a long way off. Soon it grew louder, and it became obvious that it was headed in our direction. The chatter of the assembled pupils dwindled into silence as we all listened to the raucous approach of this engine of death. Then chairs began to scrape as we struggled to our feet and began to run. Suddenly Mr. Flook leapt to his feet and jumped up onto the grand piano—an unparalleled act of musical *lèse-majesté*.

Waving his arms frantically, he yelled, "Don't panic! Don't panic; lie down! Take cover under something! All of you, lie down!"

But the whole mob of us were running to the exits, which caused Mr. Flook to redouble his exhortations to us to take cover. We were not actually panicking. We were all trying to get out of the hall as fast as possible, in order to have a look at this clanking, flying dragon, the likes of which we had often heard but few of us had ever seen. I made it out before most, because I had been the last one in. And there it was, dead overhead, not very high up, cranking its way across the sky—a small, black, ugly, angular aircraft with its engine perched on top, at the back of the beast, with a little brown smoke emitting from the rear of it. It spluttered on its way, the noise of its engine growing fainter as it disappeared from view. We all stood and watched, with more boys streaming out of the entrances as we did so. The sound grew fainter, and finally, we heard it stop. We all held our breath, counted to fifteen, and then heard the explosion, far away, somewhere over the other side of Hampstead Heath.

When this disorderly crowd of irresponsible youth eventually settled back down in assembly, we were treated to a magisterial scolding from Fruity. "Utter foolishness! Never risk your lives! Can't think what you were all doing. You know the air raid drill. Never let this happen again!" We listened politely. It had no effect at all.

September came, and with it (on the 8th) came the first V-2 (Vergeltungswaffe Zwei) rocket. It fell in Chiswick, unannounced, and silent until the huge explosion. After the explosion, one could see a vapour trail disclosing the course of the rocket. It was the world's first ballistic missile. The Germans launched almost 3000 of these missiles against England, France, and Belgium, of which three fell on Hampstead. They arrived without warning. No approaching whine allowed one to take cover. There was no defence against these things until the British Army overran the launching pads at Peenemünde.

One Saturday morning, there was a huge explosion not far down the road from the block of flats, at the top end of Holly Hill, where I lived with my parents. After breakfast, I hustled down the road looking for the bombsite. I found it, but a worried-looking police officer shooed me away. I could see considerable activity and a number of ambulances. The area was roped off. I walked around the corner, intending to return home up Frognal, and discovered that the blast had forcibly removed most of the windows from the school buildings. There were a number of students and a few masters clearing up the mess. Mr. Bennett, one of the science masters, saw me and yelled, "Hey, Roberts! Come and help us! Over here!" I did as I was bidden and spent the rest of the morning sweeping up more glass than I ever thought could exist in any one building. I never wanted to see a shard of glass ever again. The school had suffered no evident structural damage, and somewhat to our dismay, those with the power to decide (Fruity, no doubt), declared that there would be school as usual, and there was. School resumed, on schedule, the following Monday. It was a little drafty, but the weather was warm.

LOBSTERS

Sent away from Hampstead by my parents, to get me away from the Blitz, I spent a great deal of time during the first part of the war staying with my aunt Florrie, who lived in a house near Churston Ferrers, high up on a hill and overlooking Torbay. The town of Torquay was clearly visible to the east, on the other side of the bay. Aunt Florrie ran a boarding house. It was mostly for friends and relatives on holiday, but she occasionally took in strangers and had the odd permanent guest as well—mainly invalids in need of some care. She had been a nurse during the First World War and had ended up as the matron of the hospital in Malmesbury. She had a hospital matron's dictatorial personality, only somewhat modified by a kind heart. She was my father's first cousin, and therefore of Welsh peasant ancestry. She was thin, wiry, and hyperactive in the way many energetic peasant women are. She seemed to stop talking only in order to draw breath. She was a Wesleyan and a bible was never far from her reach. Aunt Florrie never learned to drive, had no motorcar, and did all her shopping by bus.

Aunt Florrie was a widow. She had married a merchant seaman, Jack Wilcox, the first engineer aboard a coaster. He had drowned when his ship was torpedoed in the English Channel during the First World War. An enormous, brown sepia photograph of him hung over the fireplace, and dominated the sitting room. Alongside was a smaller photograph of his ship—a small tramp steamer with a smoke stack that rose vertically from amidships, like a thin, tall pillar-box. I liked the look of Uncle Jack. He was photographed in his merchant navy uniform, with officer's stripes around the cuffs, and a peaked cap firmly on his head. His eyes twinkled above his bushy moustache, and the photograph revealed a faint, whimsical smile as he tried to look as appropriately stern as the occasion demanded. It was the merchant navy equivalent of the Mona Lisa.

Uncle Jack had been torpedoed twice. The first time he had managed to swim ashore, and dragged himself, exhausted, up Clapton Sands. As he hauled himself up the beach, his trouser pockets had filled with sand. Aunt Florrie had emptied the sand out of the pockets and stored it in a little

19

bottle, which she kept in a display cabinet in the hallway of her house, to show to anybody who expressed an interest. The second time his ship went down in much the same place, but either he was killed in the explosion or it sank too far from shore for him to repeat his earlier escape. Aunt Florrie never believed that he was dead. Someone had told her that the German U-boat had surfaced and was seen picking up survivors. She spent the remainder of her life making enquiries to try to find him, and firmly believed that he remained a prisoner of war. She bought the house at Churston because it was close to where his ship had gone down, and she lived there for the rest of her life, yearning for her lost husband. Aunt Florrie went to chapel in Brixham every Sunday, and would frequently work at the Mission for Seamen run by the Wesleyans.

The house was large and looked as if it had been built in the nineteen twenties. Aunt Florrie had added on bits here and there and had converted the garage into a bedroom, all to accommodate the maximum possible number of guests. In consequence, it was a warren of small rooms. I went to have a look at it half a century later, and noticed that the new owners had dismantled many of Florrie's carbuncular extrusions, and restored the garage to its original purpose.

There was a great rambling hedge at the bottom of her garden, inhabited (I was told) by poisonous adders. I was under a permanent injunction not to go near it. On the other side of the hedge, there was a huge field that always filled up with holiday-makers' tents in the summer. It rolled down to the ridge, along which ran the Great Western Railway Line, from Paddington to Penzance. This railway held a small boy's fascination, and I learned the names of most of the steam engines that hauled the trains to and from Cornwall. The engines all had names, inscribed on a curved plate above the driving wheels. "Hall class" and "Castle class" locomotives were named after the great English country houses and castles that existed within the Great Western's jurisdiction. The railway line emerged from a tunnel in a large round hill, called the Sugar Loaf. I could always hear the sound of a train approaching, and never tired of watching it burst out in a cloud of steam from the entrance of the tunnel. Beyond the railway, were steep cliffs, sandy beaches, and the sea. I knew every inch of thise stretch of coast below her house. The cliffs were full of caves. One in particular I remember, because it was lined with amethyst crystals. I don't doubt that, by now, the tourists will have stripped it bare of this beautiful stone.

I often fished off the rocks, mostly for mackerel, with a shiny silver spinner. Searching for food, the fish would come into the coves in schools and it was not difficult to hook a few, which I would triumphantly take home to my aunt. For some reason, she was under the impression that mackerel could be bad for one's health, and I think she threw a lot away while I was not looking. I was once fishing from a rowing boat off Paignton Sands and my spinner came to the surface having lost its weight. A seagull swooped down upon it and the hook got caught under its beak. I started to reel it in and it took off. There I was, with a seagull flying around at the end of my fishing line. I reeled it aboard the boat and released the hook, after some difficulty, as it fought for what it clearly perceived was its life. Before I could let it go, it threw up the entire contents of its stomach into the boat. Half digested fish were sloshing around my feet.

Lobsters were the great prize. They lived around the rocks that littered the little beaches. Our preferred way of catching them was to get a stick, tie a three or four foot length of picture wire to it, and arrange a slip knot so that it could be tightened into a small loop. A piece of mackerel was then tied to the end of a piece of string. The trick was to creep over a likely rock that had a sea-filled space below it, and drop the bait in front of this little cave, which (as often as not) provided a snug haven for a lobster. We would patiently wait until the lobster detected the bait. He would slowly emerge from his haven and creep towards the piece of smelly mackerel, antennae waving. As soon as his tail cleared the rock, the wire noose was slipped under the tail and he was hoisted ashore, to be taken home for supper.

The Heirloom

My mother's family were all Geordies—folk who inhabit the north-east coast of England. Mother's maiden name was Watson and the Watsons had owned a shipyard at the mouth of the River Wear in Sunderland. The yard was nestled between the city and the river, in that part of the old town known as Monkwearmouth. Once the site of the old abbey, it became the centre of shipbuilding in Sunderland. Now all the old shipyards are gone, and Monkwearmouth is home to the University of Sunderland.

The Watsons built ships in the days of sail, and ran a small fleet of merchantmen themselves. Their ships put to sea carrying cargoes destined for some foreign port, and returned (laden once more) after sometimes as much as two years at sea. In the interim, they would not hear from the ship until she docked back home in Sunderland. No phones in those days, no telegraphs, no radio. My mother once told me that her grandfather had told her that they felt themselves fortunate if they had lost as few as two members of the crew during such a voyage. Most fell out of the rigging. If they were lucky, they plunged into the sea, where there was a chance (a small chance) that the ship might be able to heave to, lower a boat, and rescue the unfortunate mariner. Less lucky were those who hit the deck, which brought instant death and burial at sea. The old family bible, with a family tree in the closing pages (left blank in all family bibles for that very purpose), contains information about at least half a dozen ancestors who "drowned at sea".

The family made a small fortune over the years. Then misfortune descended upon them out of this financially dazzling blue sky. Robert Stevenson invented the steam engine, Isambard Kingdom Brunel built the first ocean-going steamship, the Britannia, and (all in one year) the Watsons lost three ships: one foundering in a storm in the North Sea, driven ashore at Deptford, and two lured onto the rocks by wreckers. Both these latter events occurred on the south coast of Cornwall—a county notorious for its population of land-based pirates. These ruthless peasants would create a light on a cliff at night that mimicked the signal of a real lighthouse, thus

22

confusing the sailing master of any passing merchantman, whose ship (its position miscalculated) would end up on the rocks. The Cornishmen would then set about pillaging the wreck—as often as not, killing the crew into the bargain. They wouldn't want any witnesses. The ships were, of course, insured, but nonetheless, it was a sorely troubling blow.

The family faced a difficult decision in the mid-nineteenth century. Should they retool the shipyard and convert to building steamships or fold the business in the face of what they reluctantly realized was the inevitable demise of sail as a maritime commercial carrier? They had all inherited, or earned, enough money to permit them to retire and live in comfort. They chose to phase out the yard. Their last ship, a brig called the "Sarah Watson", was built in the latter part of the nineteenth century, and was still in use by new owners in the nineteen thirties.

Now Sarah Watson was my great-great-grandmother. A Scotswoman from Edinburgh, she was the matriarch of the family and ruled over it with a determination that brooked no opposition. My mother remembered her, for she died at the age of ninety-four when my mother was a little girl. She had been born just before the Battle of Waterloo. Mother had a photograph of her riding in a carriage, manned by a driver and a footman. She is seated bolt upright in the carriage—a lady with the figure, garb, and demeanour of Queen Victoria.

Great-Great-Grandmother owned a grandfather clock, which she had ordered to be made for her by a clockmaker in Sunderland. The face of the clock bears the legend "Jacob Joseph, Sunderland". After the old lady died, the clock found its way into my grandfather's house, and it was in that house that I became acquainted with it. Grandfather died when I was six, in 1937. He lived in Reading, where he ran a marginally successful, old-fashioned Victorian music hall, aptly named "The Reading Palace of Varieties". He frittered away his inheritance, which had been substantial when he'd received it at the turn of the century, on theatrical ventures— the last of which was the Reading Palace of Varieties. When he died, my grandmother sold the theatre, which ultimately became a cinema, and she lived on the proceeds and what was left of Grandfather's patrimony.

As a small boy on visits to the old house in Reading, I became fascinated by the grandfather clock. I listened to it chiming the hours. It boasted a distinct and unique chime. High pitched and unusually fast, it chimed at the rate of slightly more than two strikes a second. With its high pitch, it sounded hysterical. When Grandmother died, during the closing stages of the Second World War, my aunt Marjorie acquired the clock. She didn't like the chime, and bound up the striker with Elastoplast to silence it. The clock wouldn't function if you didn't wind the striking mechanism, so she had to muffle it, so its strike was reduced to a thump, as if an imprisoned elf were angrily beating on the door, striving to get out.

Aunt Marjorie eventually died a spinster, in 1970, when I was living in West Vancouver. Since both her brothers had predeceased her, my brother and I inherited her small estate. The estate included the clock. My brother told me that my niece, his eldest daughter, would like the clock and asked if I would mind her getting it. Well, yes, I would mind. It was the one thing I remembered from my grandparents' home. So I gently insisted that it be boxed up and shipped out to BC. With it came a portrait of its original owner, Sarah Watson, painted on the occasion of her wedding in the eighteen thirties. She had, in Sheridan's phrase, a damned disinheriting countenance. The portrait is of an unsmiling woman of domineering mien, used to being obeyed and not welcoming opposition.

The clock duly arrived. It was encased in a large wooden box, specially constructed for its sea voyage across the Atlantic and thence by rail to Vancouver. I lugged it into the basement and began to unpack it. As I tore away the last planks and lifted up the old clock, its strike suddenly began to function. Startled, I was taken aback by the sound I had last heard in my grandfather's house forty years past. It was an eerie feeling. Someone had unwound Aunt Marjorie's Elastoplast, restoring the strike to its former excited and high-pitched knell. We cleaned a half-century of grime from its case and its face and installed it in the hall. Some time later, it became in need of repair and I took it to an artisan who specialized in restoring grandfather clocks. For some reason he slowed down the strike to one per second. I rather missed the frenzy of its old strike.

I found, inside the case, a piece of paper glued to the inside wall, which had been half torn away. It had the figure 74, and I assumed that to be when Mr. Jacob had made it for Great-Great-Grandmother. I checked with a clock shop in Winchester, on one of our trips to visit family in England. They consulted a clock encyclopedia and verified that Jacob was indeed in business in Sunderland in 1874.

I shall have to decide to whom to bequeath the clock. There are several takers amongst my children and grandchildren, unlike the huge portrait of Sarah Watson, which all have politely declined on the excuse that it is too big to fit into any of their houses. Perhaps I will have to make it a condition that whoever gets the clock must also take Sarah Watson.

ONLY THE BABOON

For thirty-three years, until 1999, William F. Buckley Jr. hosted a public affairs television show called *Firing Line*. Buckley was highly educated, articulate, ostentatiously erudite, and seriously right wing. Had he lived long enough, he would undoubtedly have joined the Tea Party.

He would invite a public personality to each show and interview them. The guests, prodded by Buckley, would be lured into a debate, and Buckley was not above demolishing his guest if he could. He occasionally hosted the show in London, and on one of those occasions, his guest was Sir Harold Macmillan, then aged close to ninety and looking his age. What became immediately evident was that Sir Harold had retained all his faculties and was intelligent and quick-witted. Buckley knew better than to make any attempt to upstage this strong-minded old man. They fell to discussing political leadership, at some length. At the end of the show, as was customary, Buckley allowed his guest to take questions. A young woman rose and said, "Sir Harold, you have been discussing leadership in the world today and my question has to do with what has happened to the calibre of the current world leaders. Once we all looked up to Churchill, Roosevelt, de Gaulle, but now we have to put up with nonentities like Gerald Ford, Harold Wilson, and the French President who is so insignificant that I cannot remember his name. Why do we now have to endure such mediocrities?"

Macmillan was much too shrewd to answer a question like that. He said, "My dear, when I was first elected to the House of Commons, I was sitting, one evening, in my club, when a friend of my father's came over and congratulated me on my election. After a brief conversation he said, 'Of course, there's no one left of any calibre, Disraeli's gone, Gladstone's gone: just nobody left with any stature.'"

Well, my recollections of that *Firing Line* show led me to free-wheeling ruminations. One thought led to another. I am cursed with a magpie mind, or so my history teacher maintained in my final year of high school. He became exasperated by an essay I had turned in and in which I had wandered from his assigned subject. A magpie mind. It flits from branch to branch, perching on a thought here, pecking at another there—distracted by the hanging fruit on another bough and turned aside by the temptation to pick a yet different cherry on another tendril. The magpie flutters from thought to thought in unplanned pattern, easily and frequently deviating from the originally (and only vaguely) charted course. My dear old history teacher had never heard of attention deficit disorder, a buzzword the psychologists had not then invented, but I know he would have used it, with advantages, to criticize my meandering essay.

So it was that, after watching the show, I fell to musing about leadership—the subject that Buckley and Sir Harold had tossed around. This prompted me to remember the man who lived next door to the house in Edgware in which I was born, and in which I lived for the first six years of my life. Dr. John Barnett was a prominent zoologist, and he worked at the London Zoo. A kind, gentle man, he kept a hutch of Guinea pigs for his children to play with. They were always producing baby Guinea piglets and Dr. Barnett spent a great deal of time trying to find homes for them in order to stave off the serious overpopulation of his hutch. He had a decisive quality about him that one day saved his life. He was tending to a king cobra at the zoo. The king cobra is the world's largest poisonous snake, sometimes reaching eighteen feet in length. Its bite is fatal. If a king cobra bites you, you die within half an hour. Dr. Barnett was handling this particular snake when it struck and bit him in the arm. In an instant, he pulled out a Swiss Army knife that he always carried with him, tore off his shirt sleeve, and slashed his arm five times from shoulder to wrist, letting the blood flow until he was satisfied that the poison had drained away. Apart from a few days weakness from loss of blood, and an arm that took some weeks to heal, he was none the worse for this alarming mishap.

Not long after this incident, Dr. Barnett accepted an appointment as curator of the Rangoon Zoo and he and his family moved to Burma. We never saw him again. It was 1938, and we later heard that he had died while leading a group of refugees to safety across the Arakan Yoma mountain range into India, ahead of the invading and uninvited Japanese army.

Dr. Barnett's connection with the debate between Buckley and Sir Harold Macmillan had to do with an observation I'd once heard him let drop while discussing politics with my father one day. He said that a study conducted by a group of fellow zoologists had revealed that of all the vertebrates, only the baboon elected its leaders for their intelligence. All the other vertebrates, including the human race, elected their leaders for other reasons, when their leaders had not already seized power by force.

Only the Baboon

MOTHER'S AUSTIN 7

Although my mother had a driving license, she had never passed a driving test. No test was required in the days when she acquired her license. You only needed to complete an application form and contribute five shillings in order to be issued the little brown booklet that evidenced your qualification, if not competence, to drive. She had learned to drive shortly after she and my father were married in November 1917. There were two reasons why no test was then administered to applicants for a license. There was a war on, in which my father was a reluctant participant, and there was a severe shortage of manpower. There was simply no one to administer the test, let alone devise one. In addition, the motorcar was still a novelty. When the war broke out, in August of 1914, the motive power of choice and necessity was still the horse. Taxis powered by the internal combustion engine were only slowly replacing the Hansom cab. The French Army learned by bitter experience that cavalry, though it added grace to what otherwise might degenerate into an unseemly brawl, was unable to withstand the Mausser carbine, capable of thirty rounds per minute, let alone the Maxim machine gun's thirteen rounds per second. This was the great transformation wrought by the First World War—the evolution of transportation from the horse to the internal combustion engine.

Thus it was that my mother's introduction to the motorcar took place during the newfangled machine's infancy, and before there was such a thing as the Highway Code—a booklet that later became mandatory study for aspiring road users. The Highway Code was a tome from which my mother was permanently and invincibly estranged.

It must have been my father who taught my mother to drive, because none of my grandparents ever owned a car. All born in the middle of the reign of Queen Victoria, by the end of World War I, they were simply too old to learn to drive.

Now my father never took a driving test either, so his instruction of my mother was a case of the uninformed teaching the uninitiated. And it showed. My mother's method of driving a car was best, and politely, described as unconventional. She never had a serious accident, but this was largely because she always drove at the pace of a farm cart. It was unusual for her to reach a speed that required the use of fourth gear. Indeed, there was little evidence that she ever mastered the concept of the ratio between speed and gear.

Not long before the outbreak of the Second World War, my father bought my mother a second hand Austin 7. This vehicle was, to the United Kingdom, a rough equivalent of what the Volkswagon was to the Germans, and the Citroen a *deux chevaux* to the French. As its name implied, the Austin 7 had an engine that boasted seven horse-power. It had four doors and could seat four people, as long as they were of no more than average size. It was furnished with a minimum of equipment, but did have a turn signal system consisting of two trafficators. These were little illuminated orange arms, one on each side of the car. When at rest, they were housed vertically in a receptacle in the body of the car, between the front and back doors, at about shoulder height. When activated by a small lever on the hub of the driving wheel, the trafficators would flip out to the horizontal position and light up, indicating to following cars in which direction the Austin proposed to turn.

My father's cousin, Auntie Florrie, lived on the South Devon coast. We often journeyed thither to stay with her. Mother had driven down with me on one of these jaunts, with a surfeit of luggage stuffed onto the back seats. A day or so after our arrival, mother was minded to go shopping in Torquay, a resort town later elevated to fame by the *Fawlty Towers* series on BBC television. Near the harbour in Torquay there is a busy intersection where five roads converge. Because of its high traffic usage, it was always controlled by a traffic policeman, standing in a commanding position in the middle of the intersection,—an imposing figure in black uniform, helmet, and highly polished boots. Mother was driving, with Auntie Florrie in the passenger seat and me seated apprehensively in the back. Auntie Florrie, thin, wiry, and hyperactive, had in her time been the matron of Malmsbury hospital and her years of exercising authority in medical institutions had imbued her with an irresistible need to tell everybody within earshot what to do. She was at her bossy best as a passenger in a car. Mother approached the five-pronged intersection and observed that the traffic policeman was facing her with the palm of his white-gloved hand upraised towards her. Mother slowed down from fifteen or so miles per hour and prepared to stop.

"He wants you to stop, Grace." Florrie's advice was predictable.

"Yes, Florrie, I can see that. Thank you." Mother's composure had clearly frayed after twenty miles of driving under Auntie Florrie's incessant guidance. Auntie Florrie did not herself own a car, and indeed, could not drive. I detected that my mother was less inclined to accept, with equanimity, the stream of counsel with which Auntie Florrie favoured her on the subject of the Austin's navigation. Mother stopped. She wanted to turn right, so she flipped the little lever clockwise and the right trafficater duly sprang out to its horizontal.

"You need to turn right here, Grace."

"Thank you Florrie." Mother's patience was palpable.

The policeman now had his back to Mother, busy directing traffic from the other four roads. Traffic was heavy and he remained with his back to Mother for several minutes—longer than Mother thought necessary.

"The damned fool. He's forgotten I'm here. There's no traffic now. I'll just go 'round him." With this, my mother engaged first gear, and slowly drove past the policeman, leaving him on her right. She cut it too fine. As she drove abreast of him, the outstretched trafficator, unnoticed by her, clipped him on the shoulder. He bellowed at her after she had gone some distance past him. Hearing his incensed summons, she slammed her foot on the brake, and peered in the rear-view mirror to see what he wanted. Because she had begun her turn, he was not in her view in the mirror.

"What's the damned fool want me to do now?" She put the car into reverse. By now, the policeman had pivoted a quarter turn to deal with cars coming from the left. Mother backed steadily towards the policeman, her attention diverted from the rear-view mirror to the task of winding down the driver's window so that she could better deliver to the policeman the benefit of her opinion of his traffic-control technique. She misjudged her direction, as the next thing she knew, the policeman was hard up against the driver's side of the car and emitting anguished cries of pain, for she had just backed up over his feet.

MOTHER'S PEPPER POT

In the winter of 1939, shortly after the outbreak of war, there was a significant number of inhabitants of the British Isles who believed that negotiations for peace should be initiated, in order to reach some accommodation with the Germans. Surrender was not a word used in discussion, but it lurked in the minds of apprehensive folk. Even some members of the government, notably Lord Halifax—once the favourite to replace Chamberlain as prime minister—considered peace overtures to be a valid option. Then came the Battle of Dunkirk in June 1940. It is now impossible to know whether it was the miraculous evacuation of 350,000 troops, the sight of British fighters fending off the Luftwaffe, or Churchill's stirring rhetoric that stiffened the public spine, but stiffen it did. I was only a small boy at the time, but I vividly remember that, by the summer of 1940, everybody's energy was concentrated on the war effort. We were all in it for the kill.

The Germans were massing on the French coast for the invasion of Britain. Hitler called it Operation Sea Lion. In southern England, extensive measures were taken to withstand this expected assault. The beaches were mined. Pillboxes were constructed and anti-tank ditches were dug. Fields were sown with posts in order to wreck any troop-carrying gliders that might try to land. All street signs, railway station name boards, and directional signs were removed. Many inhabitants living near the coast were evacuated. Tanks full of paraffin were hidden on the shore, the lethal contents of which would be poured into the sea to incinerate any German soldiers storming the beaches. Large tracts of the coast were out of bounds to civilians.

It seemed as if the entire population had been enlisted. Nobody did much that was not connected to the war effort. A home guard was formed. At first untrained, ill equipped and over-age, it eventually became an efficient force that relieved the army of many time-consuming guard duties.

"Take one German with you," was the doctrine, coined (of course) by Winston Churchill.

Looking back, though many deride me for this view, I am convinced that a German army would not have survived once it set foot on English soil. The German army was the best trained, most efficient, and best equipped in the world, but notwithstanding that, it would probably have been decimated at the hands of a determined population.

My father had been an infantry officer in the First World War and knew a bit about hand-to-hand combat. Throughout the war, he always carried an ugly looking little dagger in his brief case.

But it was my mother's anti-invasion preparations that impressed me most. Now Mother was a small woman, a shade over five feet tall—though since she never took more exercise than carrying a shopping basket home, she had attained a rotund congibundity that did not auger well for any kind of unarmed combat. She had heard, somewhere, that the best way to disable a man was to throw pepper in his eyes. Thus it was that she hustled off one day to the grocers and purchased the largest pot of pepper she could find. Returning home, she half unscrewed the cap to facilitate the fastest possible deployment of its contents.

Now our house had two doors, both on the same side of the house. There was the front door immediately reached by the path from the gate, and the door that opened into the kitchen. It was not really a back door, because it was at the front. It functioned as the tradesman's entrance. Mother placed her pot of pepper on the shelf beside the tradesman's entrance. Naturally, she assumed that any German soldier would present himself at the tradesman's entrance, not the front door.

Despite the obvious frailties in her plan for the repulse of the enemy, what I do know for certain is that any German soldier who did attempt entry via the tradesman's entrance of our home would have instantly suffered a severe set back to his visual acuity.

My First Encounter with Injustice

The human brain is an eccentric computer. At birth, our genes furnish us with all the necessary hardware, but no operating system. This we build ourselves, with the acquisition of knowledge gained from experience. Gradually, the operating system creates a button labelled *memory*. With luck, some of us create a button called *instinct*, which is at the heart of our creative function.

Memory is a fickle archive and the memory of early childhood is the most capricious of all.

No one can remember being born, because their operating system has not yet been installed. But everyone cherishes the illusion of our earliest childhood memory, usually occurring between the ages of two and three, when enough of our operating system is in place that our memory button is beginning to function.

I believe I know the first recollection of my childhood, because it was also my first encounter with injustice. In addition to all that, it was the first (and last) time that either of my parents ever used corporal punishment as a disciplinary measure.

My mother had put me to bed in my crib. It was a cold winter's night. Our house, though recently constructed, was equipped with only rudimentary central heating, which (as I remember it) was central in the sense that the kitchen boiler was more or less in the middle of the house. To keep me warm, Mother had filled a hot-water bottle and tucked it in beside me. I was now just old enough to last the whole night without diapers—known to the English, and all their nannies, as nappies. She kissed me goodnight and retreated downstairs, leaving a small nightlight on to keep at bay the multitude of unfounded terrors by which small children are prone to be assailed in the dark.

I fell asleep, but after the passage of an hour or two, was awakened by an uncomfortable, cold feeling. My bed was wet. I stood up and began to whimper. I was cold. My nighty was soaked. I couldn't lie down, as the bedclothes were cold and soggy, so I resorted to the first solution of all small children. Clutching the rail of my crib in my little hands, I let out a wail of combined despair and anger, in one long screech spanning an octave of sharps and flats and carrying an urgent message beseeching parental assistance. At that time of life, Mummy is the cure for all ills, the solution to all problems, and the comfort for all troubles.

Mother came pounding upstairs, all five feet one inch of her, propelled upwards by the maternal fear provoked by my screams. She leaned over my crib and picked me up for a cherishing hug. Her consoling words soon turned to annoyance, as she felt my sodden nightclothes and stooped to feel the wet bedclothes with a searching hand. She was dismayed that months of carefully easing me out of diapers had suddenly become a failed project. She would have to start all over again. "You naughty little boy, you've wet your bed!" She pulled up my nighty and spanked me, quite hard. My wails of discomfort took on a different tone, delivered at a higher pitch, and with a decibel rating as loud as my little lungs could achieve. She stood me down at the end of the crib as she gathered up my wet bed-clothes and flung them to the floor. I wept, gasping for air between sobs, as I stood, banished to the end of the crib, watching Mother disassemble my bed.

Then she picked up the hot water bottle, and as she lifted it, realized that it was emitting a steady trickle of water. She had not screwed in the stopper tight enough. It had slowly leaked into the bed, until the warm water, liberated from its rubber container, grew cold enough to wake me up. Mother was mortified. She picked me up, full of apologies, bestowing a deluge of kisses and hugs of contrition. She took me downstairs, washed me, and dried me in front of the fire. I was given warm milk and biscuits, and fussed over until I was returned to a now-remade, dry, and warm bed.

I, of course, had no idea what had wet my bed. Had Mother not owned up, I would probably have thought (with uninformed infantile logic) that I had done it myself. Only when I had been covered with apologetic kisses did I realize that I had been punished unjustly. I know that I did not exactly think this through. It was a foggy realization, deduced from my mother's behaviour, that I had been done wrong, stuck there—a defenceless child in my crib. The incident must have had a considerable impact on my develop-ing mind for me to remember it still, three quarters of a century later.

CHILDHOOD MENDACITY

I was, I suppose, about thirteen years old, and living with my parents in Hampstead, which is scattered about a hill in north-west London. We inhabited an old Victorian walk-up apartment block—though in England these edifices were called blocks of flats.

I was enrolled in day school, which was (conveniently) just around the corner. I was not a good student. Consistently near the bottom of the class in every subject, except woodworking, I was impervious to the demands, pleas, and threats of every teacher who besought me to work harder and to concentrate on what was taking place in class. My end of term report card was always a disaster. We pupils were always given our report cards to take home to our parents. I knew that I faced approximately two days of my father's wrath upon my presentation to him of the dreaded report card. Once, in the junior school, it was so bad that I told the teacher I had lost it and asked for another one, which to my surprise, he wrote. I then gave Dad the one least likely to upset him.

I am sure that all children indulge in daydreaming. I know that I was endowed with a vivid imagination that sporadically erupted into the desire, and sometimes the practice, of compensating for my inept scholarly endeavours by exaggerating, and occasionally lying about exploits at school, treating my parents to tales of achievements I could never have accomplished: I would regale them with marks I had never achieved; claim to have scored goals in soccer games that I could never have scored, because I was consistently relegated to the position of goalie—the location on the field where I was least likely to damage my team. I think I must have had a fragile grasp of the concepts of right and wrong, and the need to restrict my lies to only the very whitest, to be told on occasions of exigent social necessity. I was, in truth, an infantile sociopath.

My father eventually and effectively curbed my tendency for mendacity.

It was wartime. The army had commandeered part of our large schoolyard, in which to tether a barrage balloon. These were gas-filled dirigibles that floated several hundred feet in the air in order to deter low-flying enemy aircraft. Made of some airtight grey material, they boasted three huge tail-flaps, which made them resemble three-eared, airborne elephants.

One windy day, during morning break, a small group of us ambled over to watch the soldiers struggling in vain against the wind to get their balloon down and anchored. The ungainly craft was flailing about as the wind gusted, its guy wires flapping dangerously. To our unconfined joy and gratification, the cable that secured the balloon parted and the balloon swept up into the air, turned once over the school buildings, and dipped as if in a curtsey to the school on its departure, before wafting away over northern London to disappear into the clouds.

Now, there was a boy in my class called Hoffman. The German name caused some of us (with more imagination than was good for us) to suspect him of being a Nazi spy. We would conjure up stories about him, all quite untrue, and sit around entertaining each other with them like witches around a cauldron. He was not very popular, though that was not because of our suspicions about his espionage activities. He just wasn't an interesting person. I hustled home the afternoon of the barrage balloon's escape from its anti-aircraft duties to tell my parents about it.

But I could not resist embellishing the tale. I invented a story about having found a penknife—with the name "Hoffman" printed on it. I said that it had been attached to the balloon's mooring rope and had been the instrument of its sudden and unauthorized departure. I informed my parents that I had given the knife to the headmaster, who had said that he would take the matter up with appropriate authorities. This story was vitally unbelievable, though I was too young, naive, and dim to recognize this. Dad waited an hour or two, and then, over supper, said that he was so pleased about what I had done that he had decided to go to the school the next day and talk to the headmaster about it. I was instantly terrified. I was plainly going to be shown up, to my father and to the headmaster, as a mischievous purveyor of falsehoods. My discomfort must have been evident to my parents. I was unable to finish my supper, could not concentrate on my homework, and went to bed in a state of panic. What could I do to forestall my father's impending visit? I had attempted to suggest that the episode was not important enough for him to waste his time on it. He insisted that he wanted to talk to the headmaster about my brave contribution to the war effort. I had tried the argument that the headmaster would be too busy—tied up in class, or preparing end of term reports. Dad remained adamant that even if he had to wait until the headmaster was available, he wanted to discuss with him my clever disclosure of German infiltration into the defence of the realm.

I was in a state of excruciating anxiety. I couldn't sleep. I worried. I wept into the pillow. I sat up and cast about for some way to get out of the awful mess I had got myself into. I even considered owning up to my falsehood, but simply didn't have the courage to do so, despite the fact that the consequences of not doing so would be worse. When I did finally get to sleep, I was seriously troubled by recurring nightmares, all revolving around my dilemma. Next morning, I crept in to breakfast and sat looking at my father as if I were a small mouse about to be pounced upon by the family cat. I ate little. Breakfast dragged on interminably. I expected that, as soon as it was over, I would be accompanied to school by my father. My apprehension at the outcome of the interview between the headmaster and my father grew until I became virtually paralysed with fear. Dad got up from the table and went into the hall to put on his overcoat. He returned to the breakfast table where I was still sitting in a complete funk. "Oh," he said, "I'm really sorry, but I've just realized that I won't have time to come with you to see the headmaster today." Then he turned and disappeared through the front door on his way to work.

I crept off to school, completely exhausted by this harrowing experience. The incident had the effect intended by my father. It circumscribed my childish desire to inflate my own importance by relating tall tales about activities that had occurred only in my own lively imagination.

I like to think that the portion of my imagination that survived my childhood has been a positive influence on my career. In this respect, I am with Albert Einstein, who said, "I am enough of an artist to draw freely upon my imagination. Imagination is more important than knowledge. Knowledge is limited. Imagination encircles the world."

TARZAN OF THE APES

When a boat belonging to English aristocrats is driven ashore on the coast of West Africa, the mother dies, the father is killed by a troop of natives, who then adopt and rear the couple's child as one of their own—in the jungle. The Tarzan stories, by Edgar Rice Burroughs, were the inspiration for some eighty-nine movies, six of which starred Johnny Weissmuller as Tarzan, and a scantily clad Maureen O'Sullivan as Jane. Weissmuller had been a swimming star in the 1920s, winning five Olympic gold medals (and a bronze for water polo). "Me Tarzan, you Jane." This was the line we small boys quoted from those flicks, that and the Tarzan yell. The Tarzan movies were really bad theatre. Ineptly acted, with unbelievably unlikely plots, and filmed against cardboard backdrops, they were monumental box office successes. At least the animals were credible, borrowed from the nearest zoo. The films struck a chord in the hearts of all us small boys.

It was the early days of the war. I was about ten. My mother and I had journeyed down to Devonshire to stay with Auntie Florrie, my father's first cousin. Auntie Florrie had inherited, from our Welsh peasant ancestors, a streak of single-minded stubbornness of a kind I had never encountered before, and rarely since. She was stick thin, wiry, and hyperactive. She rarely stopped talking.

I was lonely, smothered by the twin authoritarian tyranny of my mother and Auntie Florrie. I made friends with two local boys. The first, Christopher Watson, was the only child of elderly parents, who lived down the street from my aunt. The Watsons were retired middle-class folk, with a strong sense of genteel propriety. Christopher was a year or two older than I was, and in consequence, felt entitled to boss me around. All games and pastimes were conducted to his rules.

The other boy was John Soul. His widowed mother ran the local gas station and automobile repair shop, aided by her hunch-backed elder brother (always known to me as "Mr. Turner"). Mr. Turner seemed to spend the bulk of his time fly-fishing in the Devonshire streams. The Soul's menu was oversupplied with brook trout. John was way further down the social scale than the Watsons. His vocabulary was grounded deep in the vernacular of the Devonshire lower classes. He introduced me to the verb "to fart". I had hitherto only used the expression "to let off". At the time, in my childish innocence, I thought this the very depths of verbal depravity. John was not as bossy as Christopher, but was more independent minded and self assured. His mother spent most of her waking hours running the business, and had less time to devote to her son's social development.

Christopher and John had nothing in common. John attended the local grammar school, while Christopher was enrolled in a boarding school that I suspect his parents could ill afford.

The day came when the latest Tarzan movie came to town. The film had been made before the war, but it had only just reached British cinemas. We were all wrought up with excitement in anticipation of watching this jungle fairytale. The movie became the sole subject of our conversation for days in advance. Mr. and Mrs. Watson invited me to go and see it with them and Christopher. I told Mother and Auntie Florrie about the invitation and then made the mistake of telling John Soul. John was intensely jealous. He was not going to get to see this cinematic gala. His mother had neither the time nor the money to take him. Mr. Turner did not volunteer. I think he preferred the company of his trout.

I returned home to Auntie Florrie's and committed my second error. I told both of them how disappointed John was at the disclosure of the Watson's exciting invitation. They both immediately set upon me and said that I should ask the Watsons if they could take John with them. Now I was not yet at that stage in the evolution of my social consciousness that I had a firm grasp of the niceties of social etiquette. Indeed, like any small boy of ten, I was quite oblivious to the customs and mores of social interaction. On this occasion, however, my slowly budding instinct told me that what I was being instructed to do was a mistake. It would only end in tears. I knew the Watsons would be vitally disinterested in taking John Soul, the son of a garage proprietor, on this jaunt.

On the other hand, it would be inappropriate in the extreme to refuse to bend to the wishes of these two determined women. I demurred. They insisted. I wept. They said I had to approach the Watsons. I spent the whole argument in tears. I was embarrassed beyond my childish belief. It didn't occur to me to tell them to ask the Watsons themselves. Anyway, that would have been mutiny. I was too young to mutiny. I could have bluntly refused, but they were the adults in charge of my life. It would be many years before I ever mustered the courage to defy my parents outright. After close on an hour of relentless bullying, I gave in.

Of course, I put off this distasteful task. I wandered around the street, scuffing about and kicking stones. Aunt Florrie saw me loitering in the road and marched out of her house to accost me. Feet planted wide apart, one arm extended, finger pointing at the Watsons' house, she exhorted me to do my duty. She only lacked a chariot to look like Queen Boadicea urging her troops into battle. So I trudged over to the Watsons' and put the ugly proposition to them. Would they take John Soul as well? Mrs. Watson received this request with the reluctance I had expected. She suggested that if I wanted John Soul to come, perhaps my mother might be prepared to take us both. She did not think it appropriate to take John Soul. In any event, she churlishly aborted the whole expedition. I had been right. Asking this favour of the Watsons had been a bad idea.

I returned to Aunt Florrie's house, and (in tears) related to them the unhappy outcome of my disagreeable embassy. They tried in vain to console me. I had done the right thing. I was a brave boy. Mother would take John and me to see Tarzan of the Apes, as indeed she eventually did—after all, she now had no option. Auntie Florrie fished a sixpenny piece out of her battered, old black handbag and handed it to me with a torrent of sanctimonious sermonizing. To this day, I remember her bony hand extended, proffering the silver piece, grasped between skinny finger and skeletal thumb. I took the sixpence, because I had neither the wit nor the experience to think of refusing it as a matter of principle. The incident has remained lodged in my memory: The inception of the feeling of right verses wrong. I should have refused the after-the-fact bribe. I could have refused to go to the movie, but this would have deprived both John Soul and me of that pleasure. I could have stood fast and refused to approach the Watsons. This would have unleashed a torrent of invective and unwanted discipline. I was too young and too scared of these domineering women to take such a principled stand.

At the time, I thought my mother and my aunt were behaving quite unreasonably. Thinking back on it, I wonder what devastating harm it would have done the Watsons to have invited John to join us. I suspect they felt themselves a notch or three above the Souls in the social scale that was so important in England in those days—and, to a lesser extent, continues to be even now. Perhaps they expected that John, with his inadequate social graces and scruffy appearance, would somehow contaminate their precious son and embarrass them in public.

THE RECURRENT NIGHTMARE

Ever since the birth of psychiatry, in the closing years of the nineteenth century—conceived in the fertile academic imaginations of Sigmund Freud and Carl Gustav Jung—the psychiatric industry has attached significance to its patients' dreams. Before these inventive geniuses created psychoanalysis, dreams were the province of poets—a phenomenon encountered on a midsummer's night in the bosky glades of the Forest of Arden. Freud conjured up the value of dreams as a source of insight into the unconscious desires of his patients. Dreams, according to his theory, were symbolic. Freud's theories provoked squalls of criticism and controversy amongst those who professed to know about such things. He claimed that recurrent dreams are indicative of events that have created a lasting impression on the mind.

For me, it remains a mystery why, to this day, I am sometimes awakened by a dream in which I am entering an examination room, not having prepared adequately for the dreaded exam that awaits me—though it is an experience I remember all too well during my three years spent at university.

A variation on that theme is a dream I have, in which I am in court with an inadequately prepared brief. It must be admitted that it is only rarely that any counsel can honestly claim to be completely prepared for a case. It is an unfortunate fact that few cases can warrant the time and funds that ought to be expended if the absolute certainty of success is to be assured. You have to compromise and concentrate on the vital issue that marks the watershed between success and failure.

At the age of sixteen, having no idea what I wanted to do for a living, my father, anxious to see me off the payroll, cross-examined me on the subject. There were no aptitude tests in those days, and in any event, the old man seemed bent on sending me off to study law.

The School Certificate examination, taken at the age of sixteen, had won me a place in the faculty of law at University College London, because I passed it at the Matriculation level, to my surprise and to my various teachers astonishment, so I spent the last two years of high school studying history with enjoyment, but not much application, for my place in law school was already assured, regardless of the result of my exam at the end of high school.

It was my great fortune to spend three years at university in the middle of (what was then) the largest city in the world, with an unsurpassed cultural life. English theatre blossomed into life as its denizens were discharged from the armed forces. The city abounded with museums. The English movie industry was headed towards its golden age. The art galleries were treasure houses of paintings, sculptures, and frescoes, many pilfered over the centuries from their unresisting and rightful owners. My fellow students and I could, and did (with unremitting frequency) inhabit the London theatres at a cost of sixpence a seat. I played cricket and rugby until a marauding wing-forward dislocated my collarbone, necessitating a night in University College Hospital. London was then unstressed by the inundation of immigrants, uncluttered by the traffic jams in which drivers are now mired, and unsullied by the piles of odious garbage that lie uncollected at the street curbs. I usually rode a bicycle to college, and around town—a plain, sit-up-and-beg bicycle with no gears. I owned no padlock. I simply leaned the machine against a lamp post and went into lectures. It was always there when I came out.

Having been enrolled in a boys-only school, I was introduced to the magical novelty of female students, to the nurses at University College Hospital, and to entrancing damsels encountered at college hops. I fell in love on a weekly basis, and with a regularity that was not conducive to the dedicated study of law. I neglected academic work with carefree carelessness, to the dismay of those members of faculty who had the misfortune to have to tutor me.

In retrospect, my career as a student reminds me of the little quatrain penned by Edna St. Vincent Millay:

> "I burn my candle at both ends;
> It will not last the night;
> But ah, my foes, and oh, my friends—
> It gives a lovely light."

I always studied best under pressure. I found that if I left the main thrust of my efforts until the last weeks before the exams, that would ensure the requisite pressure to galvanize my concentration to the necessary fever pitch.

The university awarded degrees in three classes: firsts, upper and lower seconds, and thirds. It was very parsimonious with first class degrees. Only one was awarded in my year, and that to our only Nigerian student, Festus Adabesi Ajayi. Silent and uncommunicative, he took no part in college life. He was awarded a first in every subject in each of the three years. We all stood in awe of this aloof intellectual giant. He later became

Attorney General of Nigeria, and now at eighty-six years of age, is revered by the Nigerian legal community. Most of my friends gained second-class degrees. The college regularly failed forty per cent of the first year. After that, it seemed to lapse into a more indulgent marking system, and few of us failed after first year.

In my first year, I managed to nose past the finishing post with a third in each of the four subjects. Second year saw me achieve the same result. Third year saw me propelled into the real world with a third-class degree, but not just an ordinary third-class degree. I had achieved a third in every subject in every year—twelve thirds. I never dared to enquire, but suspect this may have been something of a record.

All this was partly the fault of a friend of my father's, who asked me if I intended to try for a first. When I told him I didn't think I was capable of getting a first, he had said, "Well then, get a third. Anything in between is a waste of time." In a sense, he was right, but he had no business telling this to an impressionable young man about to go to university. I later discovered that he had stolen this philosophy from Evelyn Waugh's Brideshead Revisited.

What remains a vivid recollection is the feeling, amounting almost to terror, that gripped me in the final few weeks approaching the exams. This annual trauma during my university years visits me still on odd occasions in my dreams. I am driven awake by the well-remembered sense of panic that I endured as a result of my charmed and misspent university career, too much enjoyed and too little dedicated to study.

Breakfast in Paddington Goods Yard

My brother, Peter, eleven years older than I, was discharged from the army shortly after the end of the war, and had embarked on a course of study in mechanical engineering. Our parents had moved to the country, leaving me, while still at school, installed in an apartment on the Finchley Road, which Father used when up in London on business. This was a daring step on their part, to leave a sixteen year old by himself while attending high school. I welcomed the solitude, out from under my parents' incessant directives. Peter's course involved some practical, on-the-job experience with British Rail, Western Region. This was that part of British Rail that had, until very recently, been the Great Western Railway, the grand dame of all British rail lines—brainchild of the eccentric genius Isambard Kingdom Brunel. Thus it was that, for a brief period of a few weeks, Peter came to live with me in the little apartment, in which I dwelt in the dust and squalor of a teenager's habitat. Before Peter moved in, I only ever cleaned it up in anticipation of a visit from Father, whose attitude toward teenage domestic chaos was unforgiving.

Peter went out each day to take part in the routine running of the railway. One day, the telephone woke us from our slumbers at about four o'clock in the morning. Peter answered it, for no acquaintance of mine would ever have called at that hour. I heard him grudgingly agree to what the caller was proposing. He rang off and struggled out of bed. Now fully awake, I enquired as to the cause of this indecently early call. He said there had been an accident in the marshaling yards outside Paddington Station, which was, of course, the London terminus of the old Great Western Railway. He had been asked to come down and help, and they wanted him to get down there right away. Since I was now wide awake, he suggested that I might like to go with him. I did not think I would be missed for half a day at school, so I got up and dressed hurriedly. We grabbed a bite to eat and clambered into Peter's old Austin for the short journey to Paddington.

It took some time for us to locate the accident. The Paddington goods yard, fanning out in a westerly direction from the great old glass-roofed railway station, seemed vast: an extensive array of rails, signals, water towers, signal boxes, cranes, platforms piled with goods, levers for hand operation of the points, and mountainous bins of coal to fuel the steam engines. On a variety of sidings stood a scattering of rolling stock with the occasional engine coupled to a train. There was not much activity. The mighty Western Region had not yet sprung to life, to haul its passengers down to the west country and carry early-morning, bleary-eyed and partially comatose commuters into the city. After a diligent search, we located the accident. It was not serious. A tank engine had missed a signal and become derailed by a set of points pointing, for the tank engine, in the wrong direction. The engine now stood on its six driving wheels, steaming and rumbling gently beside the track on which it was supposed to have been working. It had been pulling no load at the time, so it only remained for those in charge to manipulate the engine back onto its tracks. The rails, where the engine had left them, had been damaged by the unauthorized departure of the engine from the route laid down for it. Some of the railway ties (or "sleepers" as the English call them) had been badly cut up by the engine's steel wheels. Though the smallest engine in the railway's fleet, it still weighed some eighty or ninety tons and any accident at any speed, however slow, was bound to cause considerable damage. Tank engines are designed for shunting rolling stock around railway yards. Unlike long-haul steam engines, which keep their coal and water supplies in a separate tender, tank engines have a compartment behind the cab, where the coal is stored. The water supply is carried in rectangular tanks attached to each side of the boiler. Because of their limited coal and water carrying capacity, they are necessarily used for short-haul work. They have no bogies, just six driving wheels.

A breakdown crew was already in reluctant attendance—dawn was only just breaking. They had brought to the scene another tank engine, which had hauled a flat car with a crane on it, attached to which was a goods wagon full of tools and railway ties, to replace those destroyed by the errant wheels of the tank engine. A half a dozen railway personnel were standing around in desultory conversation, discussing how best to restore the engine to its track. It was not a scene of raging activity and I calculated that it might take all day before things in the goods yard were restored to normal operations. This was the era of what the public called the "British Workman". The union movement was at its apogee, wildcat strikes were a daily occurrence, and the economy was floundering under the weight of a workforce that was indifferent to the need to improve productivity. To some extent this was due to the fatigue produced by six years of war. The standard joke was to the effect that if the men did not have shovels they could lean on, then they should lean on each other.

The crew of the tank engine consisted of the engine driver and the fireman. The driver was a burly individual in grimy coveralls, sporting a few days growth of beard. The stoker, smaller and of wiry build, was garbed in identical and equally soiled coveralls. The accident was entirely the fault of the driver, who had missed the signal that (had he bothered to keep a lookout) would have warned him that the points were switched against him. He gave the appearance of being utterly indifferent to the accident, the damage it had wrought, and the fact that he was responsible for both.

He and the fireman were busy preparing their breakfast. They had taken the fireman's shovel and laid out a dozen rashers of bacon on its blade. This they inserted into the firebox until the driver deemed the bacon to be nearly cooked. Then they broke six eggs onto the shovel next to the bacon and flung the shells into the firebox. The driver thrust this improvised frying pan back into the firebox, kept an eye on it until the eggs were done, then retracted the shovel, whereupon both of them produced knives and forks and set to work devouring this feast. They had several slices of toast, which they must have cooked in a similar fashion before I noticed what they were up to. Of course, this was all perfectly hygienic as the temperature in the firebox, which can reach seven hundred degrees Fahrenheit, was quite sufficient to kill any bacteria. I fell into conversation with the foreman of the breakdown crew, who assured me that the residue of coal on the shovel added a spicy taste to this feast. "It saves you having to carry salt and pepper in the cab," he explained. He gave me the impression that this culinary performance was standard operating procedure for Western Region steam engine crews at breakfast time anywhere along the line.

HALF A PINT OF BITTER

It would be an exaggeration to describe my rugby playing career as undistinguished. While at high school, I made it into the third fifteen only once. The occasion was the temporary indisposition of one of the team's wing three quarters, which compelled the coach (my history teacher) to rummage around in the bottom of his barrel of spare players. Never chosen to play again, I suffered pangs of disappointment and mild humiliation. During my first year at law school, at University College London, I decided to re-establish my rugby career. I joined the University Wanderers—Wanderers, because they had no playing field of their own, but always played away games on other teams' fields.

My first and (as it turned out) only game for this team was a disaster. I held myself out to be a scrum half. Indeed, that was the position I had played most of the time at school, although I also played at wing three quarter. Wing three quarter requires a player fleet of foot. I fancied myself as a sprinter and thus qualified for this position at the distal end of the three quarter line. My claim to this qualification was based on the only time anybody ever timed me over a hundred yards. One school sports day, one of the masters used a stopwatch to time a hundred-yard sprint. He told me I had done the distance in eleven point four seconds. The world record, at that time was nine point six—established by Jessie Owens at the 1936 Olympics in Berlin, and, since he was black, snubbed by Adolf Hitler for his pains. I calculated that, had I been able to race against Owens, I would have finished eighteen yards behind him at the tape.

The day of my one match for the Wanderers, we were to play one of the teams from the London Welsh. As soon as I saw them trot out onto the field, I realized I had made a serious error. The members of their scrum looked as if they spent their working days hewing at the coal-face. They were huge. In those days, I stood five feet eight inches tall and weighed about a hundred and forty pounds. I was plainly outgunned. The entire Welsh team could not have looked more intimidating if they had been garbed in horned helmets, bearing Viking broadswords, and bent on pillage and murder.

It was wet and the pitch was muddy, making for a slippery ball. A loose maul resulted in the ball issuing forth from our side of the scrum. I pounced on it, looked for my fly half and promptly dropped it. Another scrum. This time I was tackled by the Welsh scrum half before I could speed the ball to the fly half. Though my height, he plainly weighed twice what I did, and to add to my serious disquiet, he resembled a villain in a Victorian melodrama. This time, a line out. The ball was knocked back and bounced towards me. Trying to grab it, I only succeeded in knocking it on. This resulted in a set scrum. Leather shod feet squirted it out from the back of the scrum. I retrieved it and succeeded in flinging a nice fast pass, which flew several feet behind my fly half. To this day I remember his rebuke, a surprisingly mild one in the circumstances: "Scrum half, do please try to get the ball out to me." The game progressed and my vivid recollection is that I failed, ever, to land a pass into the outstretched, pleading hands of the fly half.

It was surely a relief to him when I was eventually escorted off the field with a dislocated collarbone. Ten or fifteen minutes into the game, a loose scrum resulted in my bouncing the ball along the ground in the vague direction of my team's three quarter line. As the ball left my arms, the Welsh blind side wing forward, a man of truly Viking proportions, landed on me, completely winding me. When I regained my breath, still lying on the ground, I tried to get up and immediately realized that something was wrong. My left arm was no longer functional and I had an ugly pain in my throat. I crawled about the ground on three limbs in small circles attempting to assess the situation. The referee, realizing I was injured, blew his whistle. Players from both teams gathered round, mine with solicitous faces and comments, the Welsh, silent and vaguely contemptuous. Two players got me up and led me to the pavilion, where I was lain down on a sofa and given a glass of water. There wasn't anyone immediately available to take me to hospital and I had to wait till the end of the game before I could be evacuated. It is odd that in moments of crisis, one tends to remember little incidents that have little connection to the main events. I remember the team standing gazing at me, sitting in misery, and the fly half, one of my helpful dressers, asking them. "Anyone want to play scrum half next week?" There was laughter. I did not join in.

The fly half drove me to University College Hospital, which was just across Gower Street from my college. I was processed through the emergency department and examined by a surgeon—quaintly referred to in England as a "consultant" and addressed as Mister So-and-so, never as doctor. He announced that I had, courtesy of the Welsh wing forward, dislocated my left collarbone, which was sticking into my throat—to my considerable discomfort.

I was parked on a bed with curtains drawn around it. After a brief delay, the surgeon returned and drew back the curtains to reveal an array of medical students lined up to inspect my injury. Nobody had told me to expect this, least of all asked my permission. I stared at the students miserably, and endured their inspection, as if I were a freak in a travelling circus.

A nurse finally drew the curtain on my freak show and I was given a general anaesthetic. When I awoke, my collar bone was back in its rightful position. I was put to bed and given a sedative to help me sleep. My arm was now in a sling with a soft brace holding my shoulder back and my collarbone out of my throat.

In the morning, a kindly nurse told me that I would be shortly released into the care of my father, who had been phoned to come and repossess me. All the nurses were garbed alike: blue dresses, sparkling white pinafores, and the old fashioned, white starched, Florence Nightingale bonnets. This garb conveyed an air of professional efficiency, cleanliness, and incontestable authority.

Meanwhile I was to be served breakfast. Now hospital food in English hospitals is not the lightly boiled cardboard that is the current fare in Canadian hospitals—designed, I have always thought, to encourage the patient's earliest possible agreement to be discharged. I was offered a choice: eggs and bacon, porridge, toast, and marmalade, or kedgeree. Coffee came with everything. I chose bacon and fried eggs. Quite soon, the nurse strode down the aisle between the beds, bearing a tray laden with my breakfast. She helped me into a sitting position and balanced the tray on my lap. There it all was, my bacon and eggs, concealed by an aluminium cover to keep them warm, a plate with toast and a small pot of marmalade, and to the right, a cup of steaming coffee. However, on the left stood a small glass tankard. It was a gill, just as one would find in the college pub. It was filled with a dark brown liquid. At first I thought it was some potion to promote regularity. I pointed at it with an enquiring raise of an eyebrow. I asked the nurse what it was. She exhibited some surprise and said, "Well, it's a half a pint of bitter. We always serve it on the men's wards. Don't you want it?" "Oh, yes. Yes, of course," I responded, though I wasn't sure I really needed it for breakfast. I was hungry, not having consumed anything since the referee had blown his injured player whistle the afternoon before. So I wolfed down the bacon and eggs, and washed it down with the half pint of Burton's best Yorkshire bitter.

As I drained the last drop of my breakfast beer, I wondered what they served in the women's wards. Sherry? Not for breakfast, surely. I suspected that they were confined to tea. Though they had won the right to vote, I didn't think the suffragette movement would have qualified women for a beer for breakfast in a London hospital. Not so much a matter of constitutional right as one of etiquette—like the quaint disapproval of women smoking in public.

How I Celebrated My Tenth Birthday

It was April 11, 1941. At three in the morning, we had all been roused from sleep by the wailing sirens—an air raid warning. We normally didn't get up at such a summons. You noted the sirens, turned over, and went back to sleep—usually to be roused again by the all clear.

This time we did get up just a short span after the ominous sound of the sirens had faded into silence. Perhaps five minutes had passed when the sound of anti-aircraft fire could be heard, in the distance at first, and then growing closer until the guns were firing all round us. Above the din could be heard the sound I had grown used to during night-time air raids: the unique and threatening drone of a squadron of Heinkels. No other aircraft made the same noise. It was impossible to mistake it. They always flew in squadrons of about two dozen aircraft, herded together for protection against the marauding night fighters. The Heinkels were bombing Croyden Aerodrome, one of three aerodromes that surrounded us, and each of which was home to several squadrons of Hurricanes and Spitfires.

But now we were being attacked by the Luftwaffe. These lumbering twin-engined bombers bringing death and devastation in their train. Night after night they came, relentless, ruthless, and pitiless. The onslaught was designed more to break our morale than to achieve any damage of strategic value. Tonight, however, they had a specific target in mind.

Wave after wave of Heinkels droned overhead. We could hear the explosions as they unloaded their bombs around the aerodrome. We peered out of the window. A dozen searchlights probed the sky. Suddenly one picked up a Heinkel. Instantly, four or five more searchlights focused on the doomed craft. The Heinkel tried to break free of the lights, diving, turning, and weaving—all in vain. It was trapped in the shafts of light, like a blowfly caught in a spider's web. The anti-aircraft guns flung a barrage of shells at it. Eventually it turned, one wing severed from its body. It spiralled down so fast that the lights could not keep it in their sites. We saw the explosion as it struck the ground. A great bonfire of orange and yellow flames billowing thousands of feet into the sky as its fuel tanks exploded. It was not possible for any of the crew to have survived. We worried more about how many houses it had demolished as it came to its fiery end. In truth, we didn't give a fig for the poor devils in the Heinkel. They were trying to kill us and that fiery death was (we felt) only what they deserved. We did feel sorrow for the civilians inevitably killed by the crash. It was a certainty that somebody would have suffered. The area was densely populated and the aircraft must have hit some habitation.

"Come away from the window, David. If there's an explosion the glass will cut you to bits." My father was, of course, right. But I was annoyed at being denied the thrill of watching the raid. My childish mind gave no thought to the danger, in the excitement of watching this spectacular fireworks display.

Then we heard it. One lone Heinkel, droning home and approaching nearer, overhead. The odd thing was that it was not coming from the direction of the aerodrome. "Perhaps he's got lost. I hope he doesn't have any bombs left." Mother was exhibiting some anxiety, unusual for her, as she was normally indifferent to danger from an air raid—limiting herself to imprecations against the Hun. The whine of a stick of bombs caused the three of us to crouch down in the hallway. There was a series of almighty explosions, one second apart and each getting closer. Six in all. We counted as the explosions grew louder, each closer than the last. The final one landed at the bottom of our garden, wracking the big garden shed that I used as a play room. The shed had surely served to protect the house from worse damage.

All the windows at the back of the house were blown in, shredding my mother's curtains. Long slivers of cloth flapped in the breeze. There was some structural damage, discovered a few days later, when we were able to inspect the little house in the peace and tranquillity of a spring day.

"Grace," said my father, as we picked ourselves up off the hall floor, "Grace, do you realize what time it is?"

"Well, it's about three o'clock, isn't it?"

"Yes, well it's April the 11th. David was born ten years ago this very minute."

SCARRED

The jagged piece of shrapnel tore through the canvass of his tent and buried itself beneath his shoulder blade, entering his back just between the spine and the edge of the scapular. Another inch to the right and he would have been paralysed for life. Because the missile was red hot when it began its flight from its exploding shell, it carried no bacteria to penetrate the wound. And since he was lying on his camp cot, asleep behind the front line, he didn't have to contend with the bacteria infested mud that swilled about the floor of all the trenches.

The artillery barrages had destroyed the drainage systems that the French and Belgian farmers had so skillfully woven into the flat farmland during centuries of husbandry. Thus, with the drainage system ruined, rainwater accumulated where it fell, instead of flowing through the ditches into the rivers and thence out to the North Sea. It seeped relentlessly into the trenches that the two armies dug. The water turned to mud, liberally spiced with feces, blood, rat shit, and bits and pieces of human remains. It was a toxic stew. If a combatant did not die of his wounds, the chances were that blood poisoning would finish him off. Just standing in the foot of mud and slime that slopped about every trench caused a disorder the troops called "trench foot", which cost many a soldier his lower limbs if left untreated. Dysentery was a common ailment and lice were constant companions. Every soldier was accompanied by his quota of lice. No count was kept of how many died of disease, or blood poisoning after being wounded. The statistics simply listed you as killed, or missing in action.

He crawled out of his tent and stumbled to a field dressing station, where they bandaged him up to stop the bleeding, and shipped him back to a field hospital. Three days later he found himself in an old Victorian edifice in Marylebone High Street, London, converted (for the duration of the war) into a hospital.

The surgeon announced gruffly that the shrapnel had lodged hard up against the underside of his shoulder blade, right in the middle of it.

"Hard to get at. We'll have to burrow in from your spine until we find it. There's no important organ close to it, just the back of your left lung. It'll tear a lot of tissue and muscle, but there should be no serious damage."

"What if we just left it there and let it mend?"

"Oh, can't do that, old boy. Got to get it out, though nothing would happen if we left it. Just restrict your shoulder movement a bit. Nurse'll come and prepare you in fifteen minutes".

In five minutes he was dressed. In another three, he had wrestled his limp left arm into the impressive sling that had been festooned over his shoulder in France. Before the nurse reached his room, he had fled out of the front door of the hospital, hailed a cab, and retreated to his parents' modest apartment above a coal merchant's shop, overlooking Twickenham Green.

Eight weeks later, he married my mother at All Saints Church, Twickenham. After a two week honeymoon, he returned to his regiment, then stationed outside Ypres.

He had been felled by the little piece of shrapnel during the first week of the Battle of Passchendaele, and it was in its last throes when he rejoined the Monmouthshire Regiment. In just that one battle, 244,877 British and some 400,000 Germans had been killed. They had gained a few miles of muddy, battle-scarred farmland, lost it, regained some, and then ended the battle in much the same place as it started.

Some few years ago, Gill and I visited Flanders to prowl around the country where both our fathers had fought. In Ypres, on the road leading to the Menin Gate, there is a shop run by a couple of old British ex-service men. They will sell you souvenirs, mostly old shell casings, and will organize tours for you. They have a plentiful supply of books, including many regimental histories. I asked if they had a history of my father's old regiment. They didn't, but looked on the internet for me for information. To my astonishment, they said that the Monmouthshire Regiment had been a pioneer regiment. These were the men who dug the trenches and repaired them after they had been damaged by shellfire—often themselves under shellfire. They also dug the tunnels under the enemy lines, filled them with explosives, which they detonated just before an attack—the notorious mines. This made sense, because the regiment was largely composed of Welsh coal miners, used to working underground in cramped, wet, airless, and dangerous conditions.

My mother once told me that, after their honeymoon, when she bade him goodbye at Waterloo Station, she had no idea if she would ever see him again. The life expectancy of an infantry lieutenant at the front was then roughly six weeks.

They were re-united in late 1918. But she said that he was never the same man. "His nerves were shot. They called it shell shock," she said. It was the result of the appalling noise of week after week of incessant artillery fire, of leading a patrol at night crawling through the mire, skirting the mud-filled shell holes in which you would drown if you fell in:, of trying to avoid the barbed wire that could enmesh you in its grasp, of desperately keeping quiet lest the sound you made attracted a burst of machine-gun fire, of the agony of striving to bring back a wounded man without making a noise.

Shell shock, or battle fatigue, afflicted any man who served for any length of time in the front line. It is now called post-traumatic stress disorder and treated with sympathy and understanding. Then it was regarded as a weakness unbecoming a British soldier. A stiff upper lip was what was called for. Many soldiers were to be found wandering around, disoriented and confused. Senior officers felt strongly that they were malingering, when in fact they were suffering a psychiatric injury. These poor souls were accused of cowardice, or worse, desertion. No less than 306 British soldiers were shot for desertion during the First World War, when they should have been hospitalized.

My father emerged from the war a scarred man—edgy, with heavily veiled insecurities. By the time I arrived, he had largely recovered, but it was difficult to get him to talk about his wartime experience. He always changed the subject. Once, my mother persuaded him to take us to the old German movie, *All Quiet on the Western Front*. It was a mistake. The movie had a number of scenes that depicted life at the front with graphic reality. Twenty minutes into the movie, there is a scene depicting a platoon of British soldiers with fixed bayonets pouring over the top of a German trench and engaging the Germans in hand to hand combat. My Father stood up. "I'm sorry. I can't stand this," he said, and walked out of the cinema.

UNCLE GEORGE'S WAR

My Uncle George was my mother's younger half brother. He had qualified as a chartered accountant, and when I knew him, he was the comptroller of the Milk Marketing Board. He never married, though he went through a string of mistresses—all actresses or connected in some way to the theatre. These liaisons came naturally to him, as both his parents had been on the stage. I met some of them, usually at my grandmother's house, which was constantly populated by theatre people, down to the last one, charming, captivating, insincere libertines.

War broke out, and George joined up early in 1940. Because of his qualifications, he was drafted into the Royal Army Service Corps—the inglorious non-combatant section of the army that was responsible for supplying the rest of the forces with ammunition, spare parts, clothing, and (most important and often dangerously urgent) food. The fighting arms had to be supplied with a hot meal, an essential for the maintenance of morale. The Emperor Napoleon was famously eloquent on the subject of feeding armies in the field. In times of active warfare, the supply of these essentials frequently propelled the Service Corps into the combat zone, delivering supplies with uncomfortable frequency under shellfire—their trucks a common target for marauding enemy aircraft.

On April 15, 1945, George found himself in command of a group of trucks that was following hard on the heels of the 11th Armoured Corps in South Saxony. They were within a half a mile of the fighting, though the Germans were retreating fast. George, driving his jeep ahead of his convoy, suddenly found himself in the middle of a group of stationary Churchill tanks, whose crews had disembarked and were milling about the gated entrance to a compound surrounded by a sturdy barbed-wire fence. Ominously, there were wooden watchtowers set at intervals along the fence. George parked his jeep and watched as the tank crews broke down the gate. Inside he could see people, some dressed in black and white striped pyjama-like uniforms. He followed the soldiers into the compound. The ground was strewn with dead bodies. Emaciated men and women were wandering about aimlessly, ill and starving.

A strange noise slowly crept into George's consciousness. It was like the sound that a flock of disturbed seabirds might make. As he searched around to find the source of this strange noise, George finally realized that it was the sound of the more able prisoners valiantly attempting to raise a cheer—an effort well beyond the capacity of most of them. A British officer was trying to get a message back to the base, to summon medical supplies and food to be brought up as fast as possible. George asked a soldier what this place was. He was told that it was a concentration camp—Bergan Belsen.

The British soldiers were rounding up and disarming those of the guards who had not already fled. They captured the commandant, SS Hauptsturmfuhrer Josef Kramer, who was later convicted of murder. He was executed along with a half dozen of the more senior SS officers in command of the camp.

The camp was originally designed as a prisoner of war camp, but later adapted as a concentration camp to hold Jews, Gypsies, homosexuals, some Russian prisoners, anti-Nazi Christians, and Italian soldiers—deserters from their fascist army. In the spring of 1945, 8,000 women, transferred from Auschwitz ahead of the advancing Russians, were crammed into the camp and forced to work in local factories as slave labour. The camp was originally built to hold 10,000 inmates. When the British liberated it, the population had swelled to over 60,000 souls, living in misery, starved, beset by typhus, tuberculosis, typhoid fever, and (common to every inmate) dysentery. 50,00 people had died in the camp by the time the British stumbled on it in their advance into Germany. Another 13,000 died after the liberation, too weak to be saved. Anne Frank had died there the previous autumn, a victim of the ever-rampant typhus.

George knew none of this as he helped separate the living from the corpses that were scattered about the ground separating the prison huts.

George turned and watched the tank crews disarm and line up, none too gently, a group of two dozen guards. Suddenly, one of the inmates, who must have been a recent arrival, for he was in reasonably good condition, rushed forward and began beating up one of the guards. He was instantly joined by a screaming mob of infuriated prisoners. They outnumbered the guards by a factor of five or six to one. It was not long before all of the guards were dead. The British troops were so upset and so angry at what they had found that they simply stood by and let the inmates go to it, until finally the SS were all dead, down to the very last guard.

Travels Around
the Practice of Law

My Association with John Diefenbaker

I had not long been editor of the *Advocate* when a copy of it was returned, undelivered by the post office. John Diefenbaker received the *Advocate* because he was a member of the BC bar. He had joined it in 1951. He had built a considerable reputation as a criminal defence counsel on the prairies, and had been retained to defend a CNR telegraph operator against a charge of manslaughter arising from the head-on collision of a troop train, which killed twenty-one soldiers and train crew. The telegraphist had incorrectly relayed a message from Kamloops to Red Path, causing the accident. Since the blunder had occurred in BC, that was the province in which the trial would take place. Diefenbaker joined the BC bar in order to be able to defend the accused.

Diefenbaker won the leadership of the Conservative Party in December of 1956. Early in 1957, he was retained to defend one Donald Cathro, charged with a murder that had taken place in the course of the robbery of a corner-store grocery—the Macdonald Market—on Macdonald Street in Vancouver. In the course of the robbery, conducted by Cathro and three others, the proprietor, Ah Wing, was killed.

The truth is that Diefenbaker was facing a federal election, expected in 1957. He seized any opportunity to promote himself and his party in any province. This murder trial, which had attracted a great deal of publicity, presented Diefenbaker with an ideal opportunity to parade his talents before the BC electorate.

The trial came on for hearing before Mr. Justice Clyne and a jury. This was a judge who harboured no doubts about his judicial ability, and ran his courtroom with a firm hand—some would say an iron fist—but not on this occasion. I walked up to the court house on the second day of the trial, out of curiosity, to see what was going on. I slipped into the courtroom to find the prosecution presenting its case. Diefenbaker was cross-examining the crown witnesses, which he did in his domineering, jowl-shaking baritone. But he was not content with just holding the stage during cross-examination. Even when it was not his turn to speak, he would be on his

59

feet, either objecting to something or agreeing to some point, or simply interjecting for the sake of attracting attention to himself.

All the while, he managed to convey a very specific and overwhelming impression: he was there, having toiled all the way from Prince Albert, Saskatchewan, to defend this poor, innocent man who had been unjustly accused of this horrible crime, which he absolutely had not committed, and it was his task to make sure that justice would be done in this case. His body language and his voice bristled with this unspoken message, aimed directly at the jury.

There was nothing the judge could do to restrain this torrent of words. Diefenbaker never trespassed beyond the boundaries of propriety. Everything he did and said was perfectly proper. He was polite to prosecuting counsel and courteous to the judge. On the occasions when the judge did try to shut Diefenbaker down, he found himself engaged in a lengthy dialogue with Diefenbaker, who would always agree with what the judge was saying and then launch into a rambling dissertation on the subject at hand. He would not stop talking. I did not go to hear Diefenbaker's closing address to the jury, but those who did said that, while addressing the jury, he succeeded in mesmerizing them. He tried, unsuccessfully as it turned out, to place the blame for the death on one of the other robbers. He painted a scene in which Cathro had tried to intervene, to separate Ah Wing from his attacker. In the ensuing struggle, Ah Wing was supposed to have fallen with Cathro on top of him, thus injuring the unfortunate shopkeeper and causing his death. Diefenbaker addressed the jury:

"And now gentlemen of the jury, I shall show you how it happened." With this, he threw himself on the floor in front of the jury box and almost under the counsel table, writhing about in demonstration of the struggle in the store. He had disappeared from the view of the judge, who (peering down) said, "Mr. Diefenbaker, if you will come out from underneath the table, I will be able to follow your argument more clearly."

After the trial, Diefenbaker spent a few days electioneering in Vancouver. He dropped in on John Taylor, the son of hockey great Fred (Cyclone) Taylor, who was running for the Conservatives in the Vancouver-Burrard riding. Diefenbaker went round to visit Taylor in his constituency office, and spied footsteps painted on the sidewalk, leading to the office, which had a sign on the door: "FOLLOW JOHN". The John the elector were being exhorted to follow was, of course, John Taylor. Diefenbaker seized on the slogan, and turned it into a country-wide advertisement for himself, with footsteps all over the country, accompanied by the jingle "Follow John". Diefenbaker won that election, but only managed to achieve a minority government. The following year, he succeeded in establishing a sizable majority. He remained the leader until his government was defeated in 1963. He was replaced as leader by Robert Stanfield, but remained a Member of Parliament.

The *Advocate* that the post office returned was addressed to "The Right Honourable John G. Diefenbaker, PC, QC, MP." And the address was that of his law office in Prince Albert, Saskatchewan. Stamped in large letters across the address were the words "NOT KNOWN".

I found this odd, if not actually offensive, and wondered what cretin in the post office could possibly have had so little imagination as not to realize that the magazine was addressed to him who had, until just recently, been the prime minister of Canada. I sent the magazine, with its offending legend stamped on it, to Diefenbaker at the House of Commons, with a little note to explain what had happened, and suggesting that he take the matter up with the postmaster general. He replied a week later, telling me that he had raised the issue in the House of Commons, and had had some fun with the postmaster general.

The old man had recently been on a trip to Russia and I thought that readers of the *Advocate* might be interested in an article from him about what he encountered in the Soviet Union. So I responded to his letter and suggested that he write such an article. By return of mail, I received a courteous reply from him. He did not say that he would actually put pen to paper, nor did he say that he would not. He scribbled on for a page without actually saying anything. It was what I believe used to be called "the evasion courteous". The article was not forthcoming, and I put the matter aside.

Then one day I was sitting in my office, minding my own business, when the phone rang. I answered it and someone speaking with the unmistakeable voice of John Diefenbaker introduced himself. I drew breath and prepared to remind him of my request for the article about the Soviet Union. I never got the chance. He started in on some diatribe about what had been happening in the House of Commons and how "they" had committed some terrible act that he clearly felt was part of a conspiracy that was intended to create difficulties for him. I never found out who "they" were, though he mentioned them several times in the course of our conversation. I say "conversation," but that is to clothe it with a sense of our having had a dialogue, which was not the case. We were on the phone for about ten minutes, during which I think I was able to talk for somewhere around fifteen seconds. The rest of the time, all nine minutes and forty-five seconds or so, was taken up by Diefenbaker talking at me in his deep, sermonizing tones. It was not possible to interrupt to get a word in edgewise. He simply would not listen and went on talking. It was a conversation much in the nature of an evangelical diatribe.

The reason that he called was because he had been invited to give the after-dinner speech at the annual dinner of the Vancouver Bar Association. He had just arrived in Vancouver and had taken the opportunity to phone me. The late David Vickers was then the President of the Vancouver Bar Association and he went to the airport to pick Diefenbaker up and take him to his hotel. When they reached the hotel, and Diefenbaker had booked in,

David accompanied him up to his room. It was fairly late in the evening. David was tired and wanted to go home. He expected that Diefenbaker would be tired as well. He watched as Diefenbaker took off his shoes and lay down on the bed. David was about to wish him goodnight, when the old man started talking. David said that he could not get away. Diefenbaker lay on the bed and talked for two hours. He simply would not stop talking. David was eventually able to seize an opportunity to terminate the conversation, wish him goodnight, and thankfully leave for home.

My daughter Kate is a consulting psychologist, and many years later, I asked her about Diefenbaker's apparent inability to stop talking, and his disinterest in listening to anything anybody else had to say. She diagnosed him as having a narcissistic personality disorder.

I looked this up in one of my sons' high-school psychology books. It is defined as "Self-love, extreme arrogance, disregard for social convention, and the rights of others, supreme confidence, and selfish exploitation of others." This definition does not fit Diefenbaker at all corners, and there were overtones of paranoia about the man, but I thought it came pretty close to the character I had experienced in that memorable, one-sided telephone conversation.

Jayne Mansfield Takes a View

Nick Mussallem had been called to the bar at the beginning of World War II, but had immediately joined the armed forces. After the war, he resumed practice in Vancouver and steadily built up a busy criminal defence practice. Nick was good at what he did, but organization was not his long suit. He never replied to correspondence and only sometimes answered telephone calls. A written submission to the Court of Appeal would tax his intellectual capacity to breaking point. Nick was an Arab. His father had emigrated from the Lebanon at the turn of the century and settled in Prince Rupert. His ten children spread themselves throughout the Fraser Valley, all becoming successful merchants and farmers, like their Phoenician ancestors. Nick was the exception. After a long career as a criminal defence counsel, he was appointed to the Provincial Court Bench.

Nick had an impish sense of humour. To have Nick as a member of the audience, if you were making a speech, was to endure the sharp end of Nick's barbs, for he could derail any speaker not adept at dealing with hecklers. Nick was popular with his colleagues, even though it was an exasperating experience to have to deal with any lawsuit with Nick on the other side. It must have been his own recognition of his propensity for disorganization that impelled him to criminal defence work, which requires a minimum of attention to paperwork. He did not seem to have any kind of filing system. I once went to his office because I could not get a response to letters I had written him about a civil suit in which we were engaged. Shown into his office, I found him sitting behind a huge old oak desk, cluttered with files, books, and empty teacups. Two bookends stood, one at each edge of the desk. Between the bookends was jammed a collection of letters, some still in their envelopes, files, and what looked like pleadings.

I gently chided Nick for not answering my letters. He looked surprised. "When did you write me?" he enquired, eyebrows raised. I gave him a date. "Ah," he said and raised a fist with one finger extended. He waived the finger over the line up of bookended papers. "Mid-February, you say?" The finger descended and selected a piece of paper. Not the right date. The moving finger parted a few more papers until it lit upon my letter. "There," he beamed, "my filing system is by date, you see."

Puzzled, I said, "Nick, what do you do when you run out of room between these bookends. Do you move them to the credenza?"

"Oh no, I just throw away the oldest, those at the right end there."

Sometime in the early 1960's Jayne Mansfield took a swing through town. Some local lawyer of her acquaintance decided that it would interest her to be shown around the Provincial Court, which in those days was housed in the same building as the Vancouver Police Department, in the 200 block on Main Street. The more-likely purpose for this strange expedition was the self-promotion of this lawyer's standing amongst his professional colleagues. It was not known how he had come to know her. It may have been a connection with her father, who had been a successful attorney-at-law in Phillipsburg, New Jersey, though since he had died when she was three years old, this seemed unlikely.

Jayne Mansfield had studied acting at UCLA, among other drama institutions, and burst upon the Hollywood scene in the 1950s. She won several beauty contests, the most notable being "Miss Magnesium Lamp" in Tucson. Her reputation as a sex kitten earned her roles in a number of grade B movies. She did land the role of the cigarette girl in *Pete Kelly's Blues* and a major part in *Will Success Spoil Rock Hunter?*, but the qualities that made her memorable were her figure, an astonishing 39-23-36, and her platinum blond hair, not its original colour. She was killed in a motor vehicle accident in 1967. During her lifetime, she gained a reputation as the poor man's Marilyn Monroe. She was once heard to let drop the proposition that, "Dramatic art is knowing how to fill a sweater."

Her lawyer acquaintance drove her down to the Main Street courts shortly after ten in the morning—the busiest time of day for the Provincial Courts. He ushered her into courtroom 101, where all the first appearances were dealt with before the trials began in earnest. News of her presence had run around the building like a wind-driven brush fire. The courtroom filled up within three minutes of her entering it. Court staff, secretaries, police, and a sizable contingent of lawyers rapidly assembled to gawk at this thespian voluptuary. Her learned friend introduced her to the presiding judge, who seemed pleased to be presented with something more exciting than the usual population of the previous night's drunk tank—the depressing array of scruffy ladies of the night, and the evening's haul of impaired drivers, burglars, and pan handlers.

The judge greeted her with a brief, if distantly polite, little speech. He knew he was facing a busy morning and would not be able to complete the routine business of the court if he allowed this distraction to consume much more valuable time. To his evident irritation, a lawyer rose and made an over-lengthy speech of welcome to the actress, who beamed with pleasure. This provoked another lawyer to rise to the occasion with some pretty platitudes about the legal profession being closely allied to the stage. Yet a third lawyer, unable to resist his moment in the sun, spoke about the courtroom being filled with unaccustomed beauty and grace. In all, eight lawyers, police, court clerks, and one sheriff weighed in with banalities about Jayne Mansfield's acting, beauty, and stage presence.

At the back of the courtroom stood Nick Mussallem, shepherding a client charged with bank robbery. His case was scheduled to be heard at eleven. It was now a quarter past that hour, and the morning adjournments and date fixings had not even started. If Mussallem's case could not be concluded by the lunch break, he was heading into trouble, for he had a break and enter to defend, commencing immediately after lunch in another courtroom.

So there was Nick with his bank robber, fuming at the back of the courtroom, while everyone else fawned on the sex kitten. Nick elbowed his way to the front of the crowd, turned his head, and took a look at the cause of all this delay and fuss. He observed Jayne Mansfield, sitting beside where he stood, wearing a short skirt that revealed a pair of Dresden China legs, and he noticed the Niagara of golden curls that cascaded about her shoulders. One high-heeled shoe was dangling from her extended toes. She smiled up at him. The judge looked at Nick and said, "Yes, Mr. Mussallem? Do you also have something you wish to say?"

"Your Honour," said Nick, in a voice that could be heard all over the crowded room, "It's just that, never before have I had the honour of appearing before such an august body."

EDDIE SILVER

Eddie Silver was one of Vancouver's down and outs. He inhabited a one-room hovel in the basement of a grubby little house on the edge of Chinatown. Eddie was unusual for an inhabitant of the east side in that he was not a drug addict. As a result, his need for an income was relatively small, and he was able to eke out a subsistence on the welfare payments he received, together with the small stipend he generated by petty theft. His age was indeterminate, but he gave the appearance of being around sixty or so. A small inoffensive little man, he always wore a soiled beige raincoat, buttoned up to his neck. I never saw him without it. I suspect that he owned few other clothes and used the raincoat to cover his otherwise inadequate wardrobe. The only other clothing that was visible was the bottom of a pair of frayed jeans, and the sneakers that he must have bought from the local Goodwill store and were seriously in need of replacement. In my few conversations with him, I was unable to determine if he had ever been employed. He was not forthcoming about his background and history, and I wrote him off as one of the city's destitute deadbeats.

Eddie had been in the habit of supplementing his welfare payments by small time shoplifting, mostly of food for his own consumption. When he had been caught at this game once or twice, he decided to give it up in favour of a scheme he had thought up while watching someone using a public pay phone. He noticed that if the callers did not get through to the intended receiver, they would hang up, and then collect the coins used to make the call from the little chute that returned the change to the caller. In those days, it cost a dime to make a call from a public pay phone. Eddie armed himself with a dime, inserted it into the appropriate slot in the call box, dialled a deliberately wrong number, rang off and watched as his dime clattered down the chute into the receptacle designed to receive it. Then he took a piece of crumpled up newspaper and inserted it up the chute, just far enough so that he could still reach it and pull it out. He inserted his dime once again, dialled his wrong number, hung up and listened for the dime to come to rest in the chute, imprisoned by the plug of newspaper.

He retrieved the plug of paper and the dime fell out, as he expected, into the receptacle. Bingo. His scheme was working.

Over the next few days, he conducted a survey of the pay phones located around the intersection of Main and Hastings Streets—the centre of activity for the drug trade, streetwalkers, panhandlers, and the usual run of east side misfits. He carefully chose those pay phones that were close to a doorway where he could secrete himself to watch activity at the phone, and near enough that he could reach the phone quickly after a caller had hung up after an unanswered call. Retrieving a discarded newspaper from a garbage can, he tore off a strip, rolled it up, and carefully stuffed it up the coin return chute. He retreated to his doorway and waited. Several people used the phone, but to his irritation they all seemed to get through to their intended receivers. Then, finally, a burly man, who looked like a logger, hung up without speaking to anyone. The logger waited for his dime to be returned to him. Nothing happened so he banged his fist on the phone box to try to dislodge the dime. No dime. The logger stuck his finger up the chute, must have felt the paper bung and wiggled around until he dislodged it and recovered his dime. With a sour look, he pocketed the coin and went on his way.

Eddie realized that he would have to push the paper plug further up the chute. So he fashioned a small hook on the end of a shortened chopstick, returned to the phone and pushed his plug up the chute, just out of reach of prying fingers. After a half an hour's wait he hit pay dirt. A caller who did not get through couldn't retrieve the dime with the finger-poking exercise, and left after banging on the phone box. Eddie pulled the paper plug down with his chopstick and pocketed the dime.

His scheme was working, but he realized that the adjacent doorway routine was far too time consuming. He often had to wait over an hour for a caller to hang up on an unanswered call. He eventually realized that he did not need to watch each phone all the time. He made up a half a dozen paper plugs, stuffed them into a half a dozen phone chutes around the neighbourhood in the early morning, and then returned in the evening to collect his contraband dimes. He discovered that, this way, he could sometimes collect as many as dozen dimes from just one phone box in a day. A day's haul would regularly amount to nearly ten dollars. He was in business.

But Eddie got too greedy. He extended his operations to a couple of dozen phone boxes for several blocks east and west of Main Street, and north and south of Hastings—stuffing the chutes in the morning and collecting his pay packet in the evenings. After a month or two, somebody must have complained to the BC Telephone Company, for one day, as he was inserting his chopstick into a chute, a heavy hand descended on his shoulder. The arm was clothed in the dark blue of a Vancouver police officer, who was accompanied by a representative of the phone company. Eddie was booked for theft under fifty dollars, and released on his own recognizance. Legal aid got in touch with me, and asked me to do what I could for Eddie.

With some difficulty, I got Eddie to come to my office. He was evidently intimidated by the surroundings, but after a little gentle persuasion, I calmed him down enough to extract his story from him. This was not an easy task, as he was in a state of minor terror and spent much of the time in my office on the verge of tears. He had never actually been jailed for any of his previous misdemeanours. I decided that I would raise the defence that the Crown could not prove that the dimes were owned by anyone. They certainly were not the property of the phone company, as they were being returned to the callers. The court set a date for his trial, and on the appointed day, I turned up to defend him. The phone company representative gave evidence that they had received a report about the malfunctioning of the phone boxes and had discovered the paper plugs. Carefully replacing the plugs they had kept watch and observed Eddie, in the morning pushing the paper into the chutes and in the evening collecting his winnings. Enlisting the aid of the police, they had Eddie arrested and charged.

I chose not to call Eddie to testify in his own defence. He was, in any case, far too nervous to say anything that would be of the slightest use. The evidence against him was irrefutable. I only asked a couple of questions in cross-examination to try to establish that Eddie was no threat to anyone and a very minor player in the downtown crime scene. The magistrate, as these functionaries were called in those days, was Gordon Scott, an experienced judge—veteran of the First World War trenches, and sometime city prosecutor. Scott treated this case as a mildly amusing variation from his usual diet of drug addicts, housebreakers, drunken drivers, and prostitutes. He dismissed my lame defence and convicted Eddie. Then he remanded him in custody for sentencing the next day. I put up a plea that Eddie be released from custody until the next morning. "No," said Scott, "I have a reason to keep him in custody overnight." I duly appeared in court the following morning. Eddie was brought up from the holding cells below and joined a line up of miscreants who had been arrested the previous day and incarcerated overnight. He looked utterly miserable and was plainly frightened. He had been taken to spend the night in Oakalla Prison Farm, and exhibited a serious apprehension that he was going to be given a sentence that would lodge him in that inhospitable jail for a serious length of time.

After disposing of the few overnight cases, Gordon Scott came to deal with Eddie. He read Eddie a serious lecture about his sinful life of petty crime, though I detected a twinkle of amusement in the old magistrate's eye as he did so. Gordon Scott drew breath. The time had come to sentence Eddie. Eddie stood, still garbed in his tattered raincoat, head bowed, a tear in the corner of his eye, terrified and cowed. Gordon Scott gave Eddie a sentence of one month in jail, the sentence to be suspended. Eddie clearly did not understand what this meant, so Gordon Scott explained that Eddie was now free to go, but that if he offended again, it would be jail time for Eddie. It was obvious that Gordon Scott had never had any intention of sending such a harmless little misfit to prison. He had jailed him overnight just to give him a taste of what was in store for him if he repeated his offence.

Eddie left the courtroom a chastened and scared little man. We stood together for a brief moment on the courthouse steps. He turned his frightened eyes towards me and said, "Thank you." Then he melted into the rubbish-strewn back alleys of the east end and I never saw him again.

The Change of Address

A clinical psychologist, approached for a diagnosis, would favour you with the opinion that Daniel O'Byrne laboured under the disability of a schizotypal personality disorder, with vague tendencies towards bipolar disorder—the common mental ailment afflicting many street people. O'Byrne, however, was gifted with an intelligence quotient significantly above average. Thus it was that he graduated from law school in the top tenth percentile, and with above average experience at stud poker. His psychopathic tendencies perfectly suited the deceit necessary for the successful poker player. Indeed, it was by his winnings at the card tables that he had been able to supplement the income provided by his meagre earnings from summer jobs. The countrywide faculties of law had yet to devise any test that would weed out candidates for law school who were temperamentally unsuited to practise law. Thus the profession boasted its fair share of psychopaths, sociopaths, and general misfits. O'Byrne was one of these.

O'Byrne served a term of articles at Harper, Grey, Easton, a law firm that specialized in insurance defence work. Mysteriously, his hippie-like approach to life's problems did not manifest itself during articles, so the firm kept him on as a junior associate. He succeeded in dodging and weaving his way through a couple of years of practice, until the firm grew disenchanted with complaints from clients, with telephone calls unanswered, and correspondence neglected. The realization finally grew upon the partners that they had a nut on their hands. The final bell rang one day when Harvey Grey, the senior partner, walking down the corridor that passed O'Byrne's office, heard the unmistakable strains of music, a trifle off-key. Grey cast about for the source of this dissonance, and upon opening an office door, beheld O'Byrne sitting cross-legged, guru-like, on his desk strumming on a guitar. Grey, a conservative at every corner of his soul, promptly summoned a partner's meeting, which resolved to terminate this unhinged associate's no-longer valued services.

Now, I was then in about the fifth year of my editorship of the *Advocate*, the legal magazine that every lawyer in BC receives. The magazine has a

70

column entitled "Bench and Bar"—a column of newsworthy items and information. Part of this column relayed information about members of the profession who had changed firms, relocated, retired, or fled to more profitable endeavours. I had picked up the information that O'Byrne had left Harper, Grey, Easton. His new address was care of the Public Trustee. Insofar as I gave it any more than a passing thought, I weighed up this move as a benefit for Harper, Grey, as well as O'Byrne, though I harboured some misgivings about the usefulness of his services to the office of the Public Trustee. He was now a civil servant, and likely to create less disorder than if he had remained in private practice.

Six weeks later, the edition of the *Advocate*, revealing the information about O'Byrne, was published, arriving on every subscriber's desk all on the same morning. I cast a quick glance through my copy, to make sure all was in order and consigned it to my "In" box. Not fifteen minutes later, I received the first of half a dozen phone calls. The call was from Marjorie Keddy, the Law Society's chief librarian. Without the usual introductory ceremonies (the normally obligatory enquiry after each other's health), she barged straight to the point.

"David, what on earth possessed you to say O'Byrne has become employed by the Public Trustee. Really, your sense of humour has got the better of you."

"Marjorie? Sorry, but what are you talking about?"

"I'm talking about Daniel O'Byrne. You announced that he'd joined the Public Trustee's Office." "Yes Marjorie, well that's what I understood he'd done. I saw his change of address. He's left Harper, Grey, Easton." "Yes indeed, he's left that firm, but ... you clown ... why didn't you enquire a bit further? He's been committed under the Mental Health Act and now he's in Essondale! You know, the local loony bin? The Public Trustee is in charge of his affairs. That's why his address is care of the Public Trustee's office."

We discussed this now widely broadcast misinformation for a few minutes and I rang off. Scratching my head as to what to do about my blunder, the phone rang again. This time it was Alfie Watts, the Secretary of the Law Society. He carried the same message, though he was less forthright and more understanding than dear Marjorie Keddy. I fielded four more calls, all in the same vein, though as I was now in possession of the full facts, I did not need to prolong discussions.

At twelve noon, precisely, there arrived on my desk a letter, by courier. The envelope bore the name and address of the office of the Public Trustee. Now the office of the Public Trustee was, at that point in its history, filled by a particularly unpopular official. By coincidence he had moved, or been pushed, from the very same Harper, Grey firm to take a position in the Public Trustee's office, and had risen up the ranks by dint of the application of the principle of seniority (known in the British civil service as "Buggin's turn next") to become head of the organization. He was a humourless cretin, who attracted the odium of anybody unfortunate enough to have to deal with him: a nit-picker's nit-picker. The letter was brusque. It explained the unfortunate truth that I now already knew. It demanded an apology and a retraction in the next edition of the *Advocate*. I put off responding, the coward's way of sidestepping a distasteful problem in the vague hope that the problem might go away, though in truth, I knew this one was not going to disappear.

It so happened that this was a Thursday and the next day was the beginning of the Canadian Bar Association, BC Branch, annual meeting—this year to take place in Victoria. I left the next morning for this ceremonial gathering of lawyers, judges, and official busybodies. I attended the reception that was to precede the ceremonial opening dinner. I was standing chatting with some acquaintances, drink in hand, when I espied the Deputy Attorney General, Gilbert Kennedy, making a bee-line across the floor towards me. He bore in his hand a copy of the *Advocate*, which he was thumbing through in search of a particular page. I opened my mouth to greet him, but he was too quick.

"David, I have to talk to you about your piece about young O'Byrne."

"Yes, well Gilbert, I know, but you see…" I explained what had happened and how the mistake had come to get itself into such public print. Embarrassing for everybody I conceded. We mulled over what should be done. I recounted the message in the letter from the Public Trustee. We finally decided that a retraction might well do more harm and cause more embarrassment to all concerned, particularly to the unfortunate inmate of Essondale. We decided to do nothing. Doing nothing, we agreed, was sometimes the best course of action in difficult circumstances. We nodded sagely to each other, shook hands, and processed into dinner.

Back in the office the next week, I penned a reply to the Public Trustee. I recounted my conversation with Gilbert Kennedy, who was (of course) his boss, and confirmed that we had agreed that no retraction would appear in the *Advocate*. I mailed the letter. The next day my phone rang. Of course, it was the Public Trustee. His voice shaking with anger, he demanded to know why I had not dealt directly with him and how dare I go over his head to his superior. This was grossly inappropriate and called for an immediate apology. Had I deliberately attempted to humiliate him? I attempted to explain that it was not I that had approached the Deputy Attorney General, but he who had accosted me and drawn me into a discussion. Nothing would mollify the man. He still wanted a printed retraction, and yes it called for an apology—indeed now, two apologies. I somehow managed to manoeuvre the conversation to a close without promising anything (known in Victorian literary circles as the evasion courteous).

I didn't publish a retraction, nor yet an apology. The unfortunate incident thinned away into oblivion without further fuss. I never heard from the Public Trustee again, though I confess that the day of the publication of the next *Advocate*, I held my breath as I answered phone calls, wondering how I was going to justify my failure to publish his cherished retraction and his appeasing apology. O'Byrne was released from his mental institution in due course of time, and returned to private practice, to pursue a thankfully uneventful and undistinguished career at the bar, before soon disappearing from the legal scene never to be heard of again.

HARRY SULLIVAN J.

Harry Sullivan, of Irish descent, but born and educated in the United States, practised law in New Westminster until his appointment to the County Court of Westminster in 1945. An experienced and capable judge, he was acknowledged, at least by the New Westminster bar, as having the unfortunate quality of knowing with certainty that he was always right.

One rainy New Westminster morning, he found himself presiding over a run-of-the mill motor-vehicle accident case. He was trying the case with a jury. The plaintiff was a woman who had been seriously injured when the defendant ran a stoplight and hit her car broadside. She was driving her own car and was by herself. Her husband, a man in his late sixties, was also a plaintiff. He himself had, of course, not suffered any physical injuries, for he was not in the car at the time. He was advancing a claim for damages for loss of *servitium*. In the quaint practice that the law followed in those days, the statement of claim alleged the facts of the accident and his wife's injuries *"per quod servitium et consortium amisit"*. Loosely translated this means that in consequence of his wife's injuries, he had lost her company and her services. The claim encompasses the loss of her contribution to the household, her care and affection, and (buried tactfully in the translation) the opportunity to have sex with her. She was too ill.

The husband entered the witness box to testify. The clerk put him under oath and his counsel elicited the sorrowful tale of this man's efforts to tend an invalid wife with the injuries she herself had testified to earlier in the trial. Counsel came to the subject of loss of servitium. The husband explained that his wife's injuries had prevented them from indulging in the physical side of marital bliss, which had added so much to the enjoyment of their marriage before the accident. The jury, which had become visibly bored by the process of the trial, suddenly perked up.

Counsel, who was defending the case, rose to cross-examine the husband. Asked his age, the husband told the court he was sixty-nine. Counsel then launched a derisive attack on the husband's contention that, at that age, he would be physically capable of the sexual act. The jury

74

began to become restless, shifting in their seats, and the older members of the jury were seen to be whispering to each other.

Suddenly, Mr. Justice Sullivan held up his hand and pointed at counsel. "Mr. Jones," he said, in a voice that contained no little hint of disapproval. "Mr. Jones, would you mind if I asked you a personal question?"

"Why, no, My Lord," came the surprised response.

"Well, how old are you?"

"Oh, well, My Lord, I am twenty-nine".

"Yes. Well young man. There are two facts that I think you ought to understand. Firstly, I am seventy two, and secondly, you still have a very great deal to learn".

The jury grinned, down to the last man. Those with silvery hair nodded sagely at the judge, with knowing looks.

Jimmy Watson and the New Office

My partner, Graham Ladner, telephoned with the news early Saturday morning. There had been a fire at the office late that Friday night. Our little office was on the top floor of the old Birks' Building (now long-since demolished and replaced by the shiny new Bank of Nova Scotia Tower). The janitor had detected smoke drifting from beneath the front door and had called the fire department. Fortunately, since the office was shut up for the weekend with all the windows closed, there had been insufficient oxygen to permit a real conflagration with flames. Our fire was confined to thick smoke and smouldering. That was bad enough. The smoke had ruined our new and expensively acquired electric typewriters and dictating machines—the old reel-to-reel type that had recently crept into usage by the profession. Our photocopying machine was damaged beyond economic repair. This was not such a blow, because it was an early model that required liquid chemicals to develop. The copies had to be hung up, like laundry, to dry. Using money from our fire insurance policy, we replaced it with a dry model that salesmen had been lately peddling to the profession, but which we had decided we did not yet need to afford.

Mary Southin was away on holiday, on a trip to Russia. Her secretary, a plump and humourless Irish girl called Meta Pollock Stevenson, had taken it into her head, in Mary's absence, to rub down her teak desk with boiled linseed oil. It looked a grand sight, all dark and velvety and uncluttered by files and books. At the end of her refurbishing labours, Miss Stevenson had thoughtlessly flung the oil soaked rag into the tin waste-paper basket beside the desk. Friday was not a night when the cleaning staff emptied waste-baskets. That task they postponed until some time later in the weekend. The weather was cold and the building remained heated over the weekend. Heating in the old building was accomplished by old-fashioned radiators, through which flowed water heated by an ancient furnace in the basement. The waste-basket had been pushed hard up against the radiator. After a few hours of smouldering in this heat, the oil soaked rag burst into flames.

76

We enlisted the aid of those of our staff we could find on a Saturday, and spent the rest of the weekend dealing with the sooty, grime-laden remains of our office. By a blessed stroke of fortune, the building manager found for us a vacant office of identical size and location several floors below our ruined premises. By Monday morning, we were installed in this temporary haven and spent the next few days cleaning up files, desks, filing cabinets, and furniture, and trying to practise law with borrowed and rented equipment. Most clients were indulgent and accommodating, as were other solicitors. Weeks later, I remember that it was still a temptation to plead the disruption of the fire as an excuse for not getting things done on time.

Our old office was completely stripped by Mssrs Birks and sons. Interior walls vanished. Our little kitchen, which we used to brew tea (and for storing Sherry), disappeared, and we faced what seemed to us to be a vast expanse of space that we had no idea how to fill. We resisted the impulse to save time, money, and energy by rebuilding the office exactly as it had been before. By now Mary had returned. The four of us wasted several days debating whether to replicate the previous office or be daring and progressive and design something new and really efficient. Replication avoided the need to plan a new configuration. We had, after all, functioned perfectly adequately before, so why not again? Mary argued that we should grasp the opportunity to create a really functional office. The more conservative of us, Graham and Robin Brammall, wanted to know how any new plan would be formed. What would we do differently?

"It worked before; how could it be improved?"asked one. "It will take too much time," grumbled another. I voiced the problem of whom we should get to advise us. "Architects are expensive. So are office design consultants." Brammall said, "They'll just want to sell us stuff we don't need." Mary Southin was not concerned. "Surely we have enough wit to withstand the blandishments of salesmen."

The argument grumbled along for several days. I complained about the problem to my wife, Gill. After she had grown tired of listening to my whining about the plans for the new office, she suddenly said, "Jimmy Watson." "What?" I asked.

"Jimmy Watson. Hire Jimmy Watson." I remained obtusely confused. "Well, isn't that what he does for a living?" Gill asked. Jimmy Watson was an old friend of ours. In a sense, he was our oldest friend. He had introduced us to each other five or six years earlier. As such, he was the person that each of us had jointly known the longest.

Jimmy was Irish—born and raised in Dublin, and a member of Dublin's small Anglican community. He had once served in the Irish Navy, which he maintained was one of the world's smallest navies, sporting a mere handful of little warships. He said that he had served on Ireland's largest warship, which was, as I remember it, a frigate. He had the most highly developed sense of humour of anyone I had ever met, with the gift of making the most mundane story hilariously funny. Some actors have what in the theatre is known as a stage presence, the ability to make audiences listen to them. Jimmy had a comic presence. To be in his company was to be amused. He could keep a roomful of people in fits of laughter without apparent effort for as long as he chose to keep it up.

Jimmy, at the time of our fire, was employed by BC Hydro, recently created by the expropriation—by the Social Credit Government—of the BC Electric Railway Company. He was what was once known as a "time and motion study man". Such functionaries are now known by more grandiose and less explicit titles. Jimmy taught people to achieve more work in less time and with less effort.

So I consulted my partners. Mary had already met Jimmy at our house and had been charmed by his humour and his ability to play the piano like Fats Waller, even though he could not read a note of music. She took up my proposal with some enthusiasm, though with the caution that we could always veto his plans if we did not like them.

So it came about that one wintry Saturday morning we all assembled, lawyers and a reluctantly dragooned staff, in the completely barren space of our old office—now scraped clean of the detritus of the fire, and with no furniture save three old chairs and some cardboard boxes, in which we had stored temporarily unwanted files.

Jimmy showed up, precisely on time, armed with a clipboard, a pencil, and a twenty-four-foot tape measure. Within three minutes he had transformed our surly group, resentful of a wasted Saturday, into an eager, good-humoured collection of enthusiasts.

Jimmy seized one of the derelict chairs, dragged it into the middle of the cavernous office, and sat down. He crossed his knees, placed the clip board on them, fished out his pencil, beamed at us all, and said, "Well it's a grand day for you to plan your office, so it is."

We all looked at him in puzzled silence, a reaction that I suspect he expected. Our reaction to his comment provoked him to say, "Now, you are all going to set about laying out your new beautiful, functional office. It'll be the best in Vancouver. A gem. The cynosure of all eyes."

"But Jimmy," someone (Mary, I think) said, "that's what we hired *you* to do. We'd have done it ourselves, if we'd thought we could do it effectively."

Brammall added, "That's like keeping a dog and barking yourself." There was a small murmur of assent from the group huddled about him.

"No, you're quite wrong," said Jimmy. "I can't plan your office for you. Only you can do that. I don't know what you all do in here. But you do—I hope." His eyes twinkled. "You all know who does what and where they all do it." "But, Jimmy—" The protests became a chorus. We had hired this guy as an expert, and here he was claiming, emphasizing, his inability to fulfil his commitment to us. My secretary, Christine Cook (an elegant English girl and the best secretary I ever had), said, in a tone of polite complaint, "Mr. Watson, we thought your job at BC Hydro was designing offices and space for people to work in."

"Quite right," said Jimmy, "That's exactly what Hydro pays me to do. But I don't do it. The people who are going to use the space plan its layout themselves. What I do is make them think. And that is what I am going to make you do. I'm going to make you think. I shall make you all plan the best layout to accommodate what you do in here. What do you all do in here? Do you interview clients ... witnesses? How many at a time? One at a time or in groups? If you don't keep them waiting, you won't have to waste space on a waiting room, will you? If you do, you will. Do you have a receptionist? What else does she do? Answer the phone? Filing? Does she have a typewriter? What about secretaries? Outside your door or in a typing pool? What size offices do you need? Big enough to interview people? How many? Or will it be more effective to have small offices and use a boardroom for interviews and meetings? How often do you have meetings? How many people? Could you use a boardroom for other functions, like office parties or clog dancing?"

He raised one eyebrow and leaned forward, addressing Meta Stevenson with a grin that was almost a leer. "D'you do much clog dancing, now? You see, I don't know." Miss Stevenson bridled, frowned, and made some huffy response. I guessed from her expression that, a Northern Irish woman, she wished to have no truck with this buffoon from the Republic.

"You see," he continued, "if you don't often have big meetings, it might be cheaper to hire a meeting room elsewhere in the building, only as the occasion demands. Is there one? Less expensive than paying rent on space you rarely use."

And so he went on. Dragging information out of us, moderating arguments that erupted between us about our perceived needs, and occasionally, and gently, demolishing cherished and long held ideas—such as the need for a large office to prop up the prestige of the lawyer who worked in it. He ferreted out the opinion, from the secretaries, that they worked better if seated near a window, despite the apparent distraction of the view from it. So we discovered that neither filing cabinets, nor photo-copiers, benefited from a room with a view, and that a view was wasted on clients waiting in the reception area. Nor did the sink and the tea kettle command a room to themselves as had been their experience before the fire. No protest would come from the Rolodex for having to share space with the coffee percolator. We discovered that we did not have enough law books to warrant a library in a separate room. The lawyers could store books in daily use in bookcases in their offices, borrowed from time to time by each other. The remaining books, consulted only occasionally, could decorate the reception area.

Slowly, as the Saturday morning approached lunch time, the assembled information transformed itself into a plan, roughed in on Jimmy's clipboard. Graham, driven by the twin urges of hunger and information overload, suggested that we adjourn for lunch to the steak house across the road. Jimmy's polite veto resulted in the delivery of pizza and coffee. The suggestion of beer was similarly quashed. Jimmy allowed as how, although beer was one of God's greatest gifts to mankind, it did tend to blunt the edge of one's concentration and promoted irrelevant thought processes. He had obviously encountered people like us before, whose thinking would be fragmented by a heavy meal with beer.

So the day wore on until, surprisingly early in the afternoon, after our pizza was delivered and hungrily consumed, it was done. The clipboard held the plan. The tape measure's lengths were transposed into figures beside the lines on the board. We had our little office and we had designed a surprisingly efficient one. The plan was so simple and obvious that some wondered afterwards why we had needed help. But without Jimmy's relentless prodding, we would never have come up with it. Without his good-humoured and sly mediation, we would never have settled the disputes about space that each of us selfishly caused, by seeking to promote a concept in our own interest.

REAL CARRIER

R eal Carrier was a French Canadian down and out. Down and out, I
suspect, because he had emotional difficulties that rendered him
unemployable. He was an inhabitant of one of the dingier flop-houses
that infest the east end of Vancouver. It was somewhere in back of the
Army and Navy Store—a filthy, cockroach-ridden, run down, old hotel
with minimum facilities. It was one of the numerous such establishments
that the City of Vancouver ought to have closed down as an insanitary fire
trap, but could not realistically do so, as closure would simply spill the
inmates onto the street to sleep under the Georgia Viaduct and freeze to
death in winter.

There are those who are poor because they have the misfortune to lack
an education, for one reason or another. Others suffer because they have,
too early in their lives, taken on the responsibility of a family to support,
which forces them to earn wages, impeding their ability to take more training and rise up the wage scale. Yet others simply do not have the intellectual ability to earn beyond the minimum wage. And then there are the
social misfits. Their mental infirmities render them unemployable. They
lack education because they are ineducable. Enlightened governments
can, or should (given the will to do so), provide universal education, thus
ensuring a prosperous society. Generally speaking, an educated society
is a prosperous society. The most that can be done for the sociopaths,
the unhinged, and the brain damaged, is to look after them as best can
be done, so that they do not resort to crime in order to pay the rent and
support the drug habits and alcoholism that afflict so many of them, in
search of an escape from their drab lives. It is a difficult, expensive task,
and we don't do it very well. It is unrealistic to think that these desperate
souls can be gainfully employed. I suspect that Christ had such people in
mind when he said, "The poor will always be with us." At least, that is what
he is reported to have said: John 12:8

Real Carrier was one of Vancouver's unhinged.

One winter's night, the front desk at the Main Street police station
received a phone call from a frightened night clerk in charge of Carrier's

81

grotty hostel. The clerk was in a state of some hysteria. There was a commotion on the third floor. He had toiled upstairs to find out what all the shouting was about, and had been met by several dishevelled men, the more sober of whom seemed to be telling him that there was a fight in progress. The night clerk, on stepping down the corridor, realized that this was indeed so. From Carrier's room came the loud sounds of a violent quarrel: a great deal of banging, much yelling, and the sound of furniture being thrown about. Some of the yelling was obviously coming from a man in trouble—screams and cries of pain. Someone, he concluded, was being beaten up. Wisely, the clerk cut short his investigations and fled downstairs to the phone.

Two police cars arrived in short order—it was only two or three blocks from the police station. Four policemen rushed to the front desk and were directed to the third floor. The constable in the lead, ascending the stairs three at a time, was shown to Carrier's room by a scared old drunk who had been awakened by the commotion, which had now ceased. There was silence where there had been the sounds of a fight. The corridor was full of nervous, chattering, unshaven men, ineffectively gesturing towards the room and trying to detain the constable to explain what was going on. Since none seemed to know the reason for the tumult, their pathetic attempts to enlighten the constable only impeded his progress. He shoved his way through this little grubby crowd and reached the door, which was now closed.

Upon opening it, he took in a ghastly sight. Someone, who ultimately turned out to be Carrier, was sitting on his bed. He was covered in blood. Not his blood, but the blood of a man whose torso was laying half on the floor and half in Carrier's lap. Carrier looked up and beamed at the constable, and said, "*C'est Saint Jean le Baptist.*" He gestured towards the man's head. The head was now almost completely severed from the body. Carrier then resumed what he had been doing when the constable had burst into his room—diligently sawing off the victim's head with a small penknife. The constable stared in horror at this grisly spectacle. The pause gave Carrier enough time to finish his task. He sawed through the last piece of muscle, dropped the body, and held up the head by its hair for the constable to see. "*Saint Jean le Baptist,*" Carrier repeated, and began a long dissertation about the matter in French, none of which the constable understood. Blood was dripping from the head onto Carrier, the bed, and the floor, as he waved the head about. He then tossed it to the constable, who leapt back, too late to avoid the head, which hit him in the solar plexus and bounced down his pants.

The three other policemen joined the constable, and they proceeded to try to arrest Carrier and handcuff him. This was no easy task, as Carrier seemed not to want them to interrupt his biblical endeavours—whatever they might have been. They had to subdue him, and he put up a tremendous fight. They finally got him onto the floor, and while three of them knelt on his body, as he lay face down on the floor, the fourth managed to attach a pair of handcuffs to his wrists behind his back. They then had to wrestle him down the stairs and into one of the police cars. The constable was by now covered in the blood of the victim. He was bruised from the struggle with Carrier, and badly out of breath. He walked round the corner, into the alley behind the building, leaned his elbow against the wall, with his forehead on his wrist and promptly threw up.

I was told afterwards that Carrier never gave up his struggle. At the police station, it took four policemen to hold him still enough to secure his fingerprints. During this fingerprinting exercise, Carrier struggled so violently that he broke the wrist of the officer who was trying to fingerprint him. I was never sure if they succeeded in obtaining what they needed. I believe they might have had to give up and do it later, after Carrier had been sedated.

The next day, Legal Aid retained me to defend him. Armed with a pad of notepaper in my briefcase, I took the bus down to the police station on Main Street. Carrier was in a holding cell in the basement. I interviewed a police sergeant who filled me in on the details of the crime. Carrier was charged with murder. I asked to be allowed to interview him. The sergeant said that, as far as anyone could determine, Carrier spoke no English, only French. At any rate, nobody had heard Carrier say anything in English. In those days I spoke and understood French quite well—a facility that has gradually eroded by the passage of time and disuse. I explained to the sergeant that I would probably be able to communicate with Carrier, and gently insisted on seeing him.

I was taken downstairs by the sergeant and was a little surprised when he called for another officer to join us. We reached the door of Carrier's cell. There was a desk nearby. Both officers were in the blue shirt-sleeves of a police officer's uniform. Both had an array of pens and pencils in their breast pockets. To my surprise, they removed all these writing materials and laid them on the little desk. They asked me to put my own pencil and pen on the desk. I asked why. The sergeant explained that Carrier had been very violent and that, although the police doctor had sedated him, they were still afraid that he might attack us. If he did, and he got hold of a pencil, he could use it on us to lethal effect. They wanted to eliminate any possibility that I, or they, might be injured. It was at this point that the sergeant told me about the struggle over the attempt to fingerprint Carrier. "He's only a little man, but he's amazingly strong and very violent," said the sergeant. I was rather sceptical, but did as I was asked.

I was then also told that they had taken all Carrier's clothes away, and that the cell was bare. Then both officers escorted me to the door of the cell. I said something about wishing to interview Carrier alone, and out of earshot of the Police. "Oh, I'm afraid we daren't let you go into the cell," said the sergeant, "and we certainly can't let you in by yourself. You stand in the doorway, and we'll be beside you—just in case. You mustn't step inside. Okay?"

I had little alternative but to agree. I had serious misgivings about all this. I was entitled, after all, to interview any client alone, and particularly in the absence of the police. Surely they knew that. I decided that this was not the time to make a fuss. I would see how the interview went and then do something more creative later.

The sergeant unlocked the door and opened it. They stood, one on each side of me, very close, and, I could feel, poised to intervene if anything happened. The cell was completely bare except for a mattress on the floor, upon which lay a small, thin, almost emaciated man, lying on his back. He was stark naked. Not a stitch of clothing. No watch. No rings on his fingers. Nothing. The cell was lit by a pot light in the ceiling that the man could not reach. "*Monsieur Carrier?*" No reply. I tried again, explaining, in French, who I was. I was about to tell him why I had come, and took a step forward so that I would be sure he could hear me. Two very firm hands grasped my arms. The officers were not going to let me any nearer to my client than the door of his cell. I addressed Carrier again. This time, he rolled his head over and looked towards me. "*Allez vous en,*" he said I tried to engage him in conversation—to reassure him that I was there to help him, to represent him. I began to try to tell him that he had been charged with murder and that I would defend him, but that I needed to talk to him and seek his instructions. "*Allez vous en,*" was the only response. This went on for a few minutes, but Carrier resolutely refused to say anything except "*Allez vous en.*"

Eventually and to the obvious relief of the two officers, I gave up. They closed and locked the door, returned their pens and pencils to their pockets, and mine to me and took me back upstairs. There they filled me in on all the details of what had happened the night before. I read over the police reports. I began to agree with the officers' expressed opinion that Carrier was mad, to use their blunt expression. I concluded that the best I could do for him would be to raise the defence of insanity. Carrier was eventually examined by a psychiatrist, a doctor whom I knew well and who often testified on behalf of the Crown. His report confirmed my opinion. Carrier was clearly insane and dangerous.

Carrier was tried fairly soon afterwards, before Mr. Justice Trainor and a jury. John Rowan was retained by the Crown to prosecute. We discussed the case beforehand. Rowan was a straightforward lawyer whom I knew well from the days when he used to do insurance defence work and I had run personal injury claims. We both agreed that a defence of insanity was the only option available. He would not oppose it. At the trial, he called the constable, he with the queasy stomach, to testify about the affray he had attended. His other witness was the psychiatrist, who explained in detail the nature of Carrier's illness. I cross-examined each witness briefly, to emphasize the bizarre quality of Carrier's conduct. Rowan addressed the jury and conceded the defence that he knew I was going to advance. Since I had not called anyone in Carrier's defence, I was entitled to address the jury last. I explained the defence to them, and asked them to return a verdict of not guilty by reason of insanity, and that such a verdict would result in Carrier being confined to a facility for the criminally insane, until he became well enough to be released or he died. The judge rather bluntly told them that there was no other possible verdict that they could reach and sent them off to deliberate. It did not take long. The verdict sought was duly announced by the foreman, and we all went home. Carrier, who had attended the trial and meekly sat in the prisoner's box throughout, without saying anything, was taken away. He went to Colony Farm, the federal facilty for the criminally insane in Coquitlam.

Some time later, I went out to Colony Farm to see him, because he sent a message to me that he wanted to see me. When I got to the Farm, I presented myself at the front desk and explained why I was there. They were expecting me. I was taken upstairs to a comfortably, if rather shabbily furnished, sitting room and was left there while the nurse went to fetch Carrier. I am not sure what I expected, but I know that I thought he would be under guard. After a brief wait, the door opened and in walked a meek-looking little man with thinning brown hair, dressed in carpet slippers, pyjamas, and a brown dressing gown. It was Carrier. I stood up to greet him, and he proffered a hand for me to shake. He was really surprisingly small—about five feet four inches tall, and looking as if he weighed about a hundred and thirty pounds. Was this the same man it had taken four policemen to subdue, in order to take his fingerprints, and who had maimed one of them in the process? We talked for quite a long time—in English. His English was very good. Though I tried, I was unable to learn much about his background, except that he had earned a living as a general labourer and, of course, that he was from Montreal. He wanted to thank me for what I had done for him. He was quite forthcoming about his state of mind, schizophrenia, and explained that he was on medication and was perfectly all right as long as he took it regularly. He did not think that anyone would ever cure him, and he expected to remain at the Farm for the rest of his life. He seemed quite content.

Just before I left, he told me something that gave me no little disquiet. He said that he remembered me coming to see him in his cell. He remembered the two police officers. He remembered me talking to him in French. Then he told me that the reason he had ordered me to go away was because he had felt, coming over him, an uncontrollable desire to leap to his feet and kill me. We had left just in time, before he did that.

Rest and Rehabilitation

Those who know about such things, maintain that most humans can only concentrate on something for about twenty minutes. After that their attention wanders. The attention span varies depending on how interesting the speaker can make the subject. Some are better at it than others. There are those who can hold an audience's attention for much longer than twenty minutes. Actors are trained to do it, which is why President Reagan gained his reputation as "the great communicator". People forgot that he was a professional communicator. He may not have been in the forefront of the acting trade, but he was trained to keep his audience's attention. Some gifted souls have a natural talent for commanding attention. Theatre people call this "a stage presence". You can't help but listen to them, however long they go on. There are some ruses that can be used to deter the audience's mind from wandering. Shakespeare knew that. He invented the principle of comic relief. After a passage in his plays that he judged would have exhausted his audience's ability to concentrate, he would introduce a bit of farce, make the audience laugh, and then resume the real thread of the play. His audience would have had an opportunity to relax, stop thinking, and be ready for a renewed bout of concentration.

The principle is not limited to those who address audiences. All our brains function better with an occasional moment of relaxation during a spate of hard work. McKenzie, in *The Time Trap* (a great book on efficiency and time management), maintains that after a period of hard, concentrated work, one should go and chat up someone at the water cooler, walk round the office, or just do some mindless job for a brief period— answer some phone calls, sort documents, or fill in one's diary.

An occasional break from a stressful enterprise is always necessary. I was once vividly reminded of this when I was appearing before a Supreme Court judge on an appeal from a decision of the Medical Appeal Board. This is the statutory board that hears appeals by physicians who have been denied privileges at hospitals, or, once granted, lost them. My client was a surgeon who had lost his privileges at one of the smaller Vancouver hospitals. It was a difficult appeal, which lasted a whole week, and I ultimately lost it. The facts involved about ten medical procedures my client had conducted, for which he was criticized, and which ultimately led to the cancellation of his privileges. My client attended the hearing, sitting with his wife—a tall, handsome, red-haired woman, —who was also a doctor, a family practitioner who had suspended her practice temporarily in order to rear their children.

At the end of the first morning, the time came to adjourn for lunch. Usually I tried to avoid having lunch with clients during lunch-time adjournments, because it gives you no time to think and regroup if you have to talk about the case with the client until it is time to go back into court. This isn't always easy, because some clients are offended if you decline lunch. They want to discuss the case—after all they are paying to have you represent them, and are entitled to an interim progress report. Declining lunch sometimes requires the exercise of some tact, and occasionally, I would have to resort to a less than truthful excuse about having to go and look something up in the library, in order to get some peace.

Judge Macdonald adjourned for lunch. I collected up my trial book and walked out into the hallway. The doctor was standing with his wife, poised to engage me in conversation. He pounced as I emerged from the courtroom, raised a finger, and began to explain to me an aspect of the case that he thought important. I listened attentively and we fell to discussing his point. The doctor was very persistent and wanted to be sure that I appreciated the nuances of the medical procedure I had been explaining to the judge ten minutes earlier. We exhausted the subject. He raised the finger again, and immediately started on another proposition that he wanted me to be sure to put before the judge. I felt like the wedding guest, buttonholed by the ancient mariner. There must have been a fleeting look of distressed impatience that flitted across my face, because, very gently, his wife took him by the elbow, turned him away from me, and said, "Wilfred, dear, Mr. Roberts' brain needs a rest. Come and have lunch with me." She turned and looked at me, imperceptibly raised an eyebrow, smiled, and led him away like a little lost puppy.

BERT OLIVER AND THE COLOURED SOCKS

A quick consultation of *The Oxford Dictionary of Quotations* discloses that Albert Einstein let drop almost as many pearls of wisdom as did Ralph Waldo Emerson or Dr. Samuel Johnson. So often, celebrities, experts in their own fields, will unburden themselves of what they believe will become universal truths, which would wither into obscurity were it not for the fame of the authors. Einstein managed a library's worth of aphorisms that stand on their own merit, without the added authority lent by their author.

All human endeavours are enhanced by imagination. Einstein had this to say about imagination:

> *"Imagination is more important than knowledge, for knowledge is limited to all we know or understand, while imagination embraces the entire world, all there ever will be to know and understand."*

I once heard our family doctor remark that a really good GP brings imagination to his practice. This is also true of lawyers. Inspired counsel work finds its genesis in the use of imagination. I recall once sitting in Provincial Court, waiting my turn to defend some miscreant, when an old friend of mine rose to defend a routine armed robbery. Bert Oliver was an experienced and capable criminal lawyer, articulate and persuasive in front of juries, and well-versed in the intricacies of criminal practice, but it was his liberal application of imagination that he brought to his practice that earned him the extra acquittals that eluded other competent but run-of-the-mill counsel.

Bert's client, a young thug in his early twenties, had been arrested by a police officer. The defence rested on the identification of the accused. Identification is always a tricky business. So many witnesses either cannot identify those who need to be convicted, or in some tragic cases, they identify the wrong person. The identification line up is a useful, but far from an infallible, tool to avoid miscarriages of justice.

In this case, the victim of the crime had failed to pick out the accused from the line up, but the arresting officer, because of the peculiar circumstances of the case, would be able to identify him.

As was his right, Bert seated his client in the body of the court so that the officer would have to pick him out from amongst the sparse crowd scattered about the courtroom. However, the accused had brought his brother along with him, as was also his right. They were both dressed alike and they looked, for all the world, as if they were identical twins. The accused was wearing blue socks, his brother red socks. The arresting officer had been ordered out of the courtroom by the judge before the accused stood to hear the charge read, and to plead not guilty. Thus the officer was not going to know which brother was which.

Some witnesses were called, including another officer, who had been in the courtroom when the accused pleaded not guilty, so he knew which brother was which. The time came for the arresting officer to testify and the judge asked the officer who had just finished his testimony to go out of the courtroom door and fetch the arresting officer.

Now it so happened that Bert had brought along his student, who was standing by the door as the officer left the courtroom. He watched as he beckoned the arresting officer to come to testify. As they passed each other, the student heard the first officer say to the other in a stage whisper, "blue socks". The student hurried into the courtroom and told Bert what he had overheard. Bert instantly asked the judge for a brief adjournment, which was granted. Bert turned, stabbed a finger at the two brothers, then pointed firmly at the rear door of the courtroom and marched out, followed by the two puzzled brothers. Ten minutes elapsed. The brothers returned to their positions on the front bench, behind the bar of the court. Bert resumed his seat. The arresting officer swore to tell the truth and Crown counsel began to elicit his story from this witness.

Now Bert could have tried in cross-examination to pry out of the officer the fact that he had been told that the accused was wearing blue socks. This might have been denied. The police sometimes tend to be economical with the truth, and anyway it was a risk. Crown counsel asked the officer to identify the accused. The officer looked over at the two brothers and his eyes drifted down to their feet. One brother was wearing one red sock and one blue sock, and the other was wearing one blue sock and one red sock.

CHAMPAGNE FOR CHRISTMAS

The ill-fated Hungarian revolution, in 1956, which failed to cast off the yoke of domination by the Soviet Union, at least succeeded in facilitating the exodus of some 200,000 young Hungarians, famished for freedom. Desperate to establish a life beyond the suffocating oppression of communism, they fled across the border onto Austria's welcoming soil. The students and entire faculty of the department of forestry, at the University of Budapest, seized the opportunity created by the turmoil, to escape. They all journeyed to British Columbia and were taken in by the University of BC, with the result that, for a generation afterwards, you could not wander far into the forest industry without stumbling across a Hungarian forester.

The revolution really came about by accident. I once had occasion to learn what sparked this uprising from a real live witness to the event. In 1982, I was retained by Northern Telecom, as Nortel was then called, the manufacturer of some PVC-covered electrical cable, to defend a lawsuit brought against it (and a handful of other manufacturers) by Cominco. There had been a fire in Cominco's switch room in Trail BC. Although the fire was the fault of Cominco's careless maintenance, the fire had spread because the cables were all bundled together in specially designed cable trays. Though the cables were all advertised as fire resistant, this fire spread along the trays, fuelled by the cables. I needed to call one of the scientists who oversaw the design and manufacture of the cables as a witness. This scientist turned out to be a woman by the name of Dr. Marta Farrago. She was Hungarian and had been a student at the University of Budapest at the time of the revolution. Gill and I had her over for dinner. We fell to talking about the revolution. She told us that a large group of students had embarked on a protest against the government of the People's Republic of Hungary. On October 23, 1956, they assembled and paraded across the Danube down to the parliament buildings, chanting and shouting and waving placards of protest. Marta Farrago was one of these students.

This was no small clutch of students. They numbered in the thousands. The Hungarian government, instead of ignoring this minor riot and waiting for the students to grow tired and hungry and repair to their homes, sent in the state security police, backed up by an ugly, clanking troop of tanks. Some students, amongst whom was Marta Farrago, marched on the state radio building, seeking entry so that they could broadcast their grievances. The security police allowed a small group inside, but they were not allowed to broadcast. Instead the police detained them. The mob outside grew restive. Three students (two men and a girl) climbed onto one of the tanks, the girl was waving a Hungarian flag on a long pole. They were stamping about on the tank and exhorting the crew to join them. The other students began demanding the release of their fellow students imprisoned in the building, flinging rocks at the windows to emphasize their point. The police inside the building lost their nerve. Some cretin of a policeman decided that this was exactly the kind of conduct he had been trained to suppress. He took aim at the girl with the flag and shot her dead. The students, who had behaved reasonably peacefully up to that point, rose up, enraged that one of their own, and a girl at that, would be shot by a fellow Hungarian. The protest rapidly developed into a riot. The students attacked the police. Unarmed as they were, many were felled by machine-gun fire. This lethal uproar ran completely out of control, and over the next two or three days, turned into a full-scale revolution, in which most of the population of the old city took part.

It spread into the surrounding countryside, and in short order, the government fell and the revolutionaries installed Imry Nagy as Prime Minister. The Soviet Union, sensing that the communist government of its satellite was doomed, dispatched a division of tanks and snuffed out Hungary's bid for freedom, spilling much blood in the process.

Along with the foresters, many of Hungary's more enterprising youth, including Marta Farrago, fled in search of a better life than communism offered. Amongst these refugees was Bo Hejduk. Bo had no qualifications; indeed he had suffered from all the inadequacies of what passed for the Hungarian education system, and possessed no skills beyond those of a common labourer. Bo became one of the beneficiaries of the compassion and generosity that facilitated the journey of so many Hungarians to British Columbia.

I encountered Bo when he was charged with possession of an offensive weapon. He had been eking out a living in the east end of Vancouver, doing odd labouring jobs and occasionally begging when he had to. He had been in the habit of carrying a small paring knife, which he used to peel fruit and cut up his food. He got into an altercation one day with some drunk at Main and Hastings. The police broke up this tiff, for it was no more than that, but they discovered Bo's knife in his pocket. They would have been well advised to limit their endeavours to giving the combatants a lecture and sending them both on their way. But some officious constable decided to teach this inarticulate immigrant a lesson and laid the charge against him. He spent the night in jail and was remanded on his own recognizance to appear the following week to set a date for his trial. Now Bo had no money to retain a lawyer, and would not have known how to do so anyway. The Salvation Army officer on duty that day realized that Bo needed help. He contacted the Legal Aid Service, who in turn contacted me. In those days, I was on the legal aid list and did a fair amount of legal aid, just for the experience. In truth, I conducted some of my most interesting cases when I was working for free, for indigents down on the east side.

I arranged for Bo to come in to my office. I had the impression that he was a trifle overawed by this event, well outside his normal experience, and it took some effort to settle him down and make him concentrate on his case. I went over the facts with him. This was not an easy task, as his English was rudimentary and his Hungarian accent was quite heavy. When the case came to trial, I had hoped to be able to succeed without calling Bo to testify, as he would be difficult for the court to understand. My motion for dismissal, at the end of the crown's case, was on the grounds that there was no evidence to warrant a conviction, but it was unsuccessful, and this left me with no option but to march Bo into the witness box to testify in his own defence. We slowly got through the agony of getting Bo to tell his story to a judge who clearly had the difficulty I expected in understanding him. In order to induce some sympathy for Bo, on the part of the judge, I went into some detail about his escape from Hungary, and his efforts to establish a life in British Columbia—not strictly relevant to the charge, but I noticed a softening of the judge's attitude. Crown counsel didn't seem to believe it worth prolonging this minor case by getting into an argument over the admissibility of this evidence. Bo explained that he carried the knife mainly to peel fruit, and then had the wit to add that it was no different than a penknife one would fold up and keep in one's pocket. We encountered some problems with the word "penknife", but we struggled through the description and eventually the judge realized what Bo was attempting to explain. After a minor passage of arms in argument, the judge acquitted Bo.

Bo was ecstatic. After we had gotten through the effusive thanks he poured out, I realized that if this had happened in communist Hungary, he would have been unlikely to have had a trial, and would not, in any event, have stood a chance of avoiding a conviction and an indefinite stint in a labour camp, from which many never emerged, and none emerged unscarred. We parted on the courthouse steps and I watched him, his jaunty step bearing him away down the street. He experienced the same sense of door-opening freedom as he'd felt the day he set foot on Austria's unoppressed soil.

I didn't hear from Bo again until Christmas of that year. Our receptionist walked into my office bearing a bottle of cheap local Champagne, and a handwritten note. It was a gift from Bo, which he had left with her for me. She said that it had been left by a little man who looked like a street person, wearing a dirty grey woollen toque. The note, written in execrable

English, recounted, blow-by-blow, the events of the trial and ended with more effusive thanks for his acquittal.

Over the next twenty years or so, at Christmas, I regularly received a bottle of the same cheap Champagne and a note of thanks. The note never contained the traditionally obligatory return address or a phone number. I noticed over time that his English was improving markedly. I always used this gift to make Champagne and orange juice for the family at Christmas breakfast.

Then one day, I happened to have some business on Granville Island. Walking past a row of studios and small shops, I spied the name on a door: "Bo Hujduk". It was a glass-blowing works, and the sign advertised bowls, jugs, and assorted glassware. The shop was closed, but I made a note of the telephone number on the door. Some days later, I succeeded in getting through to Bo on the phone. Yes indeed, this was my old client. And yes, he was now in the glassware business. He had learned the trade and established a business adequate enough to support himself in some comfort. I did not get the impression that he had any family.

The following Christmas I did not receive the usual bottle of cheap Champagne. Instead, he left a beautiful glass vase at the reception desk. It was of high quality, sturdy and simple, but exquisitely designed. We have used it ever since as a container for flowers.

This was the last I ever heard from Bo. The next time I was down on Granville Island, I looked for his shop. It was gone. On a whim, I Googled his name. To my astonishment, I discovered that he had a studio in the West End and employed three people in his glass-blowing business.

FIRING MRS. FORSBERG

W hat, you may ask, is the quality that lies at the bottom of the tool kit that all efficient people carry. Studious observation, over nearly half a century of practising law, has lead me to conclude that decisiveness is what secures their success.

The Duke of Wellington commanded armies that were composed of foot soldiers who were largely illiterate jailbirds and social misfits. He once described them as the scum of the earth, "I don't know what effect they have on the enemy, but they terrify me." His officers had all bought their commissions and were drawn from the ranks of the aristocracy, schooled in Latin and Greek, with no prior training that prepared them to command men in battle. Thus the Duke was forced to train this rabble himself, with the assistance of those few of his senior officers and NCOs with some experience of combat. He devised a system for teaching dimwitted officers to think—a system that is still used in the armed forces today.

He bade them all, when presented with a situation that required a decision, to remind themselves of four words: aim, factors, courses, plan.

You have to form a clear idea of the objective, the aim, that you need to achieve—if only on the principle that if you don't know where you are going, you most assuredly will not get there.

Once sure of your objective, you canvass all the factors that can come to bear on the situation. Where is the enemy, what is their strength? What is the lie of the land, your strength, your supplies, your reserves, the weaponry available, the weather, and so on? Some factors will be unknown and that will create risk. Intelligence, the gathering of information, is one of the nine principles of war. Without it, an army will flounder its way to defeat. So if there are unknown factors that affect your decision, you try to gather intelligence about them. In any event you have to factor in all the unknowns and calculate the risks with care.

You then consider all the courses that are open to you in the light of the information available, and the aim. Weighing each, you finally decide which course to take—this is the plan. You go for it without hesitation. Never haver between options, once you have decided what to do. Maintenance of the aim is another of the nine principles of war.

I have run into a handful of efficient people. All were decisive, some ruthless. For the first nine years after my call to the bar, I worked for a firm called Bull, Housser, Tupper, Ray, Guy, and Merritt. The Tupper was Reginald Hibbert Tupper Q. C.. A highly respected lawyer, he ran a sophisticated corporate practice, acted for two banks, several insurance companies, and a wide array of the larger businesses in Vancouver whose owners lunched regularly at the Vancouver Club. He had been schooled at the Royal Naval College at Osbourne in England. Graduating as a midshipman, he decided to return to Vancouver to practise law. In the First World War, he enlisted with the Seaforth Highlanders of Canada, and became a major in command of a machine-gun company, but was gassed at the second battle of Ypres and invalided back home.

When I knew him, he always arrived at the office about two hours before anybody else, read the mail, and worked steadily until he had nothing further to do, which was usually around three in the afternoon. Then he had his secretary call a taxi and repaired to his home. He did own a car, but that was what his wife drove. He calculated that it was less expensive to take taxis than endure the expense of a second car. In any event, he could read in a taxi, a pursuit denied to him if he was driving. He ran his practice with consummate strictness and discipline. It may have been his military training that caused him to be utterly straightforward. You never misunderstood anything that he said. Many people in the firm were secretly afraid of him.

One day, I had occasion to go and see him about a task that I was working on for him. I had made an appointment through his secretary. I arrived at his office at the appointed hour, not late, to be sure. I knocked on his door. His secretary was in his office and called me in. "Oh, David, Mr. Tupper is in a partners' meeting, but he won't be long. Why don't you sit down and wait for him." I did as she had bidden and she left the room. Some minutes later, Reggie Tupper bustled in.

"David, I am sorry to be late. Would you mind waiting a minute. I have something I must attend to right away. It won't take long." With that, he picked up the phone and dialled a number. Three digits: an intra-office extension. "Mrs. Forsberg? Reg Tupper here. There's something I need to discuss with you. Could you please come and see me immediately." He rang off and waited. Mrs, Forsberg was the office accountant, a grey-haired woman of Scandinavian extraction; she had been with the firm for some years. She knocked and entered the office. Reggie Tupper bade her to sit down, though he himself remained standing. What followed was a scene I have never forgotten. It took all of ninety seconds.

"Mrs. Forsberg, I have a very unpleasant task to perform. The partners have asked me to inform you that we have decided to dispense with your services. You are entitled to three months notice, of course, but we don't think it would be fair to ask you to work in the firm while you are under notice, so we will pay you immediately and you need not continue here. Please clear out your desk, and leave as soon as it is convenient." With that, he walked briskly around the table, and held out his hand to her.

"The partners have asked me to thank you for all you have done for the firm while you have been here. We will, of course, give you a reference." He ushered her to the door, opened it, and she was gone.

Now, if I had been burdened with the task of firing the firm's accountant, I would have thought about it for a while, and decided to wait till after lunch. Then I would have probably gone home to have a stiff scotch and talk to my wife about what to do and what to say, and then returned to the office the next day and procrastinated, performing other business until I could put off the task no longer.

Reggie Tupper's course of action may have bordered on the hard hearted, but he got it done efficiently, and without any apparent agonizing on his part. In any case, it made no difference to Mrs. Forsberg whether she was terminated within minutes of the partner's meeting that she knew nothing about, or the next day. I never did find out why she was fired, and of course, I knew I would not be told, and had no business asking.

First Aid

The Honourable Mr. Justice Thomas Wilfred Brown was a well-known eccentric. Holidaying in Portland, Oregon, one day, he and his wife ordered breakfast in their hotel room. A seagull perched on the windowsill. Tommy Brown opened the window and fed it some bread. This inevitably attracted a small flock of gulls, all seeking sustenance from this fortuitous bird food bank. Now, Tommy Brown drank, probably more than was good for him. He extracted a bottle of gin from his suitcase, and lacing the bread with gin, began feeding this intoxicating concoction to the gulls. Unused to alcohol, the birds soon became staggeringly drunk, laying about the bedroom floor and falling about the windowsill. He picked up the phone and called the front desk to complain that his room was full of drunken seagulls, and insisted they send someone up to relocate them as soon as possible, and to clean up the mess they had created.

Superimposed on this eccentricity was a strong propensity to hypochondria. He, in fact, suffered from asthma, but imagined that he was subject to a litany of additional respiratory diseases. He had, so he claimed, stomach ulcers, acid reflux, was subject to gastrointestinal bleeds, and firmly believed, contrary to his doctor's opinion, that he also had Crone's disease.

His doctor advised him to stop drinking alcohol and to drink milk to calm his tender stomach. This was advice Tommy did not want to hear, so he compromised—he still drank scotch, but instead of adding soda, he drank it with milk. This, at least, meant that he was following half his doctor's advice.

One winter's day in Vancouver, he was presiding over a case in the old Vancouver court house. Counsel appearing before him were both women. One was Inger Hansen. Now Inger had been born in Denmark. Petite, with a mass of long blonde hair, she had the reputation of being the prettiest woman at the BC bar. Inger was in the middle of her submission, when Tommy Brown caught his breath and burst into a paroxysm of coughing. Inger stopped. The judge grew red in the face and began to have difficulty breathing. He bent double, coughing all the while, and disappeared beneath the bench. The two women stood, wondering what to do as the sounds of coughing, puffing, and seriously distressed breathing arose from beneath the bench. Slowly the eruptions subsided. The judge emerged from beneath the bench, still trying to catch his breath. There was a pause in the judge's whirlwind of respiratory difficulties, and Inger seized the moment. With a solicitous look, she asked, "My Lord, is there anything we can do for you?"

Tommy Brown paused, looked down at this vision of loveliness offering aid, and opened his mouth. Then he closed it again, and then said "Oh, yes, Miss Hansen. There is. Just a little mouth to mouth resuscitation, if you please."

JAIL TIME

Part VIII of the Income Tax Act was that portion of the statute that had to do with tax incentives for research and development. It was, even in a statute as notoriously convoluted as the Income Tax Act, a particularly difficult section to understand. Any ordinary literate citizen would have to read its opaque and obfuscatory clauses several times before its purpose was finally revealed, through its fog of sub-clauses, parentheses, and dangling participles. One sentence in Part VIII contained one hundred and thirty five words. To read Part VIII was to become enmeshed in a literary barbed-wire entanglement.

Shortly put, Part VIII permitted you to register your research and development project, spend your money, and then deduct it from taxable income at the end of the year. It started as a good idea. By the end of six months, Revenue Canada had lost over one hundred million dollars with little research and development concluded. So the scheme was abruptly terminated. A collection of wily accountants and tax lawyers had hit upon a perfectly legal scheme whereby registrants would sell their tax credits to a corporation for a large up-front payment in cash.

George Wellman stumbled upon Part VIII while casting about for financing for his food irradiation project. George had run a successful paint retailing business on the prairies and had retired at a relatively early age, to live in the Lower Mainland with his wife and two daughters. He had learned about the merits of food irradiation while still selling paint to his prairie farmer customers. Intrigued, he read all he could on the subject and arrived in British Columbia determined to make his fortune in the food irradiation business. He had discovered that by irradiating food with a short wave gamma ray, the shelf life of food is greatly prolonged. The radiation kills all the bacteria and insects, and the food will last for months without refrigeration. It would be a boon to retail stores and food transportation companies, and food would be able to be consigned to countries in the tropics with no spoilage.

The problem is that radiation, like x-rays, is dangerous, and the machinery required is expensive. Members of the public routinely object that eating irradiated food will cause cancer. George was convinced that it would not. As he pointed out, when one has an x-ray, one is not radioactive as soon as the machine is turnted off.

I did not know if he was right, but he sounded convincing. He had already built a huge concrete box of a building, the biggest structure in the neighbourhood, to accommodate his food irradiation machinery.

He was referred to me by a fellow lawyer, because he had been charged with an infraction of the Custom's Act for failing to pay duty on the picowave machine he had imported from California. The picowave machine was the arrow point of the whole operation. I saw it after George had it installed in his concrete fortress. It looked like a souped up version of a cannon from one of Lord Nelson's first-raters.

Now, a picowave machine delivers a short wave. Actually, quite short: a trillionth of a metre. Food was wheeled into a concrete enclosure in the bunker, placed on a shelf, the doors closed and the food was then zapped by the machine.

After George was acquitted of what her Majesty's customs officers perceived as smuggling, I spent the next four years defending him on various charges under the Income Tax Act. He was convicted once and then acquitted on appeal. Then the Crown hit upon the charge of tax evasion. He had sold his tax credits to a well-known eastern merchant bank for nearly two million dollars, which he spent on equipment for the picowave project. The construction and administrative costs very soon consumed this fund and his problem was that he was going to encounter difficulty generating enough income to pay his tax when it fell due, for he had sold his tax credits for the cash up front In addition, there was serious and energetic opposition from the citizens in his neighbourhood to his perceived irradiation of the population of the township. He knew he was right about the safety of the irradiation.

He was charged with offences of various kinds on three more occasions. I managed to keep him out of jail for four years. Crown counsel, who prosecuted him on these three charges, was an old acquaintance, efficient, firm, but easy to deal with and utterly fair. I spent unnecessary energy trying to convince George that I should not try to have him disqualified because of George's perception that he had a conflict of interest. The officer from Revenue Canada who was assisting Crown counsel was a hard-nosed, but decent, competent bureaucrat, with whom I was able to establish a friendly working relationship, so that eventually he would go to some trouble to find documents I needed, or information that I would find helpful. George was implacably opposed to my tactics. I had a constant struggle to withstand his efforts to persuade me to go to war with these people. To follow his instructions would have been hopelessly counterproductive.

Despite my several years of effort, George was eventually convicted on a charge of tax evasion. Then came the day when he was to be sentenced.

His partner in all these devious transactions, an accountant who had once been the president of a well-known credit union, had pleaded guilty to the charges, a step that had infuriated George, who was convinced, not without reason, that this plea had affected his own conviction. We all appeared in Provincial Court on the day appointed for his sentencing. The Crown sought a jail sentence, as I had warned George it would. I called a couple of witnesses to testify about George's character. They were not very effective. George had few roots in BC and his irradiation activities had not endeared him to his neighbours, so I had run into difficulties finding suitable witnesses to speak on his behalf. In the result, the judge sentenced George to two years, less a day, so that he would serve time in a provincial, rather than a federal prison.

George had a habit of bringing his two daughters with him to interviews in my office, and to all his court appearances. They both maintained a stolid silence on all these occasions and it was impossible to tell what either of them thought of their father's engagements with the law. His wife, who rarely accompanied him, was not appreciably more communicative, but on the occasions when I did meet her, she made it clear that she had a deep, abiding faith in her husband's irradiation project. She was of German heritage. Tall and slim, with long wavy blonde hair, she bore a remarkable resemblance to Marlene Dietrich, but without that actress' sultry vibrancy.

George had brought his whole family to this hearing—his wife and both daughters. His daughters seemed unmoved by their father's sentence. They had already heard me tell George that he was likely to go down for as much as two years, and must have been resigned to it. George had, however, obviously failed to inform his wife of the advice I had given him, for when she heard the sentence pronounced, she suddenly came to life. She shot to her feet with a cry of dismay, held her hands to her head and sobbed. The judge called a short adjournment. She struggled out of the row of chairs where she had been sitting and rushed over to where I was standing at the counsel table. "Mr. Roberts, this is terrible. Two years! That's a lifetime for George at this stage. He's almost on the verge of getting his business really going. He can't be sent to jail now. The whole thing will collapse. He must be given time to get it on its feet. Couldn't I serve his sentence for him? Ask the judge! I'm sure, when the situation's explained to him, he'll understand and let me go to jail instead." I patiently explained to her that this was simply not possible. The judge had no jurisdiction to substitute a wife, or anybody, for someone who has been sentenced to jail. It was not like having a teammate serve the two minutes for a goaltender's penalty She tried to persuade me just to ask the judge. She seemed sure that I could talk him into it. I was tempted to do as she asked, not because I thought there was the remotest chance of the judge going along with it, but because I thought the judge, whom I had known for some years, would be sufficiently startled by the request that it would become the subject of discussion in judge's chambers for days to come. But, I decided that the request was so outlandish that I really couldn't screw up the courage to make it. Ever after I regretted that I didn't make the submission. It was so unusual that it would have been fun to try it on. It was a true case of *esprit d'escalier.*

MY DOWNHILL RACING CAREER

If pressed, I would have to admit that I am not an accomplished skier. In the hierarchy of skiers, I estimate that I would fall into the category of an advanced duffer. I first donned a pair of skis at the age of fourteen. I had journeyed to Brussels to visit my French sister-in–law to be, who was about to marry my brother. Her father, a smaller version of Maurice Chevalier, and her two brothers, took me south to the Ardennes and there rented for me a pair of skis. They had kitted me out with a pair of old lace-up boots. The skis, on which they intended for me to learn, were long, wooden, had no steel edges, and attached to the boots by means of what I later learned were called rat trap bindings. I spent the better part of the day in a state of terror. I quickly learned to stop by means of the snow-plough method, and snow ploughing down the hills came to be my preferred manner of descent. "*David, il faut oser, il faut oser!*" the brothers shouted at me, exhorting me to try harder. It was all very well for them; they had spent most of the war at a boarding school in Switzerland, where their father had sent them to get them out of reach of the Gestapo, and they had spent at least part of every winter's day skiing down black diamond chutes.

My next experience of skiing was in the Laurentians, while I was living in Montreal in the winter of 1952/3. I bought my own pair of skis. Still wooden, and still without benefit of steel edges, they were made, as I recollect, by CCM. I learned the Telemark and how to turn by moving one ski over at an angle and then transferring the other ski to join it. This turn was bestowed with a special name: the stem Christie. In those days, all the books that instructed novices how to ski, employed this name. The turn was really nothing more than a jack-knifed snow-plough for turning a corner, rather than arresting descent. I considered my ability to negotiate this turn to be a splendid accomplishment, and I used it for years until some ski instructor at the Sun Free Ski School, up Grouse Mountain, taught me the more simple and elegant parallel turn.

I really began to ski properly at Mt. Baker. In the 1950s, some half dozen friends and I rented a log cabin each winter, on the banks of the Nooksack River, and we spent almost every weekend clutching the Mt. Baker rope tows and racing down its slopes. I had now graduated to a pair of Head skis, then the last word in ski technology. You measured their length by standing and curling your fingers over the tip. These skis sported a rudimentary quick release binding in case of a fall—very comforting. And then we all got married and the cabin reverted to its owner.

In the early 1980s, a group of enthusiastic lawyers in Vancouver thought up the idea of holding an annual law firm ski race. Each firm was to enter a five-member team. The sex of the members was irrelevant, but it was a requirement that each team be composed of at least one woman, and one member had to be over fifty years of age. Four members of my firm strode into my office, explained the rules of the race, and told me that, since I was the only member of the firm over fifty who could ski, I was automatically drafted as the fifth member of the team.

The day of the race, I travelled to Blackcomb with the team. The race was scheduled to start at two in the afternoon, so we spent the morning enjoying the slopes. I soon realized that the rest of the team were experts at the sport compared to me. I grew increasingly apprehensive as the morning wore on. We ate our packed lunches sitting on a snow bank near the starting gates for the race. There were two gates, for there were two runs. Two racers were to race down at the same time. A rope divided the two tracks, and each track had a rope on the outside: three ropes, two tracks. Hitting a rope disqualified you. A small woman was busying about, organizing the race, shepherding racers into the gates, supervising the starter, and organizing the timing of the racers. Each time a racer finished, their time was announced. By the time my turn came around, the fastest time was down to one minute, forty-three point two seconds, a time achieved by Bjorn Hareid, a lawyer at Ladner Downs. Of Norwegian origin, he confessed that he had started skiing in Norway at the age of three.

The day had started out mild and then grown colder. As a result, the race-tracks had become icy. By the time my turn came to race, the contestants who had raced before me had gouged serious ruts at each gate. The rest of my team, who were to ski after me, exhorted me to get to the finish line as best I could, and not worry about my time. It was, they said, more important to finish and not be disqualified than to make good time. Only the time of the fastest three would count, but if I fell and did not finish, this would compromise the time of the first three.

I was ushered to my starting gate. I looked over at the track next door and saw that Hamish Cameron, from the Bull Housser and Tupper firm, was my racing opponent. He looked supremely confident. We grinned at each other. The command to go was given and off we went. I immediately realized that the course was far steeper than the hills I was used to negotiating. I habitually chose gentle, wide-sweeping slopes that caused me as little challenge as possible, slopes that had been groomed by the nocturnal snow cat. This slope was a black diamond affair and I was soon accelerating out of control. My heart was pounding at an alarming rate, not from the exertion, but from the sheer fright of staring down at a slope that looked to me to be about sixty degrees of churned up snow and ice, which I knew I would not be able to descend at the kind of speed that I needed to achieve in order to register a respectable time.

I reached the first gate and was horrified to see that the earlier racers had gouged a deep rut around the poles. In a desperate attempt to regain some control prior to negotiating this hazard, I resorted to my old snow plough routine to slow myself down. I staggered through the gate, gathered myself together, and set off towards gate number two. Hamish had already reached gate number two and seemed to be negotiating it in grand style. He was only two years younger than me. I was, by now, in a considerable panic and feared at least one broken limb, if not two.

Hamish was now through gate number two and barrelling down to number three. I decided to go for broke and set off to try and catch him. It was at this point, as I reached a speed I swear I had never achieved before, that I glanced over the rope to my right and noticed that the small woman, who had started us off, was skiing down beside my track. She was gesturing to me, beckoning me on, and shouting, "Come on, faster, faster!" She was going faster than I was, and then I realized that she was skiing backwards. Backwards! Faster than me! I finally made it through the last gate and saw below me a hundred yards of steep, wide snow right down to the finish line. I thrust my poles under my arms and went into a tuck that I had seen real racers use. Hamish won, but I had at least gained some ground on him. The small woman, who had accompanied me backwards down the track, was already at the finish line. She grinned. "Well done." She grabbed the rope tow and was whisked back up the hill. I shuffled over to Hamish and congratulated him. "Hamish, who was that woman skiing backwards beside us," I asked him.

"Oh, didn't you recognize her? It's Nancy Greene. She runs Blackcomb's customer relations department."

Paisley

My mother, born in Lancashire, grew up in Yorkshire—Halifax, to be precise, one of the least lovely of England's industrial revolution towns. She cherished unshakeable views about many immutable truths, not always shared by those to whom she disclosed them. One of her firmly held opinions was that England is really two countries. The dividing line, she claimed, was somewhere around Birmingham. North country folk, she maintained, were kind, hard-working, generous souls. You could tell that just by the way they talk. They persist in calling everybody *love*—an endearment that illustrates their attitude toward each other. "Not," she would say, "like the snobs in the south, unwelcoming, greedy, and self-indulgent."

I took many of my mother's pronouncements with a teenager's grain of salt. Then, many years after I had come to Canada, Gill and I attended a conference of Canadian lawyers in Paisley. Paisley, of course, is in Scotland—farther north than my mother had been talking about, and in fact, a different country, but I think it fell within her definition.

It was, without doubt, the finest convention I had ever attended. Some 400 lawyers (most of them from British Columbia), congregated in Paisley to celebrate a famous lawsuit, Donaghue v. Stevenson, a decision of the House of Lords that had advanced the law of negligence.

Mrs. Donaghue and a friend had visited the Wellmeadow Café in Paisley. The friend bought Mrs. Donaghue a bottle of ginger beer and an ice cream. Mrs. Donaghue poured half the bottle over the ice cream, and ate it. She then poured the remaining ginger beer onto what remained of her ice cream. To her consternation, as the dregs cascaded onto the remains of the ice cream, disclosed to view were the remains of a decomposed snail. Mrs. Donaghue immediately fell ill, and remained indisposed for some time. She consulted attorneys in Glasgow, who issued a writ naming the Stevenson Bottling Works as defendant. Stevenson's had bottled the ginger beer and the snail with it. But they had no contractual relationship with Mrs. Donaghue. The House of Lords held that, nonetheless, she had a valid cause of action. This was a significant step in the development of the law of negligence and recognized as such to this day.

We had all congregated in Paisley to celebrate this case. There were lectures from learned professors and other distinguished legal scholars. We held luncheons, tours of local museums, and the good people of Paisley held a banquet in our honour. We all supposed that four hundred lawyers spending holiday money in Paisley justified that expense, though in truth, it was really sparked by genuine Scottish hospitality. We held a parade from the town hall to the site of the Wellmeadow Café. Four hundred Canadian lawyers marching through the streets of Paisley. All the shopkeepers came out of their stores to wave and cheer. It was all great fun.

On the final day (a Sunday), we held an ecumenical service in The Presbyterian Coates Memorial Church. The Roman Catholic Archbishop of Glasgow journeyed from his home diocese and preached a brief sermon. A Catholic cleric in a Presbyterian church? Only in Scotland.

Before the church service, I found myself standing on the church steps. A Scottish police officer stood beside me. We fell into conversation and the subject turned to the parade of the day before. He said that the parade had given grave concern to the local police. That Saturday was the occasion of the local Derby, the soccer match between St. Mirren's and Glasgow Celtic. (Presbyterian v. Catholic.) The police realized that the soccer crowds were going to disrupt the parade. It would be a disaster. They had ten days to act. Should they ask us to cancel the parade? What they in fact did was persuade the soccer clubs to re-schedule the game to start half an hour earlier, so that the soccer crowd would be firmly seated in the stadium well before the parade started. I remembered my mother's sentiments and realized that if this had happened in London, the police would have either done nothing or ordered us to cancel our parade. But we were guests in their town, so the police removed the threat to our entertainment.

Then the Lord Chancellor drove up. He himself was a Scot, Lord McKay. He was all by himself in a big black limousine. One police motorcycle out-rider had shepherded him to the church. As Lord McKay walked up the steps of the church, I turned to my friendly police officer, and for want of anything better to say, said "Oh dear, just one outrider? You're not guard-ing the Lord Chancellor very well today are you?"

He turned to me and (in his thick Scottish accent) said "Son, ye don't underrstand. The I.R.A never operates in Scotland. They think we're down-trodden like they are. They'll run guns through Stranraer, but they'll never use them in Scotland.

THE SCOTTISH BUS DRIVER

The citizens of Paisley were kindness itself and threw a banquet in the town hall for all those attending the pilgrimage. There were a number of excursions: to Robbie Burns' cottage, to the site of the Wellmeadow Café (where the pursuer drank the ginger beer), a trip down the Clyde River, and a visit to the Burrell Collection in Glasgow.

Gill went on the excursion to the Burrell Collection. Those bent on this visit boarded a bus at their hotels. The bus, now almost full, had stopped at the last hotel, the Excelsior. The hotel parking lot was full and the bus driver had difficulty finding anywhere to park in order to load the last of his passengers. He pulled his bus into a crowded spot, close to the front door of the old hotel, and waited while a handful of patrons climbed aboard. As the last one gained a seat, the hotel's doorman climbed into the bus. He was dressed in a light grey uniform with brass buttons, and wore a large peaked hat, also grey, with an imposing black visor and a bright red hat-band. He addressed the bus driver in tones and with a volume that would have done credit to a regimental sergeant major.

"Yurr blocking traffic! Did ye no see the sign? It clearly reads *no parking*! Canna ye read, ye lummocks? Get this ugly pantechnican oot o' the way. Yurr impeding access to the hotel and ithhers canna get oot! Get off wi' ye! An' dinna come back here! Yurr causing nay end o' disturbance!"

Unburdened of this unlovely denunciation and well pleased with himself, the doorman and his hat descended from the bus, shrugging his shoulders, shooting his cuffs, and marching officiously back to the door of which he was the proud custodian. He took up station, legs apart, like an infantryman standing at ease with his hands clasped behind his back, and his chin held high—as he surveyed the domain of his parking lot.

The bus driver had sat, clutching his wheel in absolute silence, staring out of the front window of his bus while this tirade had been delivered. He watched this uniformed little Hitler march to his precious hotel door. Then he turned, stood up, and addressed the assembled and aston-ished passengers.

"Weell, there ye are, ye see? That's what happens when ye gi' a man a hat." With that he sat down, engaged the gears, and drove his bus off in the direction of the Burrell Collection.

ROLF WEDDIGEN

Rolf Weddigen had a mischievous sense of humour that would bubble to the surface at sometimes unexpected moments. Sometime in the 1960s, the benchers of the Law Society held a meeting. Members of the profession were, on this occasion, permitted to attend, which was unusual in those days, when the Law Society preferred to conduct its business in stealthy seclusion. An issue had arisen over a question of advertising, which then, was a professional sin. Many law offices had signs in their windows announcing the name of the law firm. Harry Fan, a well-known practitioner of Chinese ancestry, ran a practice in Chinatown—on Gore Avenue, to be precise. It had come to the Law Society's attention that Harry Fan had installed a neon sign in his office window advertising his firm: HARRY FAN LAW OFFICE. The benchers were debating whether or not Mr. Fan should be enjoined from thus advertising. It was at least unseemly and perhaps even unprofessional. As the debate wore on, Rolf rose to address the benchers, "Master Treasurer," he said, "would it not be possible to reach a compromise in this case. Perhaps Mr. Fan could be allowed to keep his sign lit for only half the time—let's say one second on and one second off." The debate, thus derailed, ended with a decision to do nothing about Harry Fan's neon sign.

One day, Rolf had occasion to sue the government. This necessitated creating a style of cause that named the Queen as a defendant. The rules of the Supreme Court require that statements of claim contain a description of each party to the lawsuit and their address. The second paragraph of Rolf's statement of claim described the Queen as "A married woman, with a residence at Buckingham Palace, London, England".

THE SOVIET COMMERCIAL ATTACHÉ

A lexander Mikhailovitch Soronodnikoff was one of our most cherished clients. We were never certain as to his exact position, but our connection with him came as a result of our representing numerous of the Soviet Union Merchant Marine ships, which would dock in Vancouver and load grain to carry back to mother Russia. Alexander was our liaison with the captains of these vessels when they needed legal representation. These ships belonged to Morflot, the merchant marine equivalent of the Soviet Navy. It is to the high seas what Aeroflot is to the skies. All its sailors wore a standard uniform and it boasted a hierarchy of ranks similar to the navy.

Alexander was in the nature of a commercial attaché. Except that he didn't seem to be attached to anything. We believed his immediate superiors to be secreted somewhere in the impenetrable corridors of the Soviet Embassy in Ottawa, though he seemed always to report to Moscow, whence came back his instructions. Dealing with the Russians, we had found in the past, was like groping one's way through an Elizabethan maze. Nothing was ever straightforward—offence was easily given and "yes" only ever seemed to mean that they had heard what you had said. Worst of all nobody was ever able to take responsibility for a decision. Alexander's arrival in Vancouver changed all that. We were delighted to find a representative who would give us instructions, take advice, and didn't duck responsibility as a matter of routine.

We grew quite fond of Alexander. He was easy to deal with, saw to it that our bills were paid on time, and approached his duties with a wonderfully cynical attitude toward his superiors, particularly the Soviet government. His view of his government was similar to that of a weary parent whose children had not yet learned to cope with life, and who had long since given up expecting improvement.

He was always good company, so one day we decided to take him out to lunch, just for the fun of it. Three of us picked him up at his office in the Pacific Centre. We were aiming for a restaurant in the Bentall Centre and this necessitated our taking the elevator to the ground floor and going out onto Dunsmuir Street via four double-steel doors that you opened

111

outwards by means of bars across the inside, upon which you pushed—the kind of doors that are designed to facilitate the egress of large crowds in case of fire or some such emergency. We each pushed on a separate door, so that all four were activated. Assembling outside on the sidewalk, we noticed that Alexander was standing with his back to us, staring at the four doors.

"Alexander, what's up? What are you staring at?"

He turned, and with a sly smile, said, "You know. If we were in Russia, only one of those doors would work."

We reached the restaurant and ordered lunch. As an officer in the Soviet Foreign Service, he was necessarily a member of the communist party. We had always respected this and kept off the subject of politics when in his company. But this day, he produced from his breast pocket a large envelope with a blue logo stamped on it. "Gentlemen," he said, "I need to consult you on matter of some delicacy." He extracted several pages of a typed letter from the envelope. We all sat up a little, our heads tilted to one side, waiting in breathless expectation. It sounded serious. "This," he said, waving the letter dramatically about the table, "is letter I received this morning. Is from Progressive Conservative Party of Canada." He laid the letter carefully on the table and pointed a bony finger at it for emphasis. "Progressive Conservative Party asks me for donation. And," he raised his eyebrows for emphasis, "pledge of future financial support." He paused and peered round the table at us. "What do you think I should do?"

THIEVERY

A theft stalks its victims in many forms. Sometimes it is violent—bank robbery for instance, when bystanders may fall to a robber's bullet. At the other end of the scale comes petty pilfering—the surreptitious hand in the till, theft by finding, when the thief stumbles on a lost object and makes off with it when the owner could be found with little effort. Except for robbery, which is (by definition) performed in the open, theft (like fraud) is a secret endeavour. Indeed, it has been said that secrecy is the badge of fraud. Conrad Black, that dishonoured peer, was charged and convicted of fraud for entering into contracts, with purchasers of his company's newspapers, that paid him and his confederates unimaginably large sums of money in consideration of their not setting up in competition. The prosecution alleged that the contracts were a sham, and that the money paid should have gone to Hollinger, the selling company. Fraud was alleged. The problem for the prosecution was that these contracts were disclosed in Hollinger's financial statements. Not without reason, his Lordship argued that, just because those concerned did not trouble to read the financial statements properly, it did not follow that he was guilty of fraud. There were those who found this immoral, perhaps, but fraud, he claimed, it was not. It was all in the small print—the infamous small print that shrouds, at the same time as it reveals, the clause that is slipped in to the contract, as if by a literary circus magician. Now you see it now you don't.

In the days when I practised a fair amount of criminal law, I defended a significant number of thieves, by no means always successfully. Shoplifting, I thought, was some way towards the bottom of the scale of sinfulness. It rarely involved violence, for (by definition) if it did, it ceased to be shoplifting and was elevated to the status of robbery.

Two cases I remember in particular. There was the middle-aged Cantonese lady who was caught stealing clothes from a lady's shop. Hers was the classic case of mid-life, psychological instability. She didn't need the clothes, and in any event, could easily have paid for them. There was no defence. She plead guilty. I called evidence regarding her emotional condition, though the most persuasive argument was the spectacle of this small, dejected woman weeping inconsolably in court, as the judge listened to the testimony I called in mitigation of sentence. He took pity on her, gave her a lecture, and a suspended sentence.

Then there was the engaging French Canadian lad, out of work and a long way from home. He had been arrested for stealing two tins of *paté de foie gras* and a can of caviar from a delicatessen in West Vancouver. With no possible defence, I advised him to plead guilty and did my best to plead for a light sentence. As was my invariable custom, I told the judge that my client did not want to stand mute while I pleaded on his behalf, but was prepared to answer any questions the judge might wish to ask him. Only once before had a judge ever taken me up on such an offer. On this occasion, the judge did ask the accused a question directly. The judge was Alfie Watts, who had been the Secretary of the Law Society for many years and whom I knew well. Watts was not impressed by the accused, and asked him why he had stolen food that was not exactly a necessity for his bare subsistence. My client turned on all the Gallic charm he could muster, apologized at some length, promised not to do it ever again, and slyly avoided answering the question directly. Watts gave him a week in jail, enough to teach him a lesson and not enough for him to pick up any bad habits from the other inmates. Jails have a tendency to function as schools for crime. Kids, uninitiated in the fine points of vice, often leave prison indoctrinated in the ways of the underworld. The federal government's unimaginative "tough on crime" minimum sentences are destined to graduate any number of rogues with master's degrees in larceny, who might otherwise have avoided this free tuition in the fine points of theft.

One sunny Vancouver morning, I had occasion to need to purchase an item from a chandlery that sells its wares in a shop at the entrance to Granville Island. I was ambling over to the cash desk when I became aware of a conversation, between the manager of the shop and an ill-dressed, burly individual in his thirties. The burly one handed the manager some goods, in a plastic bag with a name on it that was not that of the chandlery. The manager peered into the bag, said something to the burly one, then turned to the cashier and said, in a loud voice, "This gentleman wishes to purchase these items. Please ring them up and he will pay you. You don't need to ask anything about them." The cashier took the bag. The burly one walked round the cash desk, cast me an embarrassed glance, pulled out a wallet, and extracted some bills. The cashier rang up the sale. "$49.20 please." Two twenties and a ten. He took the change—three quarters and a nickel—thanked the cashier, and made for the door where the manager had been standing watching. The manager held out his hand. The burly one shook it. The manager grasped the hand in both his hands, and said something I couldn't hear. The burly one nodded and I heard him thanking the manager again. Then he was gone. Out of the door in a flash.

I fell to imagining what had happened. Burly had obviously been agonizing over having stolen the goods. He had probably spent days screw-
ing up enough courage to return to the shop. Easier to keep the stuff and
do nothing. There would be a risk in returning in person to give back the
goods. No telling what the reaction would be. Should he slink into the
shop, deposit the goods somewhere, and leave? If he were detected doing
that it might lead to complications. He could wander round the shop and
then go through the line up for the cash register and pay as if he had just
selected them—probably the safest option. His decision to confront the
manager and own up must have been driven by some need to be shriven
of his sin—a desire for some kind of forgiveness that would expiate his
crime. He would have to risk the chance of an adverse reaction from some
unforgiving cretin. Would the relief at recovering the money owed out-
weigh the anger generated by the theft?

In the event, he was lucky. He had run into a shopkeeper with sufficient
compassion to forgive the repentant sinner. His relief was evident, though
the speed with which he fled the shop demonstrated a residual anxiety to
be out and away from any danger he had risked—and it had been a risk.

My final experience with shoplifting occurred in the West Vancouver
Safeway. Gill asked me to pick up some stores on the way home, so I
swung through the parking lot. Full. I drove around the back and parked
on the road. The Safeway was busy. Progress from aisle to aisle was slow,
impeded by shopping carts groaning with produce, pop bottles, and babies.
I didn't have to buy enough to warrant picking up a shopping basket, so
as I elbowed my way from aisle to aisle, my arms filling up with groceries. Two avocados. A can of Italian tomatoes. Two cans of olives. A pot
of basil. Bananas. Where are the bananas? As I reached for a sufficiently
ripe cluster, an elderly lady got me in the kidneys with her shopping cart.
Avocados now rolling about the floor. Perfunctory apology. I don't normally glare at old ladies. She sniffed and manoeuvred her cart towards
the lettuces. I finally reached the end of my shopping list and made for
the door.

I reached the car. Now I had to find my car key. In pocket ... which
pocket? Arms full, so I placed all the groceries on the roof of the car, pre-
paratory to fishing out my key. It was at that point that it dawned on my
stressed mind that the goods were not stowed in a shopping bag. That was
odd. I stared at the array of goods reposing on the roof. The purchases
were not in a bag because I had not purchased them. I had walked straight
out of the shop door without going through the line up for the cash register.

I swore and looked around to see if anyone had followed me out of the
shop. No security in sight. I hastily gathered up the groceries and headed
back to the store. I would just hustle inside and find a nice welcoming line
up and join it as if nothing had happened. No point in trying to explain to
a store cashier. That would only have been necessary if someone stopped
me and asked for an explanation. I paid up. The bagging boy thrust the

groceries into a plastic bag and I left, with an overwhelming sense of relief. But I'd had a nasty fright. What if I had been stopped before I could get back to the forgiving comfort of the line up?

I thought about the consequences of this incident all the way home. None of the excuses for not paying for the goods, which I had heard so often in court, would have been of any avail. Shopkeepers had heard it all before. Judges had heard it all before. I'd heard it all before. If I had been convicted, the Law Society would have been required to launch disciplinary action. I might have faced disbarment.

My anxiety—angst as the Germans call it—deepened the more I thought about it. I still think about it from time to time, always with a stressful twinge of angst.

CECIL MERRITT

C harles Cecil Ingersoll Merritt was born on November 10, 1908, on his mother's kitchen table, in his parents' house in Stanley Park, on the shores of Lost Lagoon. The house later became the park warden's house, now long-since demolished. His father was killed in the First World War. A company commander in the 16th Battalion, Canadian Scottish, he was shot by a sniper during the second battle of Ypres.

I was introduced to Cecil by Tommy Korikan, who was articled at Cecil's firm, then called Bull, Housser, Tupper, Ray, Guy and Merritt. At the time I was articled to Pete Marshall at Davis and Co. I eventually transferred my articles to Cecil Merritt, and when I was later taken on as an associate, I was number thirteen on the totem pole.

Tommy Korikan ushered me into the presence of a man of imposing stature, well over six feet tall, he was of sturdy build. Indeed, I learned later that he had been the captain of the Vancouver Athletic Club rugby team when it won the Western Canadian championship in 1931, and he had won the heavyweight boxing championship at the Royal Military College, Kingston, in which institution he was enrolled in 1925. He won a number of academic prizes, mostly for history and literature. When he returned to Vancouver, he became articled to his uncle, Reginald Tupper, QC. His great grandfather was Sir Charles Tupper, sometime Prime Minister of Canada and one of the founding fathers of Confederation. Cecil was called to the bar in July 1932.

Cecil Merritt was commissioned as a 2nd lieutenant in the Seaforth Highlanders of Canada, and at the outbreak of war, in 1939, he was appointed to the active force with the rank of major, immediately going overseas. In March 1941, he was appointed Assistant Adjutant. In March 1942, now a lieutenant colonel, he was appointed to command the South Saskatchewan Regiment. It was while in command of that regiment, later that year, that he took part in the doomed raid on Dieppe, for his gallantry during which he was awarded the Victoria Cross.

The very first edition of the *Advocate* published the citation, which accompanied the award. It reads as follows:

For matchless gallantry and inspiring leadership whilst commanding his battalion during the Dieppe raid August 19th, 1942. From the point of landing, his unit's advance had to be made across a bridge in Pourville, which was swept by very heavy machine gun, mortar, and artillery fire and the first parties were mostly destroyed and the bridge thickly covered by their bodies.

A daring lead was required. Waving his helmet, Lt.-Col. Merritt rushed forward shouting, "Come on over! There is nothing to worry about here." He thus personally led the survivors of at least four parties, in turn, across the bridge. Quickly organizing these, he led them forward, and when held up by enemy pillboxes, he again headed rushes which succeeded in clearing them. In one case, he himself destroyed the occupants of the post by throwing grenades into it.

After several of his runners became casualties, he himself kept contact with his different positions. Although twice wounded, Lt.-Col. Merritt continued to direct the unit's operations with great vigour and determination, and while organizing the withdrawal, he stalked a sniper with a Bren gun and silenced him. He then coolly gave orders for the departure, and announced his intention to hold off and "get even" with the enemy.

When last seen, he was collecting Bren and Tommy guns and preparing a defensive position that successfully covered the withdrawal from the beach. Lt.-Col. Merritt is now reported to be a prisoner of war. To this commanding officer's personal daring, the success of this unit's operations and the safe re-embarkation of a large proportion of it were chiefly due.

In June 1945, upon Cecil's return to Vancouver, The Vancouver Bar Association held a luncheon in his honour. Charles Locke QC, then Treasurer of the Law Society, gave a speech, which was reported in the June 1945 edition of The Advocate, in which he said:

"The citation is not, however, the whole story of Col. Merritt's gallant conduct on that day. Sherwood Lett ... that, of course, was later Chief Justice Sherwood Lett and who was a brigadier and Cecil's immediate

superior officer at Dieppe ... told me this: After the events described in the citation, Merritt and his second in command were making a stand, with the remnants of their men, behind a wall close to the beach at Dieppe. The vessels, which were to take the troops off, owing to the state of the tide, were not able to get closer than some 200 yards from the beach. A man from Col. Merritt's regiment, who had tried to get out to the vessels, was shot and was struggling in the water and would evidently have drowned unless rescued. Two stretcher bearers who attempted to reach him were also shot. According to Col. Merritt's second in command, Merritt, watching this, said, "That man must be saved," and proceeded forthwith to wade out into the water and to pick out and carry ashore the wounded man in the face of very heavy machine-gun and rifle fire. It is for deeds such as this that the Victoria Cross is awarded, and I think Merritt won the award twice that day".

The wounded man, along with all the troops who remained stranded on the beach, was taken prisoner. At the end of the war, he joined the Vancouver police force, in which he served until his retirement.

The South Saskatchewans had taken one or two prisoners during the operation, and when all the troops who could do so had re-embarked, Cecil sent one of the prisoners to tell his German comrades that those Canadians left on the beach wished to surrender.

The Germans rounded them up, and at one point, Cecil joined his men, all of whom were sitting or standing around, dirty, exhausted, many wounded and looking thoroughly dispirited. Cecil addressed them in parade-square tones, and reminded them that they were all Canadian soldiers and that they were duty bound to behave like Canadian soldiers in the face of their captors. He called them to attention, had them fall in and march off in proper order. He wasn't about to allow any of his men to shuffle off in disorder like a beaten rabble, even if they had been captured.

I never heard Cecil voluntarily speak of his nine hours of combat. Pride was not one of his failings, and he was very modest about his achievements. I noticed that, when others made reference to the awarding of his Victoria Cross, he would become mildly embarrassed and quickly try to change the subject.

There were a couple of occasions when he did tell me things about the raid, which I have never read in the histories written about Dieppe. He said that one of the reasons they were not able to take the Germans by surprise was that, as the landing barges approached the shore, they ran into a French fishing fleet and got entangled with some of the fish boats. The commotion had alerted the Germans to the impending attack. So, when the landing barges reached the shore, the entire defence force was standing to and manning its guns. The official histories seem to say that it was a flotilla of small German naval craft that delayed the landing. I never actually heard him criticize the planning of the operation, except to say that it had been planned some many months earlier and then shelved. When it was decided that the raid should eventually go ahead, the plans were brought out and simply implemented without any review or revision.

He also told me about the incident at the bridge, the event that won him the Victoria Cross. He said that he and his troops were pinned down by enemy machine-gun and small arms fire, so that it was very dangerous to attempt to cross the bridge. He decided that he would lead the men across in one swift rush and then try to silence the guns commanding the bridge. He told the men what he intended them to do, looked around in preparation for the command to attack, and realized, from the look in their eyes, that they were not going to follow him. He deduced that if they thought they were shielded in some way from the sight of the enemy, they would pluck up enough courage to follow him over the bridge. He decided that he needed to indulge in a little psychology, so he sent word back to his mortar platoon to fire some smoke bombs at the land on the other side of the bridge. He did not, himself, believe that this would be very effective, but thought that it would encourage the men. As soon as the smoke broke out, he gave the order to attack, leapt out onto the bridge and succeeded in shepherding the bulk of the unit across it.

I have read somewhere, in a history of the raid, that after Cecil got across the bridge and had killed the occupants of the pillbox, he ran around to the back of it and encountered a German soldier at close quarters. Neither had time to reach for his weapons and a fist-fight ensued. Cecil beat the soldier to the ground with his fists. The German must have been quite surprised, but unknown to him, he had encountered the heavyweight champion of the Royal Military College.

His was the greater form of courage. He was not one of those people with nerves of steel, who have no fear. He once told me that he never went into court without a feeling of nervousness and apprehension. In fact, he kept a bottle of milk of magnesia in his locker at the courthouse, and used to take a swig of it to settle his nervous stomach before going into court. His acts of courage were those of a man who overcame his natural fear and acted courageously in spite of it.

He taught me a sense of responsibility. When we worked together, I was never left in any doubt as to what my responsibilities were and what his were. And he made it clear that I was responsible to produce what I had been assigned.

I once gave him a memorandum I had written. There were mistakes in it and some typing errors that altered the meaning of some sentences. He was not pleased. I tried to escape his criticism by blaming it on his secretary, who had typed it for me. He asked, "Didn't you proofread it?" Then he said, "Don't ever come to me again with substandard work and try to blame others for it. You and you alone are responsible for its worth. You are responsible to ensure that work done by others, that you produce, is done properly. You are responsible to see that their work is adequate. Never let me hear you blame a secretary again for what you should have checked."

He then explained to me his philosophy of responsibility. In the army, he explained, every officer is responsible for the conduct of those under his command. Each officer is responsible to see that his troops function properly and do not make mistakes. Anything that goes wrong is that officer's responsibility, for not preventing the error and for not training the troops so that they do not make mistakes. It is my belief that if Cecil Merritt had been in command of the Canadian Airborne Regiment, the disgraceful incident in Somalia would never have happened. He would not have let it happen.

He once left a file on my desk with a note pinned to its front cover. It read, "David, take this case and win it." Those were his simple instructions, and they left no doubt as to who had responsibility for the file from that moment on.

Cecil Merritt was constitutionally incapable of a mean or dishonest act, and while he was practising, he gained a reputation for scrupulous honesty and integrity. It was his intellectual integrity that I admired. He could never bring himself to put forward an argument that he knew was in error. He was occasionally wrong, but never knowingly wrong.

He was a determined man, determined to the point of stubbornness. It was both one of his strengths and one of his weaknesses. He never gave up, but by the same token, he found it difficult to change tactics quickly when surprised by a change in the course of a case. Cross-examination was not one of his strengths, for he found it difficult to change course in the face of unexpected responses from a witness. He was amazingly industrious. I have lost count of the times that I sat with him in the library of the old firm until midnight, honing an argument until it satisfied him. I have seen him, in closing argument, by sheer persistence and determination, pull a losing case out of the fire. Indeed, closing argument was his great strength.

Once, in the Supreme Court of Canada, he was making a submission that appeared to be falling upon deaf judicial ears. Mr. Justice Abbott leaned forward and said to him, "Well, Mr. Merritt, we have your point, thank you."

Cecil immediately responded, "Well, no, My Lord, I don't think you do," and continued on with his argument for another three quarters of an hour.

Cecil was extremely loyal to his clients, to the point that he sometimes believed what they said even when what they said was not true, or at least, not accurate. This occasionally created problems for him. He expected loyalty from his juniors, but at the same time, he was also loyal to them. I appeared, on one occasion, as his junior on a chambers application. Senator Farris was appearing for the other side. Now Senator Farris was one of the leading counsel in Vancouver. A powerful force in the Liberal party, he had engineered the appointment of most of the judges in BC. Cecil did not like him, though he respected his professional ability. He viewed the Senator as a counsel who tried to win cases by force of his overpowering personality, rather than by the merits of his argument. At one point, during submissions in chambers, a point of law came up that nobody had expected. The answer to it lay in a case that could be found in the courthouse library. Senator Farris turned to Cecil, gesturing to me, and saying, "Perhaps your young friend, here, could go down to the library and fetch it for us." Cecil turned to the Senator and said, "Senator, he is not my young friend. He is *your* learned friend."

He insisted on his juniors using their initiative, by which he meant doing the right thing without being told. On one occasion, he had three of us students working on a problem—Tommy Korikan, Rolly Bouwman and me. He viewed our efforts as inept and uninspired. He besought us to use our collective initiatives. In a fit of despair, he walked over to Duthie Books and purchased three copies of *The Message to Garcia*. At the time, this was a well-known homily about initiative. Garcia was the leader of the revolutionary movement in Cuba. President Teddy Roosevelt needed to get a message to him. He asked his chief of staff who he could get to take the message. A young lieutenant was produced, who (he was told) was utterly reliable. The President handed the envelope to the lieutenant and said, "I want you to give this letter to Garcia personally, as soon as possible." The young lieutenant said, "Yes, Mr. President," saluted and left. He did not ask where Garcia was, or complain about the danger, or ask for assistance with transportation, or suggest a better method of delivering the message. He just left and got on with the job. "That," said Cecil, "is the kind of initiative I expect from you fellows in the future."

Cecil had an amazingly firm grasp of fundamental principles of law. He was, in truth, very learned. One could go into his office with a problem and come out with a clear head and a list of cases to look up. In consequence, he was in great demand for consultation by others in the firm.

After the war, he was nominated to run for the Conservative party in Vancouver-Burrard, and was elected in 1945. This was the riding that had been represented by Jerry McGeer up until then. He ran again in the 1949 election, but was defeated by the Liberal candidate, J.L. Macdougall, by 291 votes. He did not enjoy his time as a Member of Parliament. Being a back bencher in opposition presented no intellectual challenge for him, and he found the lack of creative work to be irksome. He was secretly relieved to be able to return to private practice in 1949.

From 1949, until his retirement from active practice in 1987, the law reports show him appearing in eighty-nine cases—thirty four of which were in the Court of Appeal and six in the Supreme Court of Canada. In fact, he appeared in many more, which were not reported.

His practice was confined exclusively to civil litigation and he was constantly in court. A computer search of cases, in which he appeared as counsel, discloses that he had an extraordinarily varied practice. He practised for seven years before the Second World War. These were the days when only a handful of the cases that were decided made it into the law reports, and Cecil is shown as counsel, always junior to Alfred Bull QC, in four cases.

He was quite prepared to conduct any case that a client brought him. The law reports show him as counsel in cases involving estates, municipal taxation, expropriation, and disputes over bylaws, negligence and personal injury, bankruptcy, landlord and tenant, libel, many cases involving company law and shareholders oppression, contract, family relations and Testators Family Maintenance, labour law, passing off, restraint of trade, and injunctions. However, his two specialties were banking (his firm acted for the Royal Bank of Canada, and indeed, it still does) and admiralty cases—Bull Housser acted for a number of the P & I clubs, and Cecil was involved in more admiralty cases than any other subject. Two of these cases went to the Supreme Court of Canada. In Monarch Towing v. BC Cement [1957] SCR 816, he succeeded in establishing that the negligent owners of a tug and tow could not limit liability to the tonnage of the tug alone, but their liability was computed on the basis of the combined tonnage of the tug and tow. In Western Canada Steamship Co. v. Canadian Commercial Corporation [1960] SCR 632, the *Lake Chilco*, a liberty ship, which class had a propensity for propeller-shaft failures, fractured her shaft. The ship was held to be un-seaworthy, but the owners were able to show due diligence to make the ship seaworthy. A new, eight-ton shaft was flown to Singapore, rather than sending it by sea, and the court held that the extra expense thus incurred could not be recovered in an action for general average. Cecil was unable to uphold the victory he had wrung from the Court of Appeal.

In 1961, he is found representing the Minister of National Revenue on an appeal by Isaac Shulman from the dis-allowance of a management fee paid by Shulman to a company incorporated to manage his law firm. The firm was known as Shulman, Tupper, Southin, Gray, and Worral, though Shulman alone owned the firm and employed all the other lawyers, who engaged their own secretaries and set their own charges for professional services. The judge describes a firm in administrative chaos, to which Shulman attempted to bring order by inserting the management company into the administrative routine. Cecil succeeded in denying Shulman his fee.

In 1976, he appeared before the Court of Appeal, Branca, Taggart, and Corrothers JJA, in Thornton v. The Prince George School Board, (1976) 73 DLR(3rd) 35: a vain attempt to appeal an award of damages to a student irreparably rendered a quadriplegic in an accident in the school gym. Unusually for Cecil, he had two juniors on this occasion, Brian Wallace (son of the Honourable Bae Wallace), and one B.M. McLachlin, now Chief Justice of Canada.

In 1962, he succeeded in persuading, Sheppard and Tysoe JJA (though not J.O. Wilson JA, who dissented), that the Retail Food and Drug Clerks Union, while picketing Zellers in the Whalley shopping centre, should be enjoined from interfering with the easement rights of Zellers, which gave access for its customers to its shop. The interim injunction restraining the union was upheld. (1962) 36 DLR 581.

Though the DLRs chose not to report the fact, I appeared as Cecil's junior on that occasion. One Alex B. Macdonald appeared for the union. The injunction had been granted by Judge Kay Collins. Cecil and I had consumed no little midnight oil preparing the application for the injunction. I tried to persuade Cecil that the union was committing the tort of trespass and that an injunction must be granted on that ground. After some spirited argument over the course of a couple of days, Cecil gave in (unusual for him) and agreed to include this ground in his submission—more (I think) to appease me than because he thought the argument had much merit. Collins J. gave judgement from the bench, on the ground that the union was indeed committing the tort of trespass. When the judge left the room, Cecil turned to me and in Alex's presence said, "David, you were right; I was wrong. Congratulations." It was a graceful gesture of intellectual generosity, bestowed in the hearing of his opponent. It was the gesture of a man of great intellectual integrity, which is the quality I admired in him most.

E. DAVIE FULTON

Edmond Davie Fulton, PC, OC, QC, was one of those politicians whose reach always exceeded his grasp. In so many of his endeavours, his achievements fell just short of the finish line, with somebody else always breaking the tape ahead of him. This was unfortunate, because he was an intelligent, industrious, and honest public servant, as well as a capable administrator.

He was born in Kamloops in 1916, the grandson of A.E.B. Davie, sometime premier of British Columbia. A Rhodes scholar, he earned a law degree at Oxford University and was called to the bar of BC in 1936. He started practising law in Kamloops with the firm that his father, Fred Fulton, had established in 1889. The Second World War interrupted his practice and he joined the Seaforth Highlanders of Canada, serving as a company commander, and later as Deputy Assistant Adjutant-General with the First Canadian Infantry Division in the Italian and northwestern Europe campaigns.

When hostilities ceased, he was persuaded by the Conservative Party to run for Parliament in the 1945 general election. He was elected with a margin of a mere one hundred votes. In 1956, he ran for the leadership of the party, coming third behind John Diefenbaker and Donald Fleming. When Diefenbaker won the 1957 election, he appointed Fulton Minister of Justice. He resigned from cabinet in 1963, and became leader of the BC Progressive Conservative Party. His efforts to revive the provincial Conservative Party in BC were spectacularly unsuccessful. He chose to run in a general election in Kamloops, against the Reverend Phil Gagliardi, who was then the Minister of Highways in the Social Credit Government. This courageous (but ill-considered) venture failed and he returned to federal politics, winning back his old seat in the 1967 election. Two years later, he stood once more as a candidate for leadership of the Federal Conservative Party, and once more came third, this time behind Duff Roblin and Robert Stanfield. In 1968, he lost his seat and returned to the practice of law.

Unsuccessful as he had been, he was held in high esteem by his old constituents and the bar of BC, so it was no surprise that he was appointed a Justice of the Supreme Court of BC, in 1973. He encountered some initial difficulty as a judge, for he had only practised law for a total of eight years, three before the war and five after his political career ended. He did not take long to settle in as a creditable judge, before whom it was a pleasure to appear. But then he ran into serious trouble: alcohol. Years of heavy drinking, in the smoky back rooms that politicians inhabit, had turned him first into a heavy drinker, and then into an alcoholic. It was not evident. Nobody ever saw him drunk, but one day he was apprehended by a police constable and charged with impaired driving. He plead guilty, suffered a minor fine, and a brief suspension of his driver's license. He considered resigning from the bench, but he had not been the only judge to have been convicted of impaired driving, so he carried on until in 1987, when he was arrested again and charged once more with impaired driving. A second offence carried with it an automatic jail sentence—two weeks, in his case, which he served in the home of the warden of Oakalla Prison Farm. This event gave him no option but to resign and return to practising law, this time in Vancouver.

He was persuaded by his colleagues to do something creative about his alcoholism, so he consulted Dr. Elmer Ratzlaff. Now Dr. Ratzlaff was a client of mine. I had been fighting a running battle for him with the Medical Services Commission, which eventually lasted twelve years, but was at this point in about its ninth year. Elmer Ratzlaff had been an anaesthetist, practising in Prince George. One of his patients had died, which led to a lawsuit that I was not involved in. He gave up anaesthesiology and moved to Vancouver to practise as a G.P. and specializing in the treatment of alcoholism and those with drug dependencies. I never enquired, but always suspected that Elmer was himself a recovered alcoholic. I wondered about the accident that caused the death of his patient in Prince George.

Elmer was highly successful at treating alcoholics. He worked staggeringly long hours. His wife eventually made him stop going to his office on Sundays. The Medical Services Commission took after him because his billings were so high. He was categorized as a G.P., but in truth, he functioned more like a psychiatrist, with higher billings for counselling than any ordinary G.P.. He was way out at the end of the Bell curve—the formula the MSC used to monitor the billings of physicians. We found ourselves unable to persuade the MSC that there was a reason for this: his practice differed radically from that of an ordinary G.P.. The MSC eventually ordered that he restrict his counselling fees and cut his billing rate. With callous unfairness, it ordered him to repay seven years of what it considered to be over-billings. This was income on which he had paid tax. My pleas to the MSC went unheeded; indeed most of my letters were ignored. I had crafted the letters carefully, with an eye to some judge reading them in the future. I was incensed that these bureaucrats, whose wages I paid with my taxes, could exhibit such bovine intransigence.

We petitioned the Supreme Court for a judicial review and an order quashing the MSC's order. I needed evidence, by way of affidavits to explain why his practice should not be compared to that of an ordinary G.P.. I discussed with Elmer whom we could approach to swear affidavits laying out the evidence. We found a fellow practitioner with a similar practice, though he didn't work as hard as Elmer. The business agent of one of the larger unions in BC, who referred a large number of his members to Elmer, swore a compelling affidavit. I judged that we needed one more, preferably from a patient. "Oh," said Elmer, "I know just the person. Davie Fulton." I said that I didn't think I could tactfully approach Fulton. His forced resignation from the bench had been an acute embarrassment to him, and I felt diffident about calling him up for an affidavit that would be filed in a lawsuit, whose documents anybody could access in the court registry. Elmer was adamant. Fulton was the best possible person amongst all his patients. He was quite right about that, of course. If we could persuade Fulton to co-operate, it would provide a persuasive voice in our cause.

I didn't have the courage to phone Fulton out of the blue, so I composed a tactful letter, explaining what the issue in the case was. I explained that we needed evidence from a patient of how Elmer treated alcoholics, what counselling was involved, and the kind of time that it all took. I gently suggested that Fulton might comment on what success Elmer had achieved with him.

I mailed the letter. Two days later the phone rang. It was Davie Fulton. Yes, of course he would swear an affidavit. Elmer had stopped him drinking. He hadn't had a scotch in eighteen months. He was very grateful to this dedicated and inspired practitioner. I said that I would draft an affidavit and discussed its contents with him. We talked about exactly how it should be worded. I said that I'd send over a draft as soon as I had time to complete it. I put off drafting it for a day, because I was busy. Not thirty-six hours later, by courier, there arrived on my desk a letter from Fulton, and an affidavit that he himself had drawn. He asked me to look it over and phone if there were any changes I thought should be made. I read through the affidavit. It was a masterpiece of advocacy from a grateful patient. It hid nothing. He confessed to his alcoholism, explained how he had slowly sunk into the state that had landed him in prison, explained in detail the treatment he had received, and commended Elmer on his dedication and industry. There was nothing I needed to change. What he was about to testify to was clearly the unvarnished truth. I made an appointment with his secretary and went to see Fulton to have him swear the affidavit.

I lost the case in the Supreme Court and had to go to the Court of Appeal before we won. The appeal came on for hearing one day, and for reasons I thought unconvincing, counsel for the MSC asked for an adjournment, which (to my annoyance) was granted. As we gathered our books to leave the courtroom, one of the Appeal Judges, Madam Justice Mary Southin, looked down at me with a faint smile and said, "Mr. Roberts, you have some very persuasive evidence to support your appeal."

When the appeal was eventually heard, we wrung a unanimous verdict from the court, allowing the appeal. To this day, the lawyers in the Ministry still talk about the Ratzlaff case, which they considered to be a humiliating defeat for them. The appeal was successful, (at least in part) because of Fulton' affidavit, which nobody could read without believing everything it contained.

Above all, I admired the man's courage, grace, and generosity in coming to the rescue of the man who had dragged him out of his pit of alcoholism.

THE CHRISTMAS CARD

We were spending a few days at the old Qualicum Beach Hotel on the east coast of Vancouver Island. A big, elegant, old Victorian log building, with twenty-foot ceilings, it nestled in the trees uphill from the Qualicum golf course. Both the course and the hotel are long gone, victims of a housing development. We thought we needed a respite from our four children, before the frenzy of the Christmas holidays engulfed us, and took a box of books with us.

Also staying at the hotel was a lawyer from Seattle. He was an engaging, grey-haired, African American, and was also enjoying a brief sojourn with his wife—a tall, stylish, white woman, somewhat younger than her husband. We fell into conversation with them and dined together on the last night of our stay. We were all leaving the next day. He told us that he had recently moved offices. He had found an office with a small group who worked in the building mostly occupied by Nordstrom's, the department store. The Seattle telephone company had made a muddle over the transfer of his phone number when he moved in. They had inadvertently given him the same number as Nordstrom's and had published it in the Seattle telephone directory. This was a disaster for him, as any client who phoned him reached Nordstrom's instead. The problem was solved, at least until the next phone directory was printed, by the phone company persuading Nordstrom's to answer their phone calls by announcing, "Nordstrom's department store and Amos Impey Law Office." He said that he had acquired quite a few clients who had phoned Nordstrom's, heard his name, and decided to use his services. He told us a lot about his practice, which appeared to be a very general one. He seemed to do anything that came in over the transom. His wife was quiet and volunteered little, perhaps because he was so talkative. Though evidently sociable, she was not communicative, and added little to our conversations.

We all left together the next day and caught the ferry from Nanaimo. They rented a cabin on the ferry, so we didn't see much of them on the journey. We bade them goodbye at Horseshoe Bay. I gave him my business card, thinking, *You never know, one of his clients might one day need representation in Vancouver.* He said that he had forgotten to bring any cards. I did not think that mattered. We knew how to get in touch with him. We just had to phone Nordstrom's.

It was that time of year when the Christmas card list was unearthed, and we set about writing the annual Christmas letter to insert in the cards. We decided to send the Impeys a card. Gill found their home address in the Seattle telephone directory, conveniently available in the local library. She wrote a note in the card saying how pleasant it had been meeting them at the Qualicum Beach Hotel.

Three days later, the phone rang. The voice was that of a woman with a southern accent and sounding distinctly African American. There was the sound of children playing in the background. She had just received our card. She didn't understand. Who were we? She had never been to the hotel we mentioned in the card, and just exactly what were we talking about? The date when we said we had met her, she was at home with their children, and her husband had been on a business trip to Houston, Texas. Gill had answered the call. Her antenna went up. This was trouble. And it was trouble in which we didn't need to get entangled. Gill dissembled, evaded, and lied her way out of the situation. We had obviously got the wrong address .... Yes well, the name must have been similar, but we had clearly misspelled it. After a spasm of vocal writhing, she managed to end the conversation—pleading an appointment we were late for.

Not twenty minutes later, the phone rang again. Should we answer it? No call display in those days. Well, we couldn't spend the next few days not answering the phone to avoid a situation that was not of our making. I said that I'd get it. It might be easier for me to deal with a second call from Mrs. Impey.

It was Amos Impey's voice at the end of the line. This was not the measured, lyrical baritone that we had listened to at Qualicum Beach. The voice was raised an octave and seriously stressed at the edges. "David? Amos Impey here. Listen you've got me into a terrible fix. You sent a Christmas card to my home. My wife opened it. She didn't understand what you were talking about. You see, that wasn't my wife you met in Qualicum. It was my secretary. We were taking a few days off together. My wife wants to know how you say you came to meet her on Vancouver Island. What did you tell her?" I explained what Gill had said. "Listen, David, if she phones again, please cover up the meeting as best you can." I began to feel vaguely guilty. What had we done? Then I mentally shook my head. Gill was anxiously listening to the conversation. On her face there was a frown of concern. I drew a breath. "Yes, okay, Amos. But please ... you must understand. You got yourself into this mess. There is a limited amount we can do to help, and in truth, Amos, there is a limited amount that we want to get any further involved. I think you'll have to set about mending your own fences." There was a growl of reluctant agreement at the other end of the phone line and we ended the conversation after a few polite exchanges.

Gill and I looked at each other and burst out laughing, though the situation was really a tragicomedy. We never heard from either Impey again

WILLS AND OTHER EVENTS

There was a time, in the early days of my practice, when I would set about performing any task that landed on my desk—tasks assigned by others in the firm, or cases I attracted from the clientele I was slowly forging amongst my friends and acquaintances. I would convey land, incorporate companies, draft leases, draw up complicated commercial contracts, and organize divorces for people. I also drew scores of wills. This was all quite apart from the civil litigation I conducted, and the eternally innocent victims of unfounded criminal charges that I defended, occasionally successfully. This was all in the days when it was not unusual for lawyers in Vancouver to run a general practice, before specialization became the rule. Out of town, of course, it remained the rule. Country solicitors and small town lawyers had little option but to run a practice that covered the entire spectrum of legal problems their clients encountered.

By the time I retired, I had not drawn a will for twenty-five years and I wouldn't have dared to try. The impact of taxation had created so many complexities that I decided I should leave testamentary drafting to those who actually knew what they were doing. In the early days of my practice most testamentary dispositions were uncomplicated arrangements. Husbands and wives left their estates to each other. The survivor left the estate to be divided between their children. There were special provisions for grandchildren, and it got more complicated when you had to cater for grandchildren whose parents might die before the testator.

Murray Polson was an old friend. We were both members of the Arts Club in the days when the club occupied premises it shared with the New Design Gallery on West Pender Street. His wife, Phillipa, had recently died and he made an appointment to see me, because he thought he should draw a new will. Murray was an architect and (at the time he consulted me) the Registrar of the BC Architectural Institute. We had known the Polsons for some years. Phillipa had taught English literature at Capilano College, as it was called in those days. She was tall, black haired, and a positive force, full of energy. She ran a music club, which met once a week to play whatever classical music the group had enough musical scores for. She invited me to join. She had seen Gill's piano at our home and assumed I could play it too. I had to admit that I could not read music. "Oh," she said, a faint undertone of disapproval in her voice. "Well, take this collection of folk songs. Learn to read it and when you reach 'Aunt Roedde', collect up your recorder and come and join us." "Aunt Roedde" was halfway through the book. In the event, I never reached it. The group went on its way, playing happily without me.

The Polsons were evidently not wealthy people. They lived in a modest house near the Gleneagles golf course and ran one rather elderly automobile between them. A second automobile, Phillipa contended, would be a pointless extravagance. Their pleasures in life were music, art, and literature. Murray was a creditable painter and whiled away hours creating beautiful watercolours. Murray was the quieter of the two, not so much because he was naturally quiet, but because anyone in Phillipa's boisterous presence would necessarily seem quiet. Murray exhibited a gentle determination that I noticed seemed to quell (in advance) any opposition to whatever task he might (for the moment) be engaged.

When Phillipa died, although Murray said nothing about his loss, he was obviously devastated. The anchor had slipped from his life. He himself died not long afterwards—the light had gone out of his life. It was almost as if he willed it, in order to rejoin her. They had two children: a daughter who was married to a Japanese man and lived with him and their two children in Ontario, and a son, Murray, who lived in North Vancouver. I met his daughter later on, after Murray had died. She was a tall, handsome woman who seemed to have inherited both her parents' strength of character and their disdain for material possessions. Young Murray pursued a career that I never really understood, but was connected in some way to the theatre.

At any rate, after Phillipa's death, Murray decided to draw a new will. He made an appointment and brought with him a smallish piece of paper, on which he had inscribed his notes about how he wanted his estate distributed. He handed me the notes. I was astonished to see that they were in beautiful copper-plate handwriting—utterly legible, and somewhat akin to what you might see on a wedding invitation. I discovered that he always wrote in this fashion. It took him only slightly longer to write legibly what most people would scribble in indecipherable script.

Murray's instructions were simple: the estate was to be divided equally between his children, with trusts for grandchildren should their parent die before Murray. Murray was about to go for a holiday to the Sunshine Coast. He left me an address so that I could send the draft will to him. I drew the will the next day and mailed it off to the address he had given. My covering letter warned him not to try to execute the will. The Wills Act has strict provisions about the execution of wills. Wills must be signed by the testator in the presence of two witnesses, who must sign, as witnesses, in each others' presence. Any infraction of these statutory provisions would invalidate the will. I always tried to insist that clients come in to my office to execute their wills. That way I would be sure that they didn't make a muddle of it. Somewhat bitter experience had taught me that, however carefully I explained how a will was to be executed, clients nearly always got it wrong. They either misunderstood my instructions or thought that the formality didn't matter. The most common mistake was to have someone who was to be a beneficiary act as a witness. Although that would not invalidate the will, it would automatically disinherit the beneficiary.

Murray phoned. He had received the draft. He wanted a change. Since his daughter had two children, he had decided that she should inherit a little more than his son. We discussed this at some length. I pointed out that his son may yet produce grandchildren. We settled on the change. I redrafted the will and mailed off the new draft. Several weeks went by and Murray phoned again. He was apologetic, but wanted more changes. They mostly had to do with the age at which a grandchild should inherit. He thought twenty-one was too young and suggested twenty-five. I made the changes and once again mailed off the draft. A week later, a very embarrassed Murray phoned. He would like another change. I duly redrafted the will and again sent it off. Some weeks after that Murray came in to the office. He was apologetic that he had caused me so much trouble. Had I ever had to make four changes to a will before? Well, no, I conceded, I had not. He looked embarrassed. I tried to mollify him, but he remained contrite.

"You know, David," he said, "I've come to a conclusion about people like me who need to draw a will. What we should do is make a list of all the assets in the estate. Give the list to the beneficiaries and tell them to go away and discuss it and then have them draw the will. That way there won't be any unpleasant surprises later on."

I thought it was a particularly shrewd observation. I suggested this process to several clients later on. They all thought it was an inspired idea. But, no, not one was actually prepared to do it. They did not wish to surrender control of their estates and always thought they knew better than their children what was best for them.

ROD SMITH

Rod Smith practised law in Vancouver for the best part of fifty years. For twenty of those years he was one of my partners. He grew up in Saskatoon. Fascinated by aircraft, as soon as he was old enough to do so, he joined the R.C.A.F. He was sent on the Commonwealth Air Training Scheme to train as air-crew. He wanted to be a pilot, preferably a fighter pilot. He was lucky. There were three kinds of air-crew: air gunners, navigators, and pilots. Which you were assigned to was a sheer lottery. There were no tests to determine who would perform which function best. By chance, Rod was assigned to the group who would train as pilots. At the end, again by chance, he ended up a fighter pilot. He was too late to take part in the Battle of Britain, but when he arrived in England, he found himself immediately posted to Malta, which he did not think at the time was going to be all that exciting. He reached Gibraltar, boarded the old aircraft carrier, HMS Eagle, was handed a spitfire and took off to land in Malta in the middle of the Battle of Malta.

Malta was on the route for cargo ships ferrying supplies to the Eighth Army in North Africa. It was a stopping off point, and thus a target for attack by enemy aircraft flying out of Italy. Rod, who to that point had seen no combat, was flung straight into the fray. Because of the frequency of the enemy air raids, he flew every day, with only occasional days off to rest. He flew Spitfires, which were the only aircraft available to withstand attacks by Italian bombers, which were always escorted by a seemingly endless supply of Messerschmitts.

The Commonwealth air forces considered a pilot to have achieved the status of an air ace when he had shot down five enemy aircraft. Claims to have made a kill were examined carefully to ensure that there was evidence in support of any claim. Damaging an aircraft so that it would probably have crashed was not enough. A mere claim to have made a kill was not even logged. Proof was required. By the time the attacks on Malta had petered out, and Rod was posted back to England, in December 1942, he had destroyed six enemy aircraft and had been awarded the D.F.C..

He, himself, was shot down once. His engine on fire, he bailed out at 3,800 feet. To bail out of a Spitfire, the procedure was to push the hood back, climb out to sit on the edge of the cockpit facing inwards and then fall over backwards. Unfortunately for him, the tail of his aircraft hit him on the head as he fell. Though momentarily unconscious, he managed to pull his ripcord and splashed into the sea. He had had time to switch the R/T over to emergency and called Mayday. To his relief, he heard the operator in Malta say, "We've got you." He told me that, when he hit the water, he went under and felt so tired that he simply gave up struggling. Fortunately, he was picked up by one of the resident rescue launches before he drowned.

By the end of the war, he had become a squadron leader with a bar to his D.F.C., and fourteen and a half kills to his credit. The half, he told me, was an early German prototype jet aircraft, which he and several other Spitfires encountered over Holland. Two of them fired at it and registered hits, but neither of them could tell which was responsible for its ultimate destruction. So each pilot was awarded a half a kill. Fourteen and a half was a substantial achievement. There were literally only a handful of pilots who could claim more. The record was twenty three, by Wing Commander Johnnie Johnson.

After the war, he served in the Canadian Air Force Reserve. His reward was to be caught in the slipstream of a jet fighter while he was standing on the runway. It rendered him stone deaf in one ear, an impediment that rendered him unable to do court work.

He never married, though I remember him collecting about him an endless stream of women friends. His motor yacht was called the Kestrel II, after the Rolls Royce engine that powered all the later Spitfires. He kept Kestrel II in Coal Harbour, and would take his women friends out in her for lengthy cruises. He always referred to them as "crew persons."

"Rod, how about having lunch next Thursday?"

"No. Sorry David, I promised lunch to one of my crew persons."

He retired at the age of seventy-five, and would often come into the office to visit old partners. He and his Siamese cat, Boufles, inhabited an apartment in the west end with a magnificent view of the harbour and the mountains. Not long after his eightieth birthday, he began to experience some ill health. He had an operation for a brain tumour, fortunately found to be benign. He had told a number of his friends and crew persons that he would not let himself descend into an increasingly crippled old age, but would himself terminate that struggle. Then he was diagnosed with Cerabral Amyloid Angiopathy (CAA), which causes a deterioration of the lining of the arteries of the brain. It has similar symptoms to Alzheimer's disease.

In possession of this diagnosis from his medical advisers, and leaving a note to explain his departure, he walked out onto the balcony of his apartment, heaved himself up onto the rail, and launched himself backwards

136

into space, just as he had done from his doomed Spitfire a half a century earlier in Malta.

As is normal with any violent death, an autopsy was performed, which tragically, disclosed that he did not, in fact, suffer from CAA, but only the normal changes in the brain of a man in his ninth decade.

But it was a graceful exit, one which (in his note) he explained he had taken in order to avoid the prospect of endless hospital visits, and becoming a nuisance to his friends.

MIKE HERMAN

I walked into Mike's office to find him massaging his left wrist, wrapped around which was a leather strap. I thought he must have injured it playing tennis, for he and I often played together. I asked him what he had done to his wrist. We had been partners in the practice of law for some years, but I was startled by the tale he told me and surprised that I knew so little about his life before he began to practise law.

***

He knew, as soon as he saw the black eagle and the Gothic printing on the big white envelope, that he was in trouble. He toyed with the idea of burning it, unread. That, he realized, would attract the same problem as if he read it and ignored it. So he opened it. The letter was addressed to Miroslav Frantisek Michael Herman—ominous in itself. It was from the Commandant, SS headquarters, Prague. It ordered Mike to report immediately to the SS for assignment to a labour camp. This, he knew, meant certain death.

Mike was seventeen. It was 1941. He had been born in Senohraby, Czechoslovakia. The uninvited jackboots of a rapacious and tyrannical army had occupied his country two years earlier, wrecking what should have been a comfortable teenage existence with reasonably well-to-do parents. He watched as the legal profession and the judiciary disintegrated and friends began to disappear, in the same way as their counterparts in Germany had done after 1933. Criticism was impossible and it was suicide to challenge this brutal authority. Later, in 1943, he was thrown into jail. He was never charged with any offence. He was released several months later only because the jails were too full to hold all the prisoners. In 1945, the Nazis were replaced by the equally repressive communist regime.

In 1947, Mike found himself once more in jail, this time at the hands of the communists. Though charged with an offence vaguely termed *subversion*, he was never tried and (in 1949) was released for the same reason as before. He escaped from Czechoslovakia and for the next three years he lived in refugee camps, mostly in the US zone of occupied Germany. He began to work for the International Refugee Organization and later for the US High Commission. The fact that he spoke Czech, Slovak, German, and English made him a useful employee. In 1952, he moved to London, England, where he met his wife, Jane. They both immigrated to Canada the same year.

In Vancouver, Mike worked as a labourer in the Rogers sugar refinery, as a desk clerk, as an elevator operator, and as a janitor in a skid-row hotel. Having the equivalent of a Bachelor of Arts degree from the University of Prague, he was eventually able to enrol in the law school at UBC, and he graduated in 1960. He ran a successful practice and was a bencher of the Law Society for five years. In 1991, he was appointed Honorary Consul of the Czech and Slovak republic, and two years later, Consul of the Czech Republic—Slovakia having become a separate republic.

But now, here in Prague in 1941, he was facing the bleak prospect of starvation in a forced labour camp. He took himself down into his father's basement work shop, secured his left wrist in a vice, and after a few moments of indecision, smashed it with a blow from a sledgehammer. In acute pain, he went round to see the family doctor and told him what he had done and the reason why. The doctor set his smashed wrist as best he could, encased it in a cast, and put it in a sling, both to relieve strain on the wrist and to add drama to the injury. He then wrote a letter testifying that Mike was unfit for any labour, gave him something to ease the pain, and sent him on his way.

Mike set off for SS headquarters bearing the doctor's letter with him—his passport to relative freedom. He was ushered into the presence of a black uniform with silver trimmings, the officer in charge of labour camp intake. The officer's cap lay on his desk, adorned with the usual shiny black visor and the silver death's head insignia of the SS. The officer did not look up, but went on writing, the old trick of those who seek to intimidate. Mike waited. Eventually the officer looked up. "Jah?" Mike presented the letter from the SS and the doctor's certificate. The officer read the certificate and glared at Mike. Knowing perfectly well what Mike had done, he swore at him in German, and after a brief interrogation, ordered him out of his office.

HAIDA
GWAII

JEDWAY

The Queen Charlotte Islands lie off the northwest coast of British Columbia—five hundred miles north and five hundred miles west of Vancouver. Their name has just recently changed. They are now called Haida Gwaii, which means "the islands of the people" in the language of the people of the islands. The original name was chosen by Captain George Dixon of the Royal Navy, who surveyed the islands in 1787. The change makes sense. After all, it is more appropriate to name the islands after the Haida who have inhabited them for thousands of years than after the long-since dead wife of the long-since dead King, George III. The archipelago consists of some one hundred and fifty islands—the exact number is uncertain because it is difficult to determine which rocks are large enough to qualify as islands. The two main islands, Graham in the north and Moresby running almost to the southern tip, make up the spine of the archipelago. This spine is an extension of the Alaska panhandle and continues on south under Queen Charlotte Sound to become Vancouver Island. The islands are home to an unbelievably diverse array of birds, plants, and sea life that are not found elsewhere on the mainland. The reason for this is that the glaciers of the ice age that smothered British Columbia, ten thousand years ago, never touched the islands. In consequence, the inter-tidal life and animals and birds that were killed off by the frigid, imprisoning grip of the glaciers on the mainland survived on the islands. There are those who call the islands "the Galapagos of the North".

Jedway is on the east coast of Moresby Island, in Skincuttle Inlet. The name is a corruption of the Haida term Gigawai, meaning a snare or trap. Jedway was so called because in a south-easterly storm the bay is subject to sudden sharp squalls that batter the coast. In 1862, one Francis Poole—a young mining engineer—reported, "There is copper over on those islands in paying quantities." Spurred on by this contention, a group of Victoria businessmen formed the Queen Charlotte Mining Company. However, it did not pursue its interests and abandoned the venture. During one of those south-easterly storms, Arichika Ikeda (of the Japanese fishing firm of Awaya, Ikeda and Co.) came ashore and found out what the prospectors were up to. His group staked forty-seven claims and opened a mine. The mine eventually ran out of ore and they shut it down in 1920.

In 1990, my wife, Gill, and I took a week's holiday in *The Darwin Sound*, a beautiful seventy-two foot yawl that took passengers on cruises around the islands. The yawl anchored in Ikeda Bay, and some of us rowed ashore to explore the old mine site. Needing exercise, Gill and I walked up the hill until we found ourselves overlooking a huge quarry that had been the site of the old open-cast copper mine. It must have been half a mile across and several hundred feet deep—an awesome scar in the otherwise beautiful landscape.

We slowly became conscious of the sound of birds calling: a sharp "Kack-kack, Kack-kack," interspersed by an occasional cry of "We-chew!" We paid little attention. The islands were replete with a wonderful collection of birds, most of them as noisy as a clutch of children just let out of school. Then, after a while, we noticed the cause of these strange cries. Flying about in the quarry were three birds. We saw that they were flying in erratic flight patterns. Then one dropped something it had been holding in its claws. One of the other birds swooped on the falling object and caught it. It swerved violently to one side and then dropped the object as well. The third bird changed course, with its wings beating erratically (descending on the down stroke as far as they ascended on the up beat), and retrieved the falling object. The wings of these birds were always beating. They never seemed to glide, as most birds will at times.

Bird number three gained altitude and dropped the object, which we now recognized as a dead duck. Once again, bird number two pounced upon it—this time missing its prey. The dead duck fell a few feet and was very quickly retrieved by the first bird.

We stared at this strange performance for some time. The birds seemed tireless. Then we noted that two of the birds had different plumage, and were marginally larger than the third. The two were sandy coloured, with creamy chests streaked with brown. Number three was dark brown, more or less all over. They were hawks, as was apparent from their short, curved, vicious little beaks. Our knapsack, full of useful hiking gear, also contained the indispensable *Field Guide to Western Birds* by Roger Tory Peterson, which we hastily consulted. It became obvious to us, as we thumbed through the pages on hawks, that what we were watching was a group of peregrine falcons: two adults and a juvenile. But more than that, as we continued to watch, we realized that the two adults were methodically collecting up the duck and dropping it for the juvenile to catch. We were watching a pair of peregrine falcon parents teaching their offspring to hunt. We watched this performance for quite a long time, until Mummy and Daddy had had enough and flew off with the duck, followed by junior.

There is a large colony of peregrine falcons that nest in the cliffs towards the southern end of the Moresby Island. They are jealously guarded by the local community, which is constantly on the alert for poachers who try to capture the birds for sale to those who prize them for falconry. The peregrine falcon is in danger of extinction and poaching is one more peril it does not need. The falcon is at the apex of the food chain. It eats birds and animals, which eat plants, which in the more agricultural areas are inoculated with poisons that rise through each level of the food chain to the birds of prey at the top. Adult falcons are about the size of a crow. They hunt on the wing, diving on their prey from behind at astonishing speeds— a manoeuvre known as "stooping". According to Wayne Campbell, the Associate Curator of the British Columbia Provincial Museum, the falcon's speed while diving on its prey can reach a breathtaking 320 kilometres an hour. No bird can withstand the shattering stoop of the falcon. G.H. Thayer described the peregrine falcon as "perhaps the most highly specialized and superlatively well-developed organism on our planet today, combining in a marvellous degree the highest powers of speed and aerial adroitness, with massive strength."

CONNIE WEBB

In the mid 1970s, Gill and I took our four children and two dogs on an expedition to the Queen Charlotte Islands. In those days, reaching the Charlottes was not as easy as it is now. CP Air flew in to Sandspit Airport, but enquiry revealed that CPA charged seventy-five dollars each for dogs, and required passengers to buy cages in which to confine them while en route. I phoned a friend of mine who practised law in Prince Rupert to see if he had a fisherman client who might ferry us over. No, he said, and he wouldn't trust anyone he knew to get us there safely. He recommended that I contact North Coast Airlines. I duly did this and booked passages for all of us. With some diffidence, I broached the subject of our dogs. "Oh, we don't charge for pets," he said. Remembering CPA's requirements, I asked if they would need to be caged. "Well, how big are they?" he asked. I took a deep breath. "Well, one is a Malamute and the other is a German shepherd." There was a long and ominous silence. "Oh no," he said. "Well ... okay, just hang on to them."

So we booked passages, drove to Prince Rupert, and put our old International Travelall on the Rivtow Barge to be ferried across the sound to Masset. I flew in an old Grumman Goose flying boat with Peter and Kiffa and the two dogs, while Gill and the twins were flown over in a Beaver. We stayed the night in the Singing Sands Motel in Masset. It had no view at all, let alone one of the sands, and the grass outside our units was used to store a disorderly pile of disused fridges, stoves, and washing machines. The staff were friendly, helpful, and informative about the neighbourhood. The food in the motel restaurant was good, wholesome, logging-camp fare.

The next day we collected our Travelall from the Rivtow people and drove down to the mouth of the Tlell River, where we aimed to camp for a few days. The estuary is about two thirds up the east coast of Graham Island, and flows into Queen Charlotte Sound at an acute angle in a northerly direction, creating a long, wide sandbar between the river and the sea. We were camped on the sandbar, using the water from the river for cooking and washing.

A battered, old, blue-panel truck had driven onto the sand, a little way down the coast. Its driver was a man in his late sixties with only one arm. His wife was wearing a medical neck brace. She looked as if she might be of Haida descent, short of stature and with the wide build typical of the Haida people. When we came upon them, the old man was attempting to dig his truck out of a sand dune in which it had become stuck—a difficult task with only one arm. It was evident that he was not going to succeed, so we wandered over and offered to help. With obvious relief, he accepted our offer and turned his shovel over to us. We succeeded in disinterring the truck from its bed of sand. He and his wife climbed back into the truck and drove off, only to become mired in the next sand dune. We could hear the sound of Tlell beach sand grinding its way into the wheel bearings as he vainly tried to drive out of the trench he was digging for himself.

We once again offered to dig him out. He surrendered his shovel again with obvious and fervently expressed relief. His wife climbed out of the truck and stood in silence, staring out to sea with her back to her husband's homemade disaster. It took us a little longer this time, to separate the truck from its little sandy grave. I offered to drive it onto firm land for him, and was able to get it out of the sand dunes. He was effusive with gratitude. His name, he said, was Cecil Webb, Cece for short. His wife, he said, was Connie. In about five minutes, we learned that Cece hailed from Wiltshire (and indeed I had detected a west-country accent), that he had been a BC Hydro lineman and had lost his arm in an industrial accident, that he was Connie's second husband, that she was a full blooded Haida, and that her first husband, also Haida, had died just as the second World War broke out. He told us that he and Connie lived in Port Clements and offered to take us all fishing if we would come over and look him up. In fact, he was quite insistent that we come. He was anxious to repay our efforts to rescue them from a difficult situation. There had been nobody else around who could have come to their aid. He climbed back into the truck. All this while, his wife had been standing looking out to sea, ignoring the disaster taking place behind her. She climbed into the passenger seat. "Thank you," she said. That was all she had to say during the entire episode. "Thank you." We were not a little puzzled by her reticence, particularly since her husband had been so chatty and effusive in his desire to thank us for our help.

We didn't go to Port Clements, as we wanted to explore Moresby, the next island to the south. We were away on this expedition for well over a week, but we eventually returned to Tlell. After a day we began to need to replenish our supplies, so Gill made up a list of groceries and I took all the children and drove the thirty miles into Port Clements to do the necessary shopping. Port Clements is a nondescript little town at the south end of the Masset inlet. On the way, we decided to take Cece up on his suggestion that we look him up, and see if he would really take us fishing. It was relatively easy to follow the directions he had given us, and we had no difficulty finding his and Connie's trailer. As we drew up, we could see her sitting on her porch, knitting. We filed out of the van and approached her. She instantly knew who we were. "Oh, Cece has gone into Masset. He will be disappointed to have missed you. He's been looking forward to taking you fishing, but the weather has deteriorated and it may be too dangerous for the next few days." She spoke in the slow, gentle, slightly sing-song way of the north-coast natives.

We sat down and tried to engage her in conversation, but she was once again not very communicative. She went on knitting and answered our questions, mostly in monosyllables. It was proving difficult to provoke her into conversation. She seemed very reserved. After about twenty minutes of our desultory attempts to get her talking, I decided it was time to leave and go about our errands. I began to wind up our, so far unsuccessful, interview. As I was preparing to explain that we ought to be getting along, I asked her (more to fill in a hiatus than because I expected a response) if she had lived on the Charlottes all her life.

She put down her knitting, bestowed a kindly smile on all of us, and said, "I was born in Masset. My father was a lay preacher at the Anglican church. His surname was Jones, but our real Haida name was S'qil'qeetlas."

"Do you speak the Haida language," I asked.

"It's my native tongue," she said. "I spoke no English until I was sent to the residential school in Sardis when I was fourteen."

At this point, we could not have stopped her talking if we had wanted to. She held forth for the next hour with a fascinating description of her childhood on Graham Island, her experience at the residential school, and a detailed history of the Queen Charlotte Islands from the perspective of one of its older inhabitants.

It was our first introduction to the custom of the north-coast tribes, and I suspect many aboriginals. Until they become acquainted with you, and are ready to accept you on their terms, they will keep their guard up in wary vigilance. If they have nothing to say, then they say nothing. But once they accept you as a friend, you are a friend for eternity. So it was with Connie Webb.

Connie didn't seem to have suffered any of the abuse at the residential school that we now hear so much about. She resented being made to speak English to her Haida friends, and not being allowed to speak Haida at all. She also resented the fact that all the children had to do the housework at the school, and she missed her family. However, it seems that the schooling she received was entirely adequate, as she was articulate, with a wide vocabulary for someone whose native language was not English. This may have been a result of innate intelligence, for she was a shrewd and wise old lady. She was unusually straightforward and plainspoken, and one of the least manipulative people I have ever met. What she said was what she meant. Political correctness was not something that governed her tongue. She always referred to her people as "us Indians" and to us as "you people."

She had spent four years at the residential school, returning to live in Masset when she was eighteen. She landed a job in the cannery in Masset. She told us that, in those days, the white employees were paid thirty-five cents an hour, the Japanese were paid thirty cents, and the Haida got twenty-five, with no coffee break. She evidently became a union organizer, for she said she had gone round, door to door in Masset, to get people signed up in the union. She had many a door slammed in her face, and was called a communist by many of the people she tried to get into the union. But she succeeded and eventually all employees in the cannery were paid thirty-five cents an hour and all of them became entitled to a coffee break.

Connie told us about her grandfather, who she said had died at the age of one hundred and twenty. I was unsure that he was really that old, as the Haida had no written language and would have had no way of recording his date of birth. I am not sure when Connie was born, but it must have been around the time of the First World War, for she was in her sixties when we met her in the mid-seventies. She said that her grandfather used to tell her stories about his childhood, and about his life on the Queen Charlottes. She was cross with herself, because she said that she had been a typical teenager and paid little attention to the old man. However, she did remember one story, which she related to us.

One day, when he was a young man, he and a group of his peers spied a sailing ship off the coast. They were used to these ships, which plied a vigorous trade in sea otter furs throughout the nineteenth century—that is until they killed all the otters and there were none left. This ship was out of Boston, Connie told us. Thinking to trade with the ship, a group of Masset piled their furs into their war canoes and paddled out to the ship. As they were climbing aboard, a fight broke out. Most of the ship's crew, who were unarmed as they had not expected trouble, were killed, except for some who were below decks at the time. Connie said that in the end only one was saved, the ship's carpenter, but this is not commensurate with some contemporary accounts. She said that the carpenter was held as a slave for a couple of years, and then, through the intervention of Chief Edenshaw, was returned to his people. What happened was that a chief's daughter was in one of the canoes. She was dressed in an otter-skin cloak, and nothing else. As she climbed over the ship's rail, her cloak slipped, revealing to a seaman something he had not seen since he had left Boston. With seaman-like presence of mind, he slapped her bottom. She screamed and the Masset, thinking she was being attacked, came to her rescue. The rest of the crew, thinking their shipmate was being attacked, came to his aid and thus the fight broke out. The Masset overpowered the crew, who were outnumbered as well as unarmed. The Masset, who were angry at what they perceived as a gross insult to one of their women, plundered the ship and set it on fire.

Some time later, after Connie told us this story, I researched this incident as best I could and came to the conclusion that, given the old man's probable age at the time, the ship was almost certainly the *Susan Sturgis*, a schooner out of Boston, with a master named Captain Matthew Rooney, after whom the Canadian Hydrographic Service (in 1945) named Rooney Bay, which fronts along Skidegate Village.

Captain Rooney met Chief Edenshaw in 1851. The *Susan Sturgis*, with five other vessels, arrived in Gold Harbour, which is now known as Mitchel Inlet, south of Skidegate channel. They were looking for gold, but their venture was unsuccessful and Rooney went home. In the fall he returned, but his search for gold was still fruitless, so he took his vessel to the east coast of Moresby, via cape St. James. Trading, prospecting, and exploring, he sailed north as far as Skidegate, where he met Chief Edenshaw. Rooney had heard that there might be some profitable trading in Edenshaw's territory, near Langara Island, northwest of Masset. Rooney asked Edenshaw to come aboard and pilot his ship. It was when they were off Masset that they were attacked by the Haida. Legend has it that Edenshaw prevented the murder of the crew by reminding the Masset that the Americans off the *Georgianna* had been ransomed not many years before. The *Georgianna* had been wrecked in a storm and its crew imprisoned by the Haida. They were ransomed for five blankets apiece. Connie's grandfather's story is not entirely consistent with the recorded histories of the Charlottes. Edenshaw is credited with saving the entire crew. Connie insisted that only one survived, the ship's carpenter, and that it was he whom Edenshaw had saved. Kathleen Dalzell (*The Queen Charlotte Islands, Vol. 2: Of Places and Names*) asserts that it was the Hudson's Bay Company that ransomed the crew of the *Susan Sturgis*. The HBC would certainly have had enough blankets to do so. But, whatever the truth of the incident, Connie was able to tell us what brought about the initial fight and the destruction of the ship.

As we left her to do our shopping, Connie gave us a huge string of venison sausages that she had made from a deer Cece had shot. They were the best sausages we ever tasted. She told us that, before the army came to the Charlottes, there were no hunting regulations. The islanders hunted what they needed for food. Nobody ever killed anything for fun. Then NORAD established a listening post on Rose Spit, about ten miles east of Masset, and staffed it with Canadian soldiers, who began killing the deer and much else, just for the fun of it. The islanders became concerned that the deer population would be decimated, and a steady source of food would disappear. They persuaded the government to introduce hunting regulations that had never been necessary before. The Canadian army was not a popular institution in the Charlottes.

Connie explained to us that, to those who knew what they were doing, it was not possible to starve in the Charlottes. There is such an abundance of food to be garnered from the inter-tidal waters and the forests that one can live indefinitely without much effort. It is difficult to establish ordinary farms. A number of people have tried, and failed, to set up homesteads. We encountered a herd of very strange cattle wandering around the hedgerows of Tlell. They had brown and white bodies and heads with a mass of hair and long curly horns. Connie told us that they were the descendants of two herds, one of Herefords and the other Aberdeen Angus, that had been turned loose by two families, who had brought them to the Charlottes many years before, in vain attempts to farm the land.

About two years later, Gill and I went on a cruise on a 72-foot yacht, which had our daughter, Kate, as crew. We went ashore to visit an archeological dig that some university students were conducting, close to Burnaby Narrows. Connie's assertion that you cannot starve on the Queen Charlotte Islands was proved dead right that day. The dig employed a cook, Roberta, who was a Haida girl. When we showed up, she invited us to lunch. We could see a campfire, some cooking utensils, and a huge cauldron hanging from a metal tripod, but there seemed to be no supplies: no groceries and no lunch in evidence. We wondered what she was going to do. We watched as she spent half an hour grubbing along the shore and amongst the bushes. She lit a fire, and in another half hour produced for us and the archeologists, at least two dozen people, a monumental and delicious feast. It consisted of squid, abalone, clams, shrimp, and an assortment of mushrooms and other edible vegetables she had garnered off the beach and in the surrounding forest. It was a memorable meal.

The day after our visit to Connie in Port Clements, I took Gill and the children back to see her. She was delighted that we had come and we spent another hour talking to her. She showed us, with some pride, a large collection of salt and pepper shakers she and Cece had assembled over the years. There must have been fifty pairs: an odd assortment of china picked up in junk shops and second-hand stores all over the north country. For years afterwards, whenever Gill and I came across an unusual pair of shakers, we would buy it and mail it off to Connie.

We told Connie about our stay in the run-down little motel in Masset. She, of course, knew it. She told us that there was a great deal of friction between the whites in Masset and the Masset themselves. This, she explained, was only partly due to the presence of the Canadian forces manning the listening post. There was a long-standing resentment that harkened back to the early 1860s and the outbreak of smallpox that decimated the population of the Charlottes. Nine tenths of the population was killed by this epidemic. It was attributed to a consignment of Hudson Bay blankets that was infected with smallpox and had been handed to the Haida for sale or barter. To this day, many Haida believe this infection was spread deliberately by the whites, in order to rid themselves of these unwanted indigenous people. I don't think Connie believed this. In any event, if she did, she never said so.

151

Connie told us that when her mother was a young woman, she had journeyed down to Victoria and stayed there for some time. The Chief of the Masset became upset at her long absence, and eventually assembled a crew and sent it down to Victoria in a war canoe to fetch her mother back. This all happened before Connie was born and must have been in the 1890s.

We ourselves experienced the patent animosity that infected relations between the Masset and the whites. Oddly, this was not an attitude that affected the other bands. The people of Skidegate were friendly and helpful and seemed to fit in with the white inhabitants on a perfectly satisfactory basis.

Gill had expressed to Connie an interest in Haida carving, and told Connie that she would like to buy a silver bracelet carved by a Haida. "Oh," said Connie, "my brother-in-law is a carver. He's quite good and his carvings are well known. His name is Victor Adams. You should go and see him. It's easy to find his house in Masset. It's the second house after the Anglican Church. If you can't find him, go to the band office. They'll tell you where he lives." Victor, she explained, was the brother of her first husband, a Haida who had died just as the war broke out, when he and Connie were living in Prince Rupert.

Some days later we visited Masset again and drove into the old village looking for Victor Adams. We noticed that a number of the children, who were standing about by the road as we drove by, stared at us as if we somehow didn't belong on their road. We searched for Victor's house, but couldn't quickly identify it. Not wanting to bang on people's doors, we did what Connie had suggested and walked over to the band office. Going in, we were confronted by a particularly attractive young Haida girl at the reception desk, who was typing a letter. We introduced ourselves and told her that we were looking for Victor Adams, and asked if she could direct us to his house. She looked rather blankly at us and said she didn't know him. We explained that we understood him to be a carver and that we wanted to see if we could buy one of his bracelets. She shook her head, saying nothing. All our efforts to get her to tell us where Victor lived were of no avail. We turned to leave, but as we did so I said, as a sort of afterthought, "Well, that's unfortunate. Connie Webb told us that if we couldn't find her brother-in-law, we should ask at the band office, as you would know where to send us." The girl suddenly sat up, startled, and (looking very embarrassed) said, "Connie Webb sent you? Just a minute." And she rose and fled into the office behind her desk. We could hear voices behind the partition and then a young and very handsome young Haida man emerged from the back room. "Are you looking for Victor Adams?"

"Yes," we said.

"Did Connie Webb send you to see him?"

"Yes," we said, and began to explain, but he cut us off.

"Victor lives two houses down from the church. Let me show you." He took us to the door and pointed out where Victor lived.

Victor was not at home, but his wife welcomed us in and showed us a quite large collection of Victor's carvings. She thought we should come back when Victor was home, as she didn't want to sell his carving herself. We returned later and Victor showed us more of his carvings. Gill bought one: a beautiful silver bracelet with a highly stylized carving of a raven. The raven features prominently in Haida mythology. Though the same size as ordinary ravens, you have to meet the Queen Charlotte ravens to appreciate why they are so important to the Haida. They are noisy, cheeky, arrogant birds that make a wonderful and impressive whooshing sound as the wind rushes through their wing feathers. No other ravens in the world do that. It comes as no surprise that the two clans on the Charlottes are called the Raven and the Eagle—one after the great, black, domineering raven and the other after the magnificent, white-headed bird of prey.

SMALLPOX

A ll governments build reputations. Unfortunately for the plight of their constituents, the bulk of governments (starting with a clean slate and brimming with promises and vision) stumble and totter through the terms of their mandate, until a disillusioned electorate flings them from office in the hope of doing better with the crew that spent the same term in opposition—hurling criticisms and invectives. Occasionally, though rarely, an administration will function with unusual efficiency, and will be rewarded by a thankful constituency with another term. Such were the governments of Peter Lougheed in Alberta, and the immediate post-war federal governments in Ottawa, until the build up of institutional arrogance amongst the Liberals overcame them and the people reacted predictably.

The government of Sir James Douglas, which administered the two colonies of British Columbia and Vancouver Island, ran an administration that struggled with the growing pains of a new province, and the crime, commerce, and disease that accompanied the influx of a monstrous population of prospectors—all bent on wresting fortunes from the gold that had been discovered in the Yukon and in Barkerville. This was the heyday of the Hudson's Bay Company. Douglas himself was originally a Hudson's Bay factor, and finally a governor of Vancouver Island. He built a reputation as a capable administrator. Unfortunately for him, his administration also acquired a reputation amongst the Haida far more sinister than his government may have deserved.

Gill and I were keen to visit Ninstints—the old abandoned Haida village just north of Cape St. James, nestled on Anthony Island. The old Haida name, for what is now a U.N. Heritage site, is S'Gang Gwaay Llanagaay. The yawl that had brought us down the coast (called *The Darwin Sound*) dropped anchor off Anthony Island, and we and our daughter, Kate, rowed ashore. It was quite evident why this miraculously peaceful place had become a world heritage site. Scattered amongst the trees, between the high-tide mark and the forest, were dozens of weather-beaten totem poles and some mortuary poles. Many poles had collapsed, worn away by the weather. Some were leaning over, destined soon to join their mates on the ground before slowly rotting and giving themselves back to the earth from whence they had originated. Some still stood proudly, the visages carved into the trunks gazing fixedly out to sea. The mortuary poles that still stood erect cradled small coffins near the top, waiting to return their cargo to join the poles already recumbent on the grass. The outlines of several old longhouses, each completely covered with a quilt of grass and moss, marked the place where the villagers had once lived, loved, and held their potlatches.

Small deer wandered about, grazing amongst the poles, unafraid of these interlopers from the strange land up north. No hunting is permitted on Anthony Island, and it is home to no predators, so the deer were used to living unharassed by any living being that might cause them hurt. The scene was one of mystic tranquillity. We wandered around, overawed by the cathedral-like peace that pervaded this deserted, hallowed sanctum.

Kate had visited Ninstints many times before, while she was a member of the crew of *The Darwin Sound*. The island is guarded by a Haida watchman, who occupied a little hut perched atop a small cliff, shrouded by a group of huge cedars, and unseen from the beach. Kate had struck up a friendship with the watchman, and took us over to meet him. "Wonnegon, this is my father and my mother. They have come to see your beautiful home." Wonnegon appeared to be one of those beings whose age it is impossible to guess. He could have been anything from mid-forties to sixty or so. The sun and wind had combined to weather his face and his hair was iron grey and close cropped. His broad smile radiated pleasure and welcome to the white people who had journeyed down to visit his sanctuary. He might well have been less immediately welcoming if we had not been in the company of his friend Kate. Short of stature, wide in beam, and sturdily built, like all the Haida, he exhibited the Polynesian features of his race. Our old friend Connie Webb, herself a full-blooded Haida, had told us that centuries before, some Haida had ventured across the Pacific and settled in Polynesia. Sharon Hitchcock, a renowned Haida carver we had met in our travels around the islands, told us that Connie, whom she knew well, had got it wrong. It was the Polynesians who had ventured north, some populating Hawaii and some settling in southern Alaska and the Queen Charlottes. This, she said, was accomplished in the first millennium A.D..

Kate took Gill off to see another part of the Island, and I stayed to talk to Wonnegon. Diffidently, I broached the subject of the rotting totem poles. I suggested that it was a pity that some attempt was not being made to preserve them. He gave me a look, tinged with pity at my ignorance. "Ah, well," he said in the slow, lilting tones so typical of the north-coast natives. "You see, the poles originally grew as trees out of the soil of the islands. We cut them down and carved them, standing them up in our villages, as symbols of our people and our heritage, and the mortuary poles are where we house our dead. The poles are living beings. They are born, they live out their lifespan, and then, just as we mortals do, they wither and die. They go back to the earth, from which they originally came. It would be wrong to interfere with their natural life cycle. It is ordained." I wondered about all the poles preserved in the myriad museums around the world: Vancouver, Victoria, New York, Chicago, Ottawa. I mentioned to Wonnegon that I had seen totem poles that I thought must be from Haida Gwaii in the museums in Ottawa and Victoria. "That was Wilson Duff," he said. "He came here twenty-five years ago and cut down many of the poles. Cut them up and took them to Victoria. There were some of my people with him when he did it." He shook his head in mute disapproval.

Later on, as I learned more about the Haida, I realized that this expedition had sparked a bitter controversy: should the poles have been left, to return at last to the earth, or was it right to save them and preserve them in anti-septic, air-conditioned museums? I don't know the answer. But Wonnegon did.

We talked about this and that, and then I told him that Gill and I had gone ashore at Skedans, a village abandoned by the Haida many years ago. I told him that we had eaten our picnic lunch by a small clump of trees, and that I had reached back and parted some of the branches. There, revealed to view and collected up in neat rows, I was startled to find a collection of some two dozen skulls. Human skulls. Wonnegon nodded. "Yes, well, those would be the people who died of smallpox in the eighteen sixties. There were probably too few survivors to care for the bodies properly. Someone took the skulls and hid them all together where you found them." We fell to talking about the smallpox epidemic. I knew little about it, except that the smallpox virus was capable of existing in clothing and blankets and infecting people long after it had been introduced into the host material. I knew about the legend of Lord Amherst, commander of the English forces in 1763, sending infected blankets to the Indians who were besieging Fort Pitt towards the end of the French and Indian wars.

I knew that the Haida had caught smallpox from the whites and that it had seriously decimated the Haida population. Wonnegon was eloquent on the subject. He unburdened himself of a lecture on the matter. He was keen that I learned what injury the white man had wrought on the Haida. It was deliberate, he insisted. Before the mid 1850s, the Haida population had been estimated at somewhere between 6,000 to 8,000 souls (I have heard some estimates put the population as high as thirty thousand, but Wonnegan's belief held the people at about six thousand). By 1915, it had been reduced to 588, ravaged by measles, dysentery, consumption, and worst of all, smallpox. In the summer of 1863, Wonnegon said, a large group of Haida had come south to Victoria to trade their furs for pots, pans, tools, and blankets. They were encamped around Ogden Point. It was gold-rush time. *The Brother Jonathon,* a ship full of American prospectors, sailed from San Francisco and docked in Victoria, disembarking a mob of unruly Americans, some of whom were infected with smallpox. The disease spread amongst the population of Victoria, claiming many victims. These were all treated by the resident medical profession, though a number died. The Haida, camped outside the town, were becoming an embarrassment. The whites wanted them gone. Wonnegon insisted that the Douglas government deliberately infected some of the Hudson's Bay blankets with the virus and traded them to the Haida. Many fell ill, some died at Ogden Point. Deciding to go home as fast as possible, they bundled all their trade goods into their war canoes, and paddled off up north. Many died on the way, but of course, those who made it home brought the smallpox with them, infecting their families who had stayed behind. It devastated the population of the islands. In truth, the Haida came close to being wiped out completely, as had been the fate of the Beothuk in Newfoundland, though *they* had been hunted for sport by a vicious white soldiery.

I suggested to Wonnegon that no government would indulge in such deliberate genocide. Wonnegon was adamant. Nothing I said would move him from his position. "It was definitely deliberate," he insisted. "They wanted to be rid of us, so they infected the blankets and traded them to us. Sending us off to die."

I took this subject up with Connie Webb when we went to visit her in Port Clements a few days later. Her view was somewhat modified. I did not get the impression that she shared Wonnegon's certainty about the deliberate quality of the Victoria government's actions. She conceded that nobody could now show that a deliberate policy of genocide was, in fact, the case. But she allowed that many Haida certainly shared Wonnegon's opinion. This, she asserted, was the reputation the Douglas administration had earned amongst her people. To this day, she told us, a significant number of Haida still harboured a deep resentment at the harm the government had wrought on her people: a resentment that had lasted for over a century. It may account for the hard edge to the negotiations the Haida conduct for the return of their hereditary islands, Haida Gwaii.

Highland Cattle

Fifteen thousand years ago, the great, deep sheet of ice that was the last ice age began its slow retreat from British Columbia. It began melting on the coast, and inch by inch, foot by foot, it receded north and east, leaving a vast barren moraine, bare of growth, empty of life, and filled with mountains, gorges, and deserts. Seven thousand years it took for the whole of the province to be rid of the ice, and as the earth warmed, life stirred. It followed the retreating ice until the land became filled with trees, grass, plants of all descriptions, and animals and birds migrating north in search of provender. Finally, across the land bridge that is now the Bering Straits, came the people who would become the first inhabitants of this land of plenty—a land vast and fertile enough that all could live in peace without the need to wrest crops by force from one another.

The ice age that covered British Columbia for a thousand millennia never affected the archipelago that is now known as Haida Gwaii. Five hundred miles west and five hundred miles north of Vancouver, the islands were too isolated to freeze, kept warm by the great sea that surrounded them.

As a result, for fifteen thousand years and more, birds, animals, plants, and inter-tidal life existed and flourished on the islands. Some of these creatures, to this day, are not found on the mainland, though many species that survived on Haida Gwaii, having fled the onset of the icy blanket on the mainland, have now migrated back and can be found on the coast from California to the Aleutian Islands.

Halfway down the east coast of Moresby Island, there exists a large colony of peregrine falcons, nesting on the ledges and in crannies of a long cliff face. The islanders guard these birds with no little determination. No poacher, bent on seizing a bird for sale to falconers, is ever able to come near the nests without an islander showing up to threaten their life.

Murres and Murrelets, both ancient and marbled, nest along the coasts. But more interesting, perhaps, are the Cassin's Auklet, which nest in burrows. In the early summer, their young struggle out of their underground burrows and (in a mass) waddle down to the sea to spend the next several years out in the ocean. This mass exodus occurs as if the god of winged creatures had rung a bell, summoning all the chicks to leave at the same time. Small, brown divers, they have webbed feet, which make it difficult for them to land on dry land. Their preferred method of coming to earth is to pick a tree, fly straight at it, stall at the last minute with their little webbed feet out in front, hit the tree, and fall to the ground, whereupon they will pick themselves up, give a shake, and waddle off to their nests.

In 1980, our daughter, Kate, had a summer job as crew, the only crew, on a seventy-two-foot yacht that took some dozen passengers to explore the waters of Haida Gwaii. On board, as a resource person, was Wayne Campbell—the ornithologist at the Royal BC Museum in Victoria. He and Kate both went ashore one morning, and standing at the water's edge, watched as the young suddenly left their nests and made off down the beach in a great exodus of small birds. The entire beach seemed to be moving and they could not see the sand for birds. The babies flopped into the sea and began paddling out to where their mothers were calling to them. Each mother has a distinctive cry and each junior made unerringly for its mother, to spend the next several years at sea.

One evening, they watched the Auklets returning home to feed their young. They were unable to remain standing where they were. A number of the little birds chose Wayne and Kate as their preferred vertical landing post. They were both struck by so many birds, seeking to land and reach their nests, that they had to retreat back into the woods, out of range of the little feathered missiles.

The first time we visited Haida Gwaii, in 1978, was in the days when it was called the Queen Charlotte Islands, named in 1787 by an early fur trader, George Dixon. He named the islands after his ship, which in turn he had named after the wife of his sovereign, George III. Of course, it makes more sense to call the islands by the name their inhabitants have used for centuries, than for a queen, all memory of her (except in the history books) having faded into oblivion over the past two hundred years

We camped on the beach at Tlell, close by the estuary of the river. Gill and I, four children and two dogs, a Malamute and a German shepherd. The time came when we needed to journey to Port Clements for supplies, so we loaded our troupe into the station wagon, and drove down a country road that leads to the village. Turning a corner, we came upon a herd of cattle grazing beside the road. We slowed down and then, because of what we beheld, we stopped, disembarked, and stared at these strange beasts. Most had the long horns of highland cattle, as well as the long shaggy hair (which protects them in cold weather) cascading over their eyes, so that one wonders how they see at all. But these were not normal highland cattle. Almost all of them had the bodies (and some the heads and horns) of Herefords, the brown and white cattle bred in the west of England. The beasts had interbred and the result was these bizarre animals contentedly munching grass beside the road. There were fifty or so of these weird kine, and we stood and stared at them for a goodly time. They were unmoved by our presence.

In due course, we consulted our source of all information about the Charlottes: Connie Webb. She explained that the weather on the islands was consistently wet, and even in dry weather, the skies were frequently covered with a great white sheet of clouds, obscuring the warming rays of the sun. In consequence, she said, it is difficult to bring in a crop of hay on the islands. Some time before the First World War, two families decided to homestead on Graham Island. They preempted land and established farms. One family brought a small herd of Highland cattle to live on their farm, reasoning that cattle from the Highlands of Scotland would be ideally suited to the inclement weather on the island. The other family brought a small herd of Herefords. Neither venture was a success. Both families eventually gave up in the face of a climate that was simply not conducive to farming. They packed their belongings, and with their children, returned to the mainland. Unable to take their cattle with them, they turned them loose. Over the ensuing years, the two herds met, mated, and produced the engaging spectacle we had observed by the roadside.

Connie explained that the islanders, generally gentle non-aggressive folk, who only ever kill anything when they are in need of food, left the cattle alone to make their own living—grazing on grass wherever they could find it. The islanders grew fond of these eccentric creatures, and would be appalled if anybody tried to kill them. Thus they are left to their own devices, contentedly munching their way around Graham Island.

TALES OF
OLD CAULFEILD

License Plates

Hamish and Jimmy Taite had lived in their ramshackle old house, perched uphill from the church green, for as long as anyone could remember. The Taites brought up a brood of four children in a state of genteel disorder in the old house, which endured much wear and tear in consequence. When the last of their offspring departed this shelter, Hamish retired. They sold the house, and moved to Denman. The house was bought by a Swedish couple, Odd and Gisella, who also had four children—all boys.

The Swedes are an orderly, tidy race. Swedish furniture is functional with clean precise lines and no unnecessary frills—epitomizing Mies van der Rohe's principle that less is more—that truly artistic architecture must be stripped of all pretentious ostentation.

Odd and Gisella set about renovating the old home. True to their Scandinavian heritage, they transformed it into a modern, functional (if a trifle clinical) abode. With the application of only a little imagination, one might have concluded that the whole edifice had been designed by Ikea. Odd was viewed by the neighbours as a typical Swede—reserved, formal, polite, but not renowned for a roistering sense of humour. Gisella was a slim, attractive, fair-haired woman with a quiet and sardonic sense of humour.

One day, it came about that the neighbourhood realized that Odd might not be as solemn as he appeared. He was observed driving his car with a new set of license plates. The Motor Vehicle Department had just introduced the facility for motorists to purchase license plates embossed with letters of their owner's own choice. Odd had taken advantage of this whimsical bureaucratic policy, and had bought his very own set of license plates. They bore the legend, "I AM ODD". Opinion amongst the neighbours was divided. Had Odd meant to be funny? Or had he not realized that what would be a perfectly normal proposition for a Swede would translate into English as an ambiguity?

We all giggled about this for a few weeks, and then (to our unconfined hilarity) it was observed that Gisella had also been down to the Motor

163

Vehicle Department and acquired her own plates. There was no ambiguity about what they announced; "I AM NOT"

COMMODORE ROGER AND
THE PRISON HULKS

During the Second World War, a strange phenomenon was noticed about the survivors of merchant ships sunk in the Atlantic by German U-boats. Those who survived tended to be the old salts rather than the younger seamen. Those who know about such things concluded that this was because the more experienced seamen knew that they could drive themselves well beyond the normal and expected limits of human endurance, whereas the inexperienced fledglings gave up in the face of too much adversity. Out of this conclusion was developed the Outward Bound School—boot camps where merchant seamen went through rigorous training to harden their morale and survivorship skills.

In the early 1960s, the British Columbia Corrections Department hit upon the idea of creating a type of Outward Bound School for the juvenile delinquents consigned to its care. Lighthouse Park, five miles from the entrance to Vancouver harbour, had been used during the war as a location for searchlight batteries and some coastal artillery. The gun emplacements can still be seen down by the lighthouse at Point Atkinson, and the huts that were home to the gunners are still there, used (on and off) by the boy scouts and for various worthy endeavours. The Corrections Department perceived these huts and Lighthouse Park as the ideal location for the correction and training of its juvenile wards.

The implementation of this plan was set in motion, with true bureaucratic insensitivity. The neighbourhood found out about the project by accident, and the news spread through Caulfeild like a brush fire across dry savannah. Strident presentations were made to the Corrections Department. Incensed letters were fired off to *The Lion's Gate Times*, the local newspaper. Members of the Legislative Assembly were inundated with complaints, and the assistance of the West Vancouver council was urgently invoked. There was a high incidence of hysteria in the neighbourhood. Local dudgeon was high.

Then the blessed Corrections Department realized that it had forgotten the diplomatically necessary step of consulting the neighbourhood in advance of its penal project. An emissary approached the vicar, at that time a gentle, kindly, ex-social worker with a strongly ingrained sense of naiveté. Pressed by the Corrections Department for help, he leapt to the conclusion that the proposed school was an ideal solution for West Vancouver's juvenile delinquency inmates, which it was—except that the location of this project had not been thought through. The department decided that it had become necessary to mend some fences. It proposed a meeting in the hall of the church of St. Francis in the Wood. There and then, the department would explain the project to the parishioners, inspire support, and subdue the growing opposition. We would all easily be influenced to adapt to the department's point of view.

Both the vicar and the department had misread the local concern. There was fear that the park would become unsafe for women and children to walk in. The thought of dozens of male youths, some convicted of unpleasantly violent crimes, stalking the pathways of Lighthouse Park was not a welcome one.

The meeting was duly convened. The church hall was overflowing and it was standing room only for any latecomers. The meeting was opened by the vicar, who made an eloquent speech in support of what he viewed as a worthy and truly Christian approach to juvenile delinquency. His plea was received in stony silence. Then the Director of Corrections rose to explain the project. His name was Selwyn Roxbourough-Smith, an experienced senior administrator in the department. His accent gave away the country and culture of his birth. A tall man, dressed in a three-piece Harris Tweed suit, he addressed the assembled crowd with his thumbs inserted in the arm holes of his waistcoat. With the lofty superiority fostered in the English public school system, he embarked on an explanation of the project designed to suppress the opposition that had been brewing. He was very soon overwhelmed with questions, and assailed by arguments against the chosen location. As the evening wore on, he grew visibly more harassed. One could discern a look on his face that revealed his own gradually forming realization that his project was doomed. His thumbs vacated their resting places, and he began to use them (and his hands) in gestures of supplication. The vast bulk of his constituency was invincibly opposed. His embassy was a failure.

Then Commodore Roger rose to speak. Now Commodore Roger had never darkened the church door before. A Scotsman, he was an ex-Royal Navy officer who had served as a midshipman in the battle of Jutland. He lived with Frances Baker in the house next door to us. They had moved in just before we bought our house and they kept very much to themselves. Rarely socializing with the neighbours, they maintained a hermit-like existence. Everyone was surprised to see them at the meeting at all. The Commodore was a short, bulky individual with an expression that had certain martinet qualities about it. His little speech disclosed that he had no understanding of the problems of (or solutions to) juvenile delinquency, and he had clearly not been listening to the explanation of the basis for the philosophy of the Outward Bound movement. He was against crime. He was for punishment *as* punishment, and he would have no truck with these newfangled, fancy ways of dealing with prisoners.

"When I was a boy in Edinburgh," he said, in a voice that was clearly more accustomed to the quarter deck than a church hall, "and first went to sea, we used to deal with prisoners very effectively. We had a number of old ship's hulks that we moored in the Firth of Forth. Prison hulks. Two or three were enough. They were impossible to escape from. Prisoners could not jump overboard. The North Sea was too cold. You'd only survive for five minutes and then the cold got your heart. We had no trouble with prisoners once they got aboard the hulks. I don't see why you can't find somewhere around here to moor some hulks. You should be able to buy some old hulks cheaply enough. That would solve your problem. Just take my advice. Mark my words: you'll have no more trouble with these young knaves." He resumed his seat, satisfied that this gift of wisdom, bestowed upon the neighbours and the Corrections Department, had solved the problem. There was nothing more to be said.

His dissertation was received in complete and astonished silence. Roxborough-Smith stared at the Commodore in bewildered disbelief. His eyes flickered around the room as if he were looking for the culprit who had put the Commodore up to it as a joke. The rest of us looked at each other, almost in embarrassment. We all thought prison hulks had gone out of use in the days of Pip's convict, Magwitch, in *Great Expectations*. There was a momentary and edgy shuffling of feet, a few whispers, and then the meeting slowly wound up and we all went home.

The Department did not buy any hulks. It abandoned Lighthouse Park as a location for Outward Bound and moved it to Porteau Cove, a few miles up the east side of Howe Sound, where it has functioned in peace ever since. The Commodore and Mrs. Baker returned to their home to resume their troglodyte existence, and their daily intake of rum. It had been their first, last, and only involvement in local affairs.

The Starlight Express

The Starlight Express was the wheeled gem of BC Rail's transportation system.

It was a dinner train that ran on summer evenings from North Vancouver to Porteau Cove and back. You booked a table and boarded the train at the old P. G. E. station in North Vancouver. It was one long restaurant car. The wine was of superior quality. Aperitifs were available pre-repast, and Cognac and liqueurs afterwards. All was served by neatly turned-out staff, who were efficient, cheerful, and surprisingly knowledgeable about both the food and the wine. A jazz band, playing on the platform, welcomed passengers aboard, accompanied the train on the trip to Porteau Cove, disembarked, and played while passengers danced on the platform.

In July of 2004, the Canadian National Railway Company bought BC Rail, and to the dismay of the population of the lower Mainland, killed the Starlight Express. No consultation. No apology. No explanation. What had been a serious tourist attraction was now stone dead. The assets were sold off. The staff were fired, a couple of dozen student summer jobs were lost, and the band was forced to go in search of other summer gigs—all victims of the corporate bottom line, ruthlessly pursued.

My brother, Peter, some eleven years older than I, had been an engineer and worked for British Rail. In the few years before he retired, he had been in charge of the brakes on B. R's locomotives. His wife, Giséle, was French. They had met in Brussels just after its liberation, when Peter was in the army and in command of a light-aid detachment, which gathered up damaged tanks, fixed them, and returned them to service on the front line. Not long before Canadian National delivered its coup de grace to the Starlight Express, they came to visit us. Because of Peter's interest in railways, I suggested that they land in Quebec and take the train across Canada. This they did. I asked my sister-in-law what she had made of the French Canadian accent. "Oh," she said, "it's a Norman patois." This made sense, because most French Canadians came from the maritime areas of France.

Alert to Peter's obsession with railways, we decided to take them on the Starlight Express. We booked a table for four and duly turned up at the North Vancouver Station on an unusually hot summer evening. We parked, and as we got out of the car, were greeted by the strains of sprightly music. We found the jazz band playing a lively tune on the platform, which had the effect of putting all the passengers in a jolly mood. We were shown to our table by a hostess who admitted that she, like all the waiters and waitresses, was a UBC student, and that this was her summer job, paying enough to put her through one more year—a sly hint that tips would be appreciated. The tables were set with crisp white tablecloths, napkins folded into little tents, shining cutlery, and glass wear. Each table was decorated with a candle. An artistically conceived menu held out the promise of a sumptuous meal. After everyone had clambered aboard, and settled into their places, the train set off. It trundled slowly through the marshaling yard between the station and the Capilano River, and then through Ambleside Park. We were viewing west Vancouver from an unusual perspective. Another student served us cocktails. We were beginning to enjoy our journey and looked forward to the dinner, which we had just ordered from the elegantly printed menu.

As we approached the police station, there was an ugly sounding noise from up front and the train slammed on its brakes, lurching to a halt and sending a quantity of cutlery and glasses across tables into laps and onto the floor. Trains, like ships, take some time to come to a halt, but we had only been doing about twelve miles an hour so the deceleration, in this case, was fairly quick. The diners were all craning to see what had happened, and asking any passing waiter for information. It was quite a long time coming, but eventually our student hostess came by with the news that the engine had struck a car at the level crossing by the police station at 12th Street. "The car tried to beat the train across the crossing," the hostess informed us. "He didn't make it. They've called an ambulance and the police are questioning the driver."

"I bet he's Cantonese," I said. We had to explain to Peter and Gisele that the Cantonese were generally viewed by the population of the lower mainland as bad drivers—never looking where they were going, and having the bad habit of driving while talking on their cell phones.

The train was stopped for a good hour. Ambulances came and went, their sirens heightening the drama. A tow truck was observed dragging away a battered automobile. Because the train was stopped, the air-conditioning system ceased functioning. We all grew hotter and sweatier in the still, humid air. The windows in the dining cars were not designed to open, so the temperature rose relentlessly to our increasing discomfort. The kitchen had suspended service temporarily, though we were supplied with more drinks, on the house, to mollify our collective irritation. I opted for a cold lager in an attempt to beat the heat. After what seemed an eternity, the train started up again and rumbled at no great speed through Lawson Park. It gained speed along the coast.

We were still overheated, encased as we were in our sealed carriage. The air conditioning was slow in reducing the temperature that had been generated while we were stationary at the accident site. We emerged from the tunnel above Eagle Harbour and passed above Horseshoe Bay. Strangely, the train began to slow down and eventually it stopped at Lion's Bay. Once again the air conditioning switched off. Sweaty time again. Another ambulance drew up, though we could not see what business it was bent on conducting. Our cheerful hostess came by and explained this, once again unscheduled, stop. A pregnant passenger had gone into labour, and they had phoned for the ambulance to take her to hospital.

Just as we were about to start up again, we heard a scream from the next carriage and no little commotion. In her anxiety to see what was going on, one of the female passengers had been leaning over her table peering out of the window. She leant too close to the candle on her table, which set her long, brown, curly hair alight. The flames raced up one side of her face until another student waiter had the presence of mind to grab a jug of water and fling its contents at her head.

This misfortune called for the summoning of yet another ambulance, which took another half hour to arrive and take the girl to hospital to tend to her burns. Meanwhile, the air conditioning took another sabbatical while the train remained stationary.

Finally, two hours late, we reached Porteau Cove. Our dinner, interrupted as it had been, was finished and all the passengers climbed down onto the platform and into the cool refreshing air of Howe Sound. The band emerged, clutching their instruments, assembled on the platform, and began to play. This went some considerable way to restoring our morale, which had deteriorated sadly in the face of the accidents, the delays, and the stifling heat. Most of us danced—to Stan Getz, Count Basie, Dizzy Gillespie, and Sidney Bechet. It was an accomplished and lively band.

Peter vanished. I was left to dance with my sister-in-law. We found him later, down at the front of the train in an animated conversation with the engineer. The train crew, anxious to get back on schedule, ushered us all back into the hot carriages before we were really ready to go, and we set off back to North Vancouver. Thankfully it was an uneventful return trip and the air conditioning kept us at a comfortable temperature.

Some days later, Peter and Gisele returned to the UK. The next edition of the *North Shore News* contained a short account of the accident at the 12th Street crossing. The article ended by disclosing the name of the driver of the offending car: Bangki Chang. I cut out the article and sent it to Peter. "What did I tell you! Cantonese."

FLICKERS AND OTHER ACCIDENTS

The bird population around our old house is in constant flux. Over the fifty-one years we have inhabited the old place, it has seen an impressive array of dogs, cats, children, and birds. Only the rats have maintained any consistency. To repel these, we installed high-pitched sound devices in the basement, along with several generations of cats. Unfortunately, the cats also number the birds amongst their prey, though we try to foil their instinctive desire to massacre birds by making the bird feeders cat proof.

When we first moved into the house, with our one small son, we were blessed with a flock of barn swallows and the occasional cliff swallow. They built mud nests on the sides of our house and under the eves. We welcomed them for their feeding habits, for they consumed an unimaginable number of mosquitoes and other summer pests. It was always a race to see if the swallows stayed around long enough to harass the flying ants that emerge from the wood in all the neighbourhood houses in the fall, or if they would leave before that on their winter migration south.

In those days, it was not unusual to see a pheasant in the woods along the beach. They did not last long. They left in the face of too much urban sprawl. What was sad was that, over the span of a few years, the number of swallows gradually diminished as well, until (some twenty-five years ago) they were gone completely. We suspect the crows drove them off. Crows were a rarity at first. Then they must have discovered some secret about the real estate around Caulfeild, for they now live here in abundance—murders of them. We wish they didn't, for they have a vicious habit of raiding the nests of other birds, as we suspect they did to the swallows—like some hoard of rapacious horsemen out of Mongolia.

The flickers are relatively new to the neighbourhood, or maybe (when we first moved in) we just didn't notice them. The Northern Red-shafted Flicker lives up to his grandiose name. A big bird, he has a brown-speckled breast, a black bib beneath his beak, and a red slash at his throat—as if in imitation of a rainbow trout. He wakes us up in the morning, because he has a habit of laying claim to his territory by clinging to a branch and banging on it with his beak. His favourite percussion perch is one of the telephone poles at the bottom of our garden. He will cling to the top of the pole and bang on the tin cap that Telus nails on top of the poles to stop the rain from rotting them. It sounds like an old Gatling gun in intermittent use.

We are blessed, however, with a variety of other birds, some new to the scene. A kingfisher comes in the summer to shout angrily while flying around the cove. A clutch of oyster catchers fly daily from Sandy Beach to their nesting ground by the lighthouse. We have as many as sixteen bald eagles nesting in Lighthouse Park, along with a dozen ravens. And, of course the herons fish off the rocks and croak angrily if disturbed. We have one old heron who will come on cold mornings and sit on the next door chimney pot, drying his wings in the warm draft of air that ruffles his feathers.

Our chimney pots don't get the use they used to. We used to have, and regularly used, three wood fireplaces. We collected firewood off the beach and split it to size. But then we replaced them with two gas fireplaces. There is something romantic and cosy about a wood fire that gas fires can't rival, but they do save the labour of hauling logs off the beach.

When we installed our first gas fireplace in our bedroom, we discovered that we used it more than the old wood-burning grate. It has a device that turns the fire on at night, in time for bed, and then off again a while later. In the morning, it comes on again, so that we can towel ourselves off in front of its enveloping warmth after a morning shower.

This fireplace had been installed only a few months when it began causing trouble. I noticed a disturbing rattling noise on occasion. Well, you don't want to fool with devices that can cause the summoning of the fire department, so after several futile attempts to fix the problem myself, I called up the people who had installed it. An earnest mechanic showed up and I explained the problem to him. He spent half an hour fiddling with the fire: turning it on, turning it off, raising and then lowering the temperature, peering into its inner workings, and adjusting nuts with a long monkey wrench—all while I bent anxiously over his shoulder making unhelpful suggestions, which he ignored. He eventually rose, stuffing his tools into his box, and announced, with no little irritation, that the fire was working perfectly. There was nothing wrong with it. He would send me a bill.

It continued to rattle intermittently and I continued to worry about it. We had a fire detection device in the bedroom, but should I install a fire extinguisher—just in case?

Some weeks after this, and early one morning, I went up to the greenhouse to water some newly purchased tomato plants. As I was doing so, I was startled to hear the familiar Gatling gun sound, as if it were working overtime in battle. I emerged from the greenhouse door, with my watering can poised. I looked around. Nothing. Then the raucous sound broke in again. The noise was coming from our bedroom chimney. There, clinging to the brickwork, was our friendly flicker. He was diligently claiming his territory by banging his beak, at full bore, on the tin cowl on top of the chimney.

There had been nothing wrong with the gas fire, as the mechanic rightly claimed. I found myself unable to summon up the nerve to call him up and tell him what the cause of the rattling gas fire actually was.

LUMUMBA

January 1961. We had been married for twelve weeks and were living in the old Red & White store at the head of Caulfeild Cove. Patrice Lumumba, the newly minted President of the Republic of the Congo had been refused aid by the United States, turned to the Soviet Union instead, and was promptly assassinated at the hands of the CIA.

Gill had lived in so many places all over the world that she had never had the opportunity to own a dog. Now was her chance, and it had to be a German shepherd. One of my mother's many odd notions had to do with German shepherds. She wasn't afraid of much, but shepherds made her nervous. She said that they were untrustworthy and often turned on their owners. She had assembled a collection of grim stories to support her contention. Having harkened to this chant throughout my childhood, I had been infected by Mother's fear. We have had six German shepherds—all faithful and affectionate animals, down to the last paw, proving how misguided my mother had been.

We read an ad in the paper for German shepherd puppies, inserted by one D. Gilbert at an address in Burnaby. So we drove to Burnaby to inspect a three-month-old puppy. He was a large dog for his age and his legs were too big for his body, as if he had borrowed a set of legs from a much larger dog. I gave D. Gilbert a cheque for the $25 he was asking. We put the puppy in a cardboard box, drove him home, and named him Lumumba, after the President of the Congo who had died the previous week at the hands of hired assassins.

House training was surprisingly easy. He was a bright dog. We grew very fond of him. However, one day Lumumba and I were collecting firewood off the beach in the cove when we encountered something that permanently altered Lumumba's outlook on life. That "something" was a big man with an accent that sounded as if it had been nurtured in the British army. He was collecting wood too. Lumumba scrambled over the logs to talk to him. The man seemed to harbour my mother's fear of shepherds, for he ordered the dog away. Lumumba merely wagged his tail in response. I called him over, but he insisted on establishing friendly relations with the

Brit, who picked up a large two by four and shouted at the dog. Lumumba thought he was going to throw the two by four for him and let out an enthusiastic bark. The Brit thought he was being attacked, and swung the bar of wood, hitting Lumumba on the head. He let out a scream of pain and lay down, briefly stunned, on the pebble beach. I rushed over and picked him up, shouting at the dog's assailant. "You stupid idiot! What did you do that for?"

I carried Lumumba back to the house, followed by a stream of invective from the incensed Brit. "You people … think you own the cove … Keep your dog under control …report you to the police … have him put down!" I slammed the front door on the torrent of unpleasantries and we set about tending our poor dazed dog.

After that, Lumumba became quite unnecessarily protective. He hated any man on sight (even those not carrying a two by four), and if not restrained, would attack. Children he tolerated, but grownups were the enemy—to be treated as such. This became a problem, as we had to ensure that he was corralled in the house or the garden at all times, and we had to shut him away before answering the doorbell. The problem was exacerbated by the fact that he grew into a very big dog. In his prime, he weighed 140 pounds. He was well known and not much loved in the neighbourhood. By actual count, over his twelve-year life span, he bit five of our neighbours. Of course, we should never have kept him, but we could not bring ourselves to have our faithful companion, and the guardian of our children, put down.

When Lumumba was just over one year old, we bought a house across the road and moved into it with him and our old cat. There had been a path through the backyard of our new house, by which the neighbourhood children habitually took a short cut to the beach. Lumumba's reputation was such that, the very day we moved in, usage of the path ceased.

One day, we had some old friends come to stay. Although we introduced them to Lumumba, the husband remained nervous about him. Some years after, he told us that he had needed to go to the bathroom in the middle of the night, but was scared to open the bedroom door. So he had to relieve himself by peeing out of the bedroom window.

In due course, as our children grew old enough to look after them, we bought them two guinea pigs. They soon became a family of guinea pigs. We used to let them run loose on the back lawn, which was sufficiently fenced that they could not escape. They ate the grass, so that we never needed to mow the lawn, and did their business outside as well, acting as fertilizers *and* lawn mowers. Lumumba believed he was responsible for the safety of these charming little creatures. Whenever we let them out onto their lawn, he would trot out, lie on the grass, and guard them.

Phil Collings was one of the only family friends Lumumba tolerated. Whenever he and his family came to see us, Lumumba would greet them with a great show of affection.

Phil's four children, who well knew Lumumba's reputation, remained steadfastly nervous of the dog. After Lumumba died, we learned that all Phil's children persistently referred to Gill as "Mrs. Dog".

THE UNINVITED LUNCHEON GUEST

The real estate agents call our little village "Olde Caulfeild"—a tacky name that the inhabitants detest. The real estate agents certainly seemed to have sold the raccoons on Olde Caulfeild, because before the raccoon population was decimated by distemper, we were all plagued by an oversized and energetic population of the cheeky little procyons. They were pestilential. They overturned garbage cans in search of food. They dug up and ate bulbs carefully planted in the gardens against the coming of spring—tulips seemed to be their favourite. They ate everybody's grapes just as they were at the point of ripening, and terrorized the neighbour-hood cats. One year they nested beneath our playroom floor, tearing out all the flooring insulation to build their nests. We had to smoke them out with a bee smoker. They vacated these premises reluctantly and with ill grace, grumbling their way up the fir trees in the back garden.

They are equipped with thumbs, which (although they cannot close them on their index fingers) allow them to open garbage cans, boxes, and other such containers. They are omnivorous; they will eat anything. Like the coyotes, they have adapted to the presence of humans, enlarging their range, despite the encroachment of mankind into their original territory.

The name "raccoon" comes from an Algonquin word, "Arakum', which means "he who scratches with his hands". They are clever and mischie-vous and seem to be completely unafraid of anything. Although they have an engaging appearance, with their black-ringed eyes, striped, bushy tails, and grizzled grey bodies, they can be quite vicious. Like coyotes, they are well known for their propensity to seize cats and carry them off for supper. They are best left well alone.

Nancy and Chris Ashton have lived, for some thirty years, five doors east of us. One day Nancy set about baking bread. She laid out the fresh loaves to cool on her kitchen table and went upstairs. She heard an odd noise in the kitchen and came back downstairs to investigate. She beheld a raccoon, on the kitchen table, busily devouring one of the loaves she had just baked. She advanced on the beast and banged on the table with a wooden spoon, the first weapon to come to hand. The raccoon glared at her over the loaf, evidencing an edgy attitude that deterred her from any attempt to lay hands on it. The pointed teeth and (more intimidating) long sharp claws, gave warning that she should conduct only very cautious negotiations over title to the loaf. She banged her wooden spoon repeatedly on the table and shouted at the creature in uncomplimentary language. The raccoon stood up on its hind legs and glowered at her with its big, black, button eyes. It emitted a growl, a surprisingly loud baritone. The beast clearly had a flair for the melodramatic, for it bobbed up and down and continued its menacing growls, ranging over a whole octave, while Nancy continued to bang on the table, advancing the spoon towards the raccoon. This seemed to achieve the desired result, for the raccoon dropped down from its upright *en guard* stance and picked up the loaf in its jaws. It turned and wobbled, with its characteristic rolling gait, to the edge of the table, dropped the loaf onto the floor, and leaped down after it. Grasping the loaf again in its mouth, it hastened to the back door, which had a cat door let into it, through which the raccoon had gained entry in the first place—attracted by the smell of newly baked bread. Now, the loaf was too wide to go through the cat door, and though the raccoon tried to exit with the loaf in its mouth, he soon discovered that it was not an option. The raccoon dropped the loaf and bustled off through the cat door, which swung back to its closed position.

Nancy walked round the table and over to the door. She stooped to pick up her now ruined loaf. As she did so, to her astonishment, the cat door slowly opened inwards and a skinny, hairy hand was thrust through it, groping about for the temporarily abandoned loaf. The hand, locating its objective, grasped the loaf and tried to turn it round. Nancy seized the battered loaf. The claws opened and closed as the raccoon sought to retrieve its prize. Nancy bent down and peered through the cat door. Her gaze was met by two angry black eyes glaring through the door. It eventually withdrew its hand and the cat door closed with a decisive click, leaving Nancy clutching her now ruined loaf. She opened the back door and watched the raccoon hopping over the rocks in her back garden. It stopped once, cast a resentful glance over its shoulder, and disappeared into the bushes.

THE END

They made an odd couple. She was tall, raw-boned, and energetic, and had run a successful antique business in Vancouver. A woman of deeply held conservative opinions, she had been known to send packing, and in tears, any charity canvasser who knocked on her front door. Except that she was tall, rather than stout, she bore some resemblance to Gertrude Stein. Butch and authoritative, she possessed an artistic flair and had filled their house with exquisite furniture and paintings that any gallery would envy. She was kind, despite her reactionary views—frequently expressed and strongly reminiscent of the more reactionary of Charles Dickens' villains.

She had never learned to drive. At the height of her business career, and tired of riding buses and paying taxi fares, she had advertised for a chauffeur. Stewart Gordon responded to the ad. She hired him and he faithfully drove her around, ran errands for her, and delivered and picked up antiques traded in the course of her business. Stewart was some years younger than Olive, though when we came to know them it was difficult to guess their ages. Either could have been any age between fifty and seventy. Stewart was American and had served a term (apparently as a cook) in the US Navy. This was surprising, as he was well read, had evidently benefited from a good education, and had a sensitive appreciation of the arts. He did not exhibit the normal attributes one would expect in an American ex-serviceman. Shorter than Olive, he was mildly overweight, and carried about him the limp-wristed gestures (with voice to match) of a member of the gay crowd.

After several years in the relationship of employer/employee, they married and moved into the little house, tucked in between the beach and the road, at the head of Caulfield Cove. Local speculation had them either sleeping in separate rooms, or in the same room in separate beds (or in an emperor-sized double bed); nobody knew for sure. They certainly seemed to live together in contented retirement, though their relationship, as viewed by the Caulfield villagers, appeared more akin to that of brother and sister than a married couple. For years, they would throw a grand

179

Christmas party; their dining table would be groaning with a sumptuous feast of Christmas fare. Stewart would never admit to cooking any of it. He served drinks in liberal proportions, and we all ate and drank and shouted at each other, as one does at parties held in a confined space. There was always a lively log fire—the logs garnered off the beach and dried over the summer. Stewart's loud and slightly effeminate voice could be readily heard above the hubbub, chatting up the local ladies and plying his guests with drinks.

Stewart collected ducks. Every morning, at exactly eight o'clock, he would stride out onto his deck, and quacking loudly, would fling handfuls of birdseed out onto the beach, attracting flocks of merganser, goldeneye, bufflehead, and scoter, which would come winging in for breakfast—summoned by the sound of Stewart's voice. The downside of this avian charity was that the exercise also attracted an unwelcome population of rats. This did not go down well with the neighbourhood, and the local Home Hardware store experienced a sharp increase in the sale of rat-traps and poison. Stewart waged an incessant and unsuccessful war against the rats, but he refused, against all the frequently expressed entreaties to desist, to give up his morning ritual of breakfast with the birds.

The Gordon's lived their peaceful and uneventful lives for upwards of forty years at the head of Caulfeild Cove. We all grew fond of them. They never crossed the threshold of the little Anglican church, only a stone's throw across the green from their house, though they always invited the vicar to their parties.

They both grew old and frail, and the east wind got into their bones. Stewart developed diabetes and was eventually forced to take to a wheelchair. One by one, they found themselves relinquishing the little pleasures in life, each insignificant in itself, that made for a contented retired life. Olive grew increasingly fragile, and they were finally driven to give up their Christmas parties.

After a lingering illness, Olive died. The funeral, attended by most of the neighbourhood, was a graveside service in the West Vancouver Cemetery, conducted by the Anglican vicar. We all crowded around for this rite of passage of our old friend. Stewart, silent in his wheelchair, was clutching a long-stemmed red rose. The service wound to an end with the traditional casting of earth onto the coffin. Ashes to ashes, dust to dust. There was a moment's silence. Stewart wheeled his chair up to the side of the grave. He shouted at the top of his voice, "Goodbye my Darling! God bless you!" Then he flung the rose into the grave. We all wept.

TRAVELS
IN FOREIGN PARTS

CAMBRIDGE CIRCUS

It was dark, raining, and cold—a standard London winter's evening. My wife, Gill, and I were on holiday in London sometime in the early 1960s. We decided to go to the theatre.

We had dined at a little restaurant close by the theatre, which was just off Cambridge Circus—a large roundabout with five or six streets converging into it. In the middle of this roundabout was an island with an iron fence around it, interrupted by gaps for pedestrians to pass through from the zebra crossings. In the middle of the island, two sets of stairs led down to the underground public toilets, one for men and one for women.

We reached the circus and aimed for the theatre, whose brightly lit, elegant, Georgian entrance was filled with a boisterous, jostling crowd of theatre-goers. I needed to go to the bathroom, having foolishly neglected to do so before leaving the restaurant. Because I judged that the theatre's toilets would be clogged with patrons seeking urgent relief, I left Gill by the theatre entrance and walked across the road to the public toilets. I descended the stairs entitled 'Men' and entered the gloomy, ill-lit, and only moderately clean toilet. Being underground, it was dingy, cold, and damp. I took up position at the nearest urinal. I then noticed a man who materialized at the urinal beside me. Subconsciously, I noted that this was odd, because there was a row of about ten urinals, all of which had been empty when I arrived. Normally men will not use a urinal right next to one that is in use, if others are available. They will use one that is at least one removed. This is not a recognized or conscious etiquette, but some subconscious instinct having to do, I suspect, with a desire for privacy.

The man took up station beside me. He was impeccably turned out. His hat was stylish and black, with a wide brim that gave it a theatrical air—something that Richard Wagner might have worn. He had on a well-cut black overcoat with an Astrakhan collar. A tightly furled black umbrella was tucked under one arm. As I finished with the call of nature, I inspected this apparition out of the corner of my eye, trying not to appear intrusively inquisitive. I did not succeed. The man caught my eye, turned towards me, and began to engage me in conversation. I do not now remember

183

anything he said, and I suspect that I was not taking it in at the time. I was startled and embarrassed at being caught eyeing him. His face assumed an ingratiating smile, as he launched into something I realized he intended to develop into a dialogue I did not welcome. I took fright, hastily buttoned up, and fled back up the stairs.

As I emerged into the drizzle on the island, I began to realize that the man's face was familiar to me. I dared not stop, either to puzzle over his identity or wait for him to emerge so as to get a better look at him. I hastened back over the zebra crossing, all the while trying to remember where I had seen that face before.

I returned to where Gill was waiting for me, close by the theatre entrance. She looked at me in some surprise as I arrived breathless and in no little haste. As she began to ask why I had been hurrying, I burst out, "Gill, I think I have just been propositioned by John Gielgud."

PARIS

It was the end of my first year at law school. It would be at least another seven weeks before the dreaded exam results were posted, in the yard behind the London University building. I had ahead of me the sublime prospect of a month in the country. Not Russia, but the peaceful loveliness of the Dordogne countryside, with its abundance of medieval *chateaux*. My French sister-in-law's family came from La Force, a small village ten kilometres northwest of Bergerac. I had been invited to come and stay with them. Even the most humble country farmhouse in the Dordogne will have its conical turret and stone door lintels, built in the style that Eleanor of Aquitaine inspired. Local legend has it that when God was distributing his quota of *chateaux* around the Dordogne, the bottom of the sack, in which he carried these exquisite masterpieces, caught on the point of the turret of a chateau he had just put in place. It tore open the sack and before God knew what had happened, he had scattered the whole sack-full of *chateaux* all over the valley of the Dordogne.

On one of these jaunts, I was joined on my journey as far as Paris by three friends, architectural students from the Bartlett School of Architecture, which was attached to my college. Their intention was to spend some time in Paris inspecting its architecture. They persuaded me to delay my trip to the Dordogne and accompany them on their pilgrimage around Paris. This trio consisted of Mike Garrett, a tall taciturn man with a gannet-like appearance, and a set of twin brothers—always known as the Hennessy twins. They were identical, and had a sense of humour derived from their Irish ancestry, which was capable of creating boisterous anarchy out of the most mundane situations. They claimed that their family came from the Channel Islands, whither it had been driven as a result of some scandalous indiscretion that had been committed when the family lived in Ireland. I doubted this tale, as it was always accompanied by a claim to be related to a brandy distilling family, about which they knew so little that it cast in doubt their claim to kinship. Their attitude to the French was one of gentle, sly derision.

We crossed the Channel on a ferry to Deauville, in what must have been gale-force winds. Most of the passengers were seasick. All four of us were driven, by the smell of illness, to sleep on deck in the lee of some cabins. We huddled together and got very wet, though we seemed to be able to sleep well enough. As we approached the harbour, I remember standing with a group of passengers close by the point of disembarkation. I was struck in the face by several buckets-worth of water from a stray wave. I let out an oath, used mainly by students and foot soldiers, and was acutely embarrassed at the stares of disapproval from assembled company.

We finally disembarked in the rays of a watery French sun, and took the train to Paris. It was pulled by a French steam engine. Compared to the small, neat, businesslike English engines, this was a monster. Large, black, and muscular, it noisily emitted clouds of steam. It seemed to have all its plumbing on the outside, being festooned with pipes, iron ladders, taps, and gauges. It stood rumbling and shuddering like an angry bull that was impatient to be on its way. Just as we four were climbing into our carriage, immediately behind this behemoth, it emitted a whistle—a warning to passengers that farewells must be curtailed and it was time to be off. The whistle was not up to the expectations aroused by the engines belligerent appearance. One would have expected a rousing booming voice from this monster, something akin to what an ocean-going liner might employ. Instead this fierce, medieval, clanking, wheeled tyrant let out an effeminate soprano-like whistle—almost a squeak—that one would expect to be used by a referee at a small boys' soccer match. Clearly this arrogant product of the industrial revolution had feet, or at least wheels, of clay. Its voice was not up to its muscle. One of the Hennessys wondered if, like English engines, it had been given a name. "I shall call it Fifi." He announced. Fifi duly set off and hauled us (at an alarming speed) through the beautiful, warm French countryside to arrive surprisingly quickly at the dingy cavern of the Gare du Nord.

This station is now clean, bright, and shiny, bustling with passengers and serviced by numerous restaurants and snack bars that sell surprisingly good food. Of course, the French have an inbred and invincible sense of priorities. Good food and wine are very near the top of the list, second only (I suspect) to liaisons, *dangereuse* and otherwise. But our visit to Paris was not long after the end of the war, and things were not quite yet back to normal.

Through the students' union, we had booked rooms in the Sorbonne. It was spartan student accommodation, two floors up and overlooking a quadrangle. One communal bathroom served the needs of the whole floor, which made morning ablutions a frustrating and time-consuming procedure as a floor full of itinerant students (all talking languages foreign to each other) tried to urge others to more speed. We soon fell to bathing later in the day, though this led the Hennessys to fall foul of the concierge, whose duties seemed to include a relentless campaign to prevent any use of hot water above that absolutely necessary for the removal of a minimum amount of grime. This short, round, determined woman commanded us to use no more than four inches of water for a bath, and in order to save on the heating bill, tried to encourage us to share these shallow puddles with each other. Most of her instructions were delivered in French at lightning speed. When at first we appeared not to understand her, she merely said it all again, louder, but without reducing the speed of delivery. Since each sentence seemed to end with the phrase *"Parce que ca coute cher,"* we eventually caught on to the gist of her message: it was too expensive not to do as she insisted. We decided that our natural desire to ignore her instructions was not worth provoking her terrible wrath. It would be like deliberately attempting to face down our steam engine; we would simply have been run over. Our contractual rights as paying guests counted for nothing in the face of the strength of her view of what was expected of us, and what was *"defendu"*. She exhibited the strength of character and determination of a regimental sergeant major of the Imperial Guard. Without precisely saying so, she made it quite clear that she could make our stay quite unpleasant unless we adhered strictly to her requirements. It was Mike Garrett who eventually saved us from the consequences of our instinctive desire to buck the discipline of this wrathful harpy. Over the three days of our stay, he wooed her in surprisingly intelligible French, with blandishments, compliments, and praise, none of which he meant or believed. We did not think that she believed him either, but she seemed to enjoy the flattery, delivered with the skill and grace of an Asian diplomat. Perhaps she was so unused to politeness from students, however insincere, that she enjoyed being the recipient of it. Nonetheless, even Mike Garrett could not get us more than a four-inch bath, inspected by Madame each time we ran one.

I spent the next three days being shown the architectural masterpieces of Paris by these three scapegraces. They indulged in an unlovely habit each time we visited a Roman Catholic church, which (of course) was every church we visited. It started in *La Madelaine*. After we had inspected its vast and dark interior, and I had been educated by them as to its attributes of architectural interest, the three of them grouped together at the end of the main aisle and softly chanted a little ditty, to the tune of the old English carol *"In Dulci Jubilo"*. The libretto was as follows:

From the crypt of the church of St. Giles',
Came a scream that sounded for miles;
Said the bishop, "Good gracious, Dear brother Ignatius,
Forgets that the vicar has piles,
Forgets that the vicar has piles."

Then these three intellectual bandits would cross themselves and walk quickly, with affected dignity, out of the church. Oddly, they chose not to intone "St. Giles" before the tomb of Napoleon in *Les Invalides*—I suspect not so much out of respect for the Emperor as for their apprehension about the numerous *gendarmes* keeping a watchful eye on the gawking tourists. To my discredit, I joined them in this boorish ritual at the end of our visits to other churches, including Notre Dame—where we deliberately intoned it beneath the cardinals' hats suspended from the roof of the chancel.

At that time, the chancel of Notre Dame had dozens of the round, red hats (worn by cardinals) suspended from the ceiling along each side of its entire length. Legend has it that when a cardinal of Paris dies, his hat is hung from the ceiling, and he cannot ascend to heaven until it falls to the ground. We were told by a *curé* that, since the ropes that held the hats were quite stout, no hat had yet fallen to the ground. Fifty years later, my wife and I visited Paris. Upon entering Notre Dame, I noticed that the cardinals' hats were no longer hanging from the ceiling. They could not all have fallen in fifty years, and I concluded that they must have been taken down. I enquired of the people selling post cards at a kiosk, and of several priests wandering around the cathedral, but none knew what I was talking about. They had never heard of the cardinals' hats.

I did learn a great deal about architecture from my rascally friends as they raced around Paris inspecting buildings of interest. They had planned the tour well in advance, and we wasted no time searching for what they wanted to see. We saw a magical production of Carmen from the gods at the opera. We all enjoyed, for the first time, the enchantment of a real continental breakfast, eaten while seated at a table on the sidewalk, beneath an umbrella inscribed with the legend "PERNOD", which was an anise-flavoured liqueur and seemingly inappropriate for breakfast. We watched long-stemmed French beauties walking their poodles as we consumed hot croissants, with butter and strawberry jam, with huge cups of that marvellous beverage that, at that time, only the French knew how to make properly—*café au lait*. This coffee had a taste that fulfilled all the gastronomic promise of its smell. Good coffee has that aroma that only the French can translate into its equivalent in taste. The English were, and remain, constitutionally incapable of brewing good coffee. They make it taste like brown boot polish. Americans can generate a respectable cup of robust quality, but only the French can serve that indescribably delectable *café au lait* at breakfast that sets the gastronomic tone for the rest of the day.

We all four quickly awoke to the French sense of priorities. Food, and how to cook and present it, is a major art in France. It seemed to us that, however humble and grubby a restaurant might be, the food served was of a quality far superior to the surroundings. Our finances only permitted us to sample the most modest of Parisian restaurants, and we were therefore not able to compare the fare we were served with what we might have eaten had we been able to dine at Maxim's, which (incidentally) we examined from the outside like workhouse children hungrily eyeing forbidden fruit. Maxim's is just off the *Place de la Concorde*. I was strangely affected when I realized that the obelisk in the centre of the Place stood on the exact spot where Marie Antoinette had been guillotined a hundred and fifty years earlier.

We often ate at a tiny, ill-equipped, untidy *estaminet* around the corner from our digs. I would guess that, if what we ate there were to be served on Sevres china by a waiter in a dinner jacket, on tables covered in spotless damask, and if the same wine were served in long-stemmed glasses at Maxim's, it would not have tasted significantly better. Our little restaurant seemed to be run single-handedly by its proprietor. His daughter, aged about sixteen, was usually present, but she seemed to spend most of her time reading a fashion magazine or chatting up some youthful male customer who caught her eye. She would occasionally receive an irritated exhortation from Papa to lend a hand, but this was invariably met with a shrug—the kind of shrug denoting indifference. This was the shrug of France. It can only be properly executed by the French. I do not believe that it is deliberately taught to children. Rather they pick it up by example from their parents and other relatives, and from shopkeepers who reserve it for occasions when they run out of wares, there is nothing they can do about it, and (more significantly) they do not much care. This is the shrug that starts somewhere around the small of the back, working its way up to the bottom of the cervical spine, whereupon it activates the shoulders to heave towards the ears. It is accompanied by an almost imperceptible motion of the arms, which causes the hands to turn palms upwards. It is a gesture that means "*Je m'en fou*", which is a phrase that cannot be adequately translated into English without losing its surly, dismissive overtones.

Papa, the proprietor, was cook, waiter, bus boy, and maitre'd all rolled into one. Though very busy, he still seemed able to carry on several quite-animated conversations with customers all at the same time. He wore a large apron that reached his shoes, and would have been white if it had not been so soiled. In the three days that we dined there, the apron never changed. It became neither cleaner nor dirtier. One of the Hennessys thought it had been pre-printed to look as if it had yesterday's meal spilled down the front. Papa used it to wipe his hands, to clean off table tops, and once we caught him breathing onto a wine glass and polishing it on a corner of his apron—holding the glass up to the light for inspection. He always sported a two-day growth of beard—never more, and never less. Brian Hennessy thought that he must shave daily with a razor with a wheel on each side, elevating the blade so that it cropped the beard to exactly a two-day worth of growth. We were driven back to dine there the third evening, partly out of curiosity to see if the beard had grown. It had not.

By the third evening, we had become fast friends with Papa, though somewhat to our dismay, his daughter never evinced any interest in us whatsoever. Indeed, she seemed not to acknowledge our presence at all. We concluded that she disliked foreigners. The magazines commanded her attention, and only French-speaking youths warranted even her cursory examination. Papa would hail us with a cheerful shout of "*Ah, mes jeunes amis Anglais. Asseyez vous, s'il vous plaît,*" and before we had time to do as he asked and sit down, four glasses of delicious claret would arrive to greet us. The wine came from barrels kept at the back of the shop, and was of a quality I hardly ever experienced again. He never seemed to charge for the wine. When we tried to point out that our bill, a grubby piece of paper with indecipherable writing in pencil, did not include a charge for wine, he merely resorted to a politer version of his daughter's shrug, and (with a chesty rumble) would mutter something about it being "*tout compris.*" We never saw any sign of Mama. He frequently filled our wine glasses from an unlabelled bottle, which he replenished from the barrels. The food was magnificent—French country food—though he had insufficient time or energy to provide a very varied menu, which was chalked on a large slate pinned to the wall.

On our last evening, he had the radio on. We recognized a large orchestra playing a spirited rendition of Schubert's "Great C Major Symphony". He was cooking in time to the music, and between bursts of conversation with his customers, would conduct the radio with whatever implement he had in his hand at the time. When the symphony was over, a voice (which was not speaking French) made an announcement. The accent seemed to be Scottish. Mike Garret asked Papa where the concert was coming from. "*Ah,*" he said, spreading his arms wide, "*Ça vient de Glasgow. C'est le Festival d'Edimbourgh.*" Mike could not resist explaining that the Edinburgh Festival was held in Edinburgh, not Glasgow. "*Oui, Glasgow,*" repeated Papa, beaming with benevolence. "*C'est pour vous, especialement.*" Mike gave up for fear of giving offence. I never hear the "Great C major" without thinking of that dear little, noisy, dirty restaurant, and Papa's superb peasant cuisine that was cooked so delicately in such an administrative shambles.

But that night it was demonstrated to me that Paris is a city of a sophistication un-duplicated anywhere else in the world. No city can match its civilized worldliness—what some call *panache*, and others call *élan*.

Our rooms, guarded by *Madame la concierge*, were at one end of a long dark street made up of four and five storey student residences, which were originally built a hundred or so years earlier as private homes. We were sauntering home from our meal of *boeuf Bourguignon*, claret, and Schubert, chatting about this and that and the superiority of inexpensive French cuisine over English meat and two vegetables. It was quite dark. The streetlights were few and cast little light. Slowly, we each became aware that there was a figure walking ahead of us. It was a girl. Dim though the light was, we could see that she had long wavy hair that reached below her shoulders, and that she wore a beret, saucily perched to one side of her head. She was quite tall and carried a bag slung over her shoulder on a long strap. Her gait had a slightly provocative swing about the hips.

Though unhurried, she was walking quite fast, with a sense of purpose in her stride. It must have been this—what people now call 'body language'—that caught our attention. We did not have to wait long to find out what bent those footsteps towards their destination.

As she came abreast of a doorway leading into a courtyard, she turned and looked up at some windows. She slowly raised both hands, extending the little finger of each and inserting each into a corner of her mouth. She then emitted a piercing whistle that wavered over an octave. She removed the fingers and peered up at the windows. Nothing happened. She reinserted the fingers and gave an even louder whistle, this time short and much sharper. She looked up again. One of the windows on the third floor opened. There was a moment's hesitation and then a hand appeared and dropped a small object. It fell upon the stone pavement below with a little metallic clatter. She bent, picked it up, walked to the door, and inserted the key in the lock. She pushed the door open and took a step inside. As she did so, she turned and looked at us four, still approaching, but now only a few paces away. She raised her chin imperceptibly and elevated one eyebrow, without otherwise changing her expression. And then she was gone. The door closed with a soft click.

There was a century of guile in that momentary glance.

MISTRAL

February, as the medical profession would say in its quaint circumlocu-
tory way, was contraindicated as the ideal month to visit Provence.
Gill and I were staying with our daughter, Kate, in Carqueiranne, a little
town on the Mediterranean coast, about twenty kilometres east of Toulon.
Kate and her husband had borrowed a condominium for the year, which
her husband's uncle used as a summer place. Kate had enrolled her two
boys, aged seven and ten, in the local village school, and by the time we
arrived, they were both speaking French like native Provencals. We used
them as mobile, two-legged dictionaries, as we puttered around the village.

Two days after we arrived, we decided to visit Toulon on a shopping
expedition. The boys safely delivered to school, we set off for a half-day's
jaunt. The weather was odd. Overcast, cool, and windy, it carried an
oppressive quality that seemed to make everyone depressed and edgy.

Arriving in Toulon, we fed a parking metre with enough Euros to last
till after lunch and set off on our shopping spree. We immediately realized
that it was unusually windy; indeed, we seemed to be in the middle of a
serious storm. There was no rain, but the wind was, by my estimate, gale
force—somewhere around sixty miles an hour. We had to be careful crossing the roads for fear of being blown over, and at times we grasped railings
for support. None of the inhabitants seemed to be paying much attention.
We espied an appealing-looking art gallery and went inside, partly to find
some shelter from the gale that was assaulting us. An attractive middle-
aged French woman greeted us and bade us to take our time looking
around. I commented that it seemed to be very windy. She shrugged, "*Ah,
oui,*" but made no other comment. Several paintings were tempting, but
beyond our means, so we bade Madame "*au revoir*" and walked farther
down the hilly street to the sea front, poking about the shops we encountered on the way.

Toulon is France's Mediterranean naval base and we could see a sizable
collection of sea-grey warships berthed in a dockyard that was surrounded
by a formidable fence, and guarded by a platoon of intimidating "*flics*",

police armed with what looked like assault rifles. There was no way that we were going to be allowed a closer look at the French Mediterranean fleet.

The Romans originally established a signal station in the bay of Toulon, and Henry IV founded the naval arsenal in the late sixteenth century. In 1940, the bulk of the French fleet was concentrated in Toulon under the command of the Vichy government. In 1942, the Allies invaded North Africa, which provoked the Germans into occupying Vichy France. The Wehrmacht attempted to seize the French fleet, which would have been a serious disaster for the Allies, had they succeeded. Admiral Laborde took matters into his own hands and ordered all seventy-two ships scuttled.

The old town was largely destroyed during the war, leaving just a few tantalizingly quaint 17th century portions, and much architecture dating from Napoleonic times. Its industries, warfare apart, consist mostly of fishing and (of course) making wine.

On the waterfront, the wind battered everything with full force, unhampered by the buildings through which we had threaded our way to the harbour. Until we reached the vast expanse of *La Place de La Victoire*, the gale had not troubled us all that much. I wondered how many victory squares there were, gracing the towns and cities of France. This one was huge. It would have comfortably accommodated a dozen rugby fields. In consequence, the wind, which was out of the north, dipped over the tall buildings standing at its north end and whipped with vicious force across its expanse, gusting round the stone cherubim cavorting in the granite enclosed pools that decorated the northerly end. At the southeast corner, a newspaper vendor was defending his kiosk against the unwelcome gale. His papers and magazines, all tethered by a variety of bulldog clips and pieces of string, flapped about wildly, and occasionally some sprang loose and whirled across the road, gathering in corners and doorways where the eddies corralled them. *Monsieur le vendor* made no attempt to retrieve them; it would have been a pointless and futile effort.

There was a surprisingly big fleet of sailboats in a vast marina next to the naval base. The wind roared through the rigging and this collection of craft gave off a high-pitched whine, accompanied by a percussion of lines flapping against the masts. The water was churning in an ugly chop. Some flags were still tethered to flagpoles in the marina. Each stood out at right angles from its pole, shuddering violently in the wind. Without doubt, none would last till sunset.

We were at first puzzled that none of the good citizens of Toulon seemed to be paying any attention to this gale. A wind like this in London, Vancouver, or Williams Lake would have sent its inhabitants into a panic and greatly excited the media. Then it finally dawned on us that this was not an unusual event for Toulon. It was, in fact, a mistral, a strong, cold, dry wind common to the region. They get them with some frequency in the winter, and people are so used to them that they simply pay no attention. Damage seemed to be non-existent, because they have (over the centuries) arranged the city so that the wind caused no damage. In the little square in front of the opera house, people were sitting at tables outside, drinking coffee and aperitifs as if it were a balmy summer's day.

The mistral is one of the seven great winds of the Mediterranean. These winds cause it to be an unusually dangerous body of water. A dangerous swell can get up in a surprisingly short time. Yachtsmen have to be cautious about sailing more than a day's distance from land. The mistral originates on the western slopes of the Swiss Alps. When the air cools over the mountains, in the presence of high pressure, it slides down the Alps into France, gathering speed across the Massif Central until it encounters the Rhone Valley. Then it veers south—the "Venturi effect" causing it to accelerate down the valley in a funnelling effect that causes it to reach gale force speeds of over sixty miles an hour. The Rhone debouches into the Mediterranean at Marseilles, but the mistral spreads out in a delta of wind from Montelimar in the west to Toulon in the east. It is a katabatic (or downhill) wind impelled by force of gravity. It cools over the mountains so that it becomes more dense than the warm air below and slides downwards, gathering speed as it falls. It is cold, fierce, and relentless. The mistral we encountered lasted three days, but the locals told us that they can last up to five days. Mistrals reach out over the Mediterranean as far as Sicily and Malta.

The mistral has a deleterious effect on people. Three or five days of cold, incessant gale have a serious psychological impact. In France, the influence of an ongoing mistral constitutes a genuine legal defence for crimes, even murder.

In winter and early spring, the Rhone Valley can be bitterly cold. Avignon is notorious for its chilly climate. If you are intent on buying a holiday cottage in France, don't go for the Rhone Valley. Try the River Lot instead, or the sunny climes of the Loire Valley.

The Wine Shop at Carqueiranne.

And on the eighth day, God created wine.

He first created red wine, and when he saw that it was good, he created white wine. And when he saw that was good, he created rosé. Then God waxed enthusiastic, for he saw that he was onto a good thing. And he created fortified wines, Sherry, port, and Madeira. For the peasants, for whose welfare he harboured great concern, he created beer and then ale, lager, stout, and bitter, and for the Irish, of course, he created Guinness, which he decreed should be brewed from the waters of the Liffey—despite its high coliform count.

Spirits came later, and caused no end of trouble that God had not foreseen.

And then, disheartened at man's abuse of his creations, God created the hangover.

Now all this creation took place in Babylon, the cradle of civilization. It is probable that the first wines were fermented and imbibed before man learned to write, so the exact origins are not well known, and certainly not documented. There are those who claim that mead was the first alcoholic beverage. Some farmer stumbled upon a nest of bees that had been inundated by rain, and so the honey had fermented. Drinking the result, the farmer discovered the euphoric effect of this potion and took to experimenting with his domestic bees. I say farmer, but it could as easily have been a monk, because the monks kept bees—not just for the honey but also (and mainly) for wax for the candles in their monasteries. Gradually the fermenting of wine spread around the Mediterranean, and it was discovered that the soil and climates of Italy, and then France and Spain, provided a better location to make wine. So the industry flourished and the wine became better and more pleasant upon the palate.

Today, superb wine is produced in the Americas, the Antipodes, and countries that have hot summers and cold winters. The best Burgundy in the world is produced in the wineries of the Willamette Valley in Oregon, except that the French get upset and resort to litigation if the Oregonians call it Burgundy, so the Oregonian vintners call it Pinot Noir and Pinot Gris.

Even though there is currently a world-wide glut of wine, because of the taxes, that has not reduced its price to the consumers. The canny French keep their best wine for themselves, and export their second-rate wines at overblown prices. I have always avoided French wines in the local liquor stores. You get an inferior product at elevated prices.

This was vividly brought to my attention when our daughter took it into her head to take our two grandsons, then aged seven and ten, to live in France for a year. Her husband's uncle owned a summer place in a small village, Carqueiranne, on the Mediterranean coast, thirty kilometres east of Toulon. We visited them twice. The wine was of materially better quality than the French wine on the LCB shelves in Vancouver, though only slightly less expensive. We soon found the local wine store, secreted away in a little street just off the village square and next to the *boulangerie* where we bought croissants, and baguettes by the foot. We purchased an assortment of local product from Madame, who ran the wine store. After our third visit to the store, I noticed that just inside the door there were three large steel tanks, each as tall as I was. Then I noticed that each displayed a sign, suspended by a piece of string—*Rouge, Blanc,* and *Rosé.* I asked Madame what was in the tanks. Her face betrayed an expression of derision, as if any fool should have known what the tanks contained. "*Vin du pays,*" she said.

"*Combien coute cet vin?*" I asked

"*Un Euro, cinquant par litre. Voulez vous goutez un verre?*" I said that I would, and she produced a wine glass. "*Rouge, rosé, ou blanc?*" She waived the glass in the direction of the tanks.

"*Oh, rouge, s'il vous plaît.*" I responded, politely asking for red. She bent and filled the glass from a small tap at the base of the *rouge* tank, and handed it to me—now brimfull of promising-looking liquid. I sniffed it. Its aroma certainly held out the promise of things to come. I tasted the wine. It was delicious—an unpretentious, chewy Bordeaux. I handed the glass to Gill. Her eyebrows shot up. "Get a litre. Let's take it home for lunch." For the rest of our stay, we ceased buying bottles of wine with labels marked "*appellation d'origine contrôlée*"—which was a French certification of origin—and took our litre bottle down on a daily basis to have Madame fill it for us at a cost of the equivalent of three dollars a litre. It was the best value for wine I had ever come across. Madame told me, upon enquiry, that each tank held 625 litres of wine, made locally in the *departement.* We did notice that the glass tube attached to the tank, which showed how full it was, went down at quite a pace each week, to be replenished over each weekend.

One day we emerged from the wine store, clutching our precious litre bottle of wine. As we stepped onto the sidewalk, a Citroen (*a deux chevaux*), the French equivalent of the German Volkswagen stuttered to a halt, parking with its right wheels on the sidewalk just outside the wine shop. An elderly Frenchman struggled out of the driver's seat. He wore the obligatory black beret and walked with a serious stoop. He shuffled round to the back of his Citroen, opened the hatchback, and took out one of those big, red, five-gallon gasoline cans—twenty-two litres. He entered the wine shop, greeted Madame, and placed his gas tank on the floor beneath the rouge wine tank. Producing a long plastic tube, he attached it to the wine tank's little tap and turned it on, syphoning off the red liquid treasure. He spent the next ten minutes filling his gas tank with wine. Finishing this task, he paid Madame, and heaved up his tank now laden with red wine. Hardly able to manage it, he tottered out to the Citroen, grasping the red tank with both hands and carrying it resting against his stomach for extra support. Bent over nearly double, he heaved the tank up and into the Citroen. Slamming the hatch, he shuffled round to the driver's seat, and driving at no small speed off the sidewalk, disappeared, bearing away his twenty-two litres of *vin rouge*. I wondered how he had managed to scrub his tank clean of gasoline. He might, I supposed, have bought it specifically for the purpose of storing wine. I hoped so. Wine overlaid with the odour of gas would be unacceptable, not to say unhealthy.

I still refuse to buy French wine at the local liquor store. My original opinion that its prices are overblown was confirmed by the contents of the tank of exquisite and robust *rouge*, from which Madame daily filled our litre bottle for €1.50.

CHINA DIARY

November 11, 1986
Breakfast in our room. We were the first to board the bus, which was out of character for us. It took us to the airport in the dark and the rain. Unpacked our films and cameras, and passed them through security for fear of the damage the Chinese x-ray machines might inflict on them. One uses up a surprising amount of energy on journeys, with all this logistical luggage problem solving. There was a German group at the airport making a fuss. They had 48 people and only 47 tickets! An auburn-haired German girl was their leader. She was wearing leather trousers and motorcycle boots, and bore a striking resemblance to Joseph Goebbels. She leaned over and turned off the computer at one point, when the attendant was trying to adjust it. Plane delayed by fog at Chungking. Scheduled to leave at 7.50 a.m..

Finally left at 9:00 a.m. on a different aircraft than originally scheduled. We were boarded onto a two-engined, Russian turbo-prop, AN-24, that had been manufactured in China. 48 seats. We discovered later that fog had not been the cause of the delay. We had simply been bumped. Nobody explained why.

In the cold, Soviet-built airport, we bought beer, ate cheese and crackers, and re-boarded for our flight to Guilin, China. Taken to our hotel by bus, but our luggage had disappeared. Queenie Chang, our tour guide (who runs a travel agency in Vancouver's Chinatown) had what seemed like an endless, and not very diplomatic negotiation, with the CTIS girl about the absence of our luggage. She eventually achieved its delivery. As is the habit with tours in China, it was dumped in the hotel lobby and covered with a huge net to discourage theft. It was the sort of net that one sees wielded by gladiators in movies about Rome.

Watched from our hotel bedroom window as a platoon of workmen were building a road. They were using an undersized, antique cement mixer, and were wheeling the cement about in wheelbarrows. Another group was squatting by the road with short-handled sledgehammers, breaking rocks. In the evening, we attended an operatic Chinese ballet.

Beautifully dressed Chinese girls with exquisite voices sang lovely Chinese songs and danced for us. One of them played a sort of harp held horizontally, while another accompanied her on a mandolin. Both were accomplished musicians. Male dancers and singers joined the girls, and some played what looked like panpipes. The whole show consisted of a series of scenes or vignettes. In the last scene, 12 men, all in colourful costumes and each wearing a different mask, were joined by two girls, also masked, in an elegant dance. The show was magical, and one of the most delightful theatrical events we had ever experienced. So different from the Beijing opera, with its dissonance, clashing cymbals, gaudy dress, and silly plots shouted at full lung-power.

Bought a tape of the performance, for 5 yuan—the equivalent of $2.00.

NOVEMBER 13TH

And now comes the rain, like a whole monsoon season in one night. We had never encountered rain like this. It was a downpour of Biblical proportions. It flooded the streets and turned the grass to mud. Nobody could go out in it. You were soaked in half a minute. This kept up for 36 hours. It closed the airport, and this created a serious problem.

NOVEMBER 14TH

Still raining, but not as hard. We hear that there are 2000 tourists backed up in Guilin, and nothing is flying in or out of the airport. We all hung about the hotel waiting for news. We are now a day late, and probably won't make it to Canton. May have to fly directly to Hong Kong in order to catch our flight back to Vancouver. Queenie maintains a calm appearance, but is busy trying to get us a flight. She can be seen either on the phone or shaking a Cantonese finger at one or more of the CTIS staff. The hotel is crammed with disturbed tourists and worried tour guides all bent on getting their charges on their way. Queenie loaded us onto a bus and we made our way to the airport. It was congested with a monstrous, undisciplined, milling crowd of anxious, and stressed travellers. The decibel level endangers the ears. Queenie told us, at one point, that we were supposed to be on the next plane out. But it left without us, full of other tourists. At lunch time, Queenie disappeared and we began to get nervous without her reassuring and competent presence. She reappeared an hour later. She corralled us all into a corner and then produced 22 boarding passes. "Take these," she said in a hushed voice. "Don't, whatever you do, lose them, and say nothing to anyone." Ten minutes later we were through security, which had deteriorated into a perfunctory procedure in the turmoil and confusion. Our luggage miraculously appeared on an old wooden gurney, and we followed it to an aircraft and scrambled aboard. Some of us began pestering Queenie with questions. She waved us down. "Later," she said sternly. We all settled down in a group at the front of the plane.

The plane had reached its cruising altitude when Queenie rose from her seat, right behind the pilot's cabin. She held up an imperious hand for silence. "All right," she said, addressing her mystified flock. "Now you all owe me twenty dollars each, and if you don't mind, I'll collect it now." She explained that she had realized that, with the chaos caused by the torrential downpour, 2000 tourists were not going to get out of Guilin inside a week. We had given up our hotel rooms and now faced the prospect of sleeping over several nights in the inhospitable airport lounge. She had decided that she had to do some creative negotiations with those in charge at the airport. She had marched into the airport manager's office, shut the door, put her fist on his desk and said, "How much will it cost to get 23 Canadians on the next plane to Canton?" Without any hesitation, he made a two-second calculation on his abacus and said, "$400, in cash." He then handed her a booklet of boarding passes and said, "Put the money in the booklet and hand it to the attendant at the baggage counter." Queenie did exactly as instructed, and the requisite number of boarding passes were turned over to her. She took one for herself, and then did as she was told, distributing the rest amongst us and telling us to be ready to board the aircraft designated in the passes.

We had intended to spend 2 days in Canton and then fly to Hong Kong, but the delay in Guilin forced us to skip Canton, and as we had missed our flight, we took the train down through the new territories to Hong Kong. On the train, we all fell to discussing Queenie's remarkable and decisive style of diplomacy. One of the group said, "Well, that's not surprising. You know who her brother is, don't you?" Of course, no one knew, so we asked. The answer made a lot of sense. "He's David Lam." David Lam later became the Lieutenant Governor of British Columbia.

THE BRIEFCASE

K owloon was the obvious place to buy the briefcase. I wanted one like Morley Koffman's—bigger than the slim affair that businessmen carry, but not as large as the capacious one-foot wide cases that lawyers stuff full of files and need a porter's trolley to transport. Morley said that he had bought his in Hong Kong.

Flying in to Kai Tak Airport, I was presented with a foretaste of the kind of city I was about to experience. The aircraft lost altitude, with its landing flaps down in readiness for landing. As I looked out of the window, I was startled to see that we were coming down below the level of the top floors of a huge complex of apartment blocks, some of which were only a couple of wing spans away. They were full of people. Washing festooned most of the balconies. It was a high-density area. They had crammed as many people as possible into this small space. The aircraft descended through what appeared to be a landing path that had been clear cut out of a forest of apartment blocks. The airport itself consisted of one runway laid out on a man-made peninsula jutting out into Hong Kong harbour.

Our eldest son, Peter, had been in Hong Kong the previous year. Hotels in Hong Kong are expensive and he recommended that we stay at the YMCA on Salisbury Road, next to the Peninsula Hotel, one of the world's most elegant and costly hotels. He assured us that the Y was very comfortable and looked out over Hong Kong harbour, the same view as from the Peninsula Hotel. So I had phoned the Y and booked a double room. We took a taxi from the airport and checked in at the Y. It was late at night when we arrived, and we couldn't see the harbour. The Y was busy, full of young Chinese people. We were given a key and told the number of our room, and no, they did not have a bell-hop to take our bags, so we lugged them to the elevator and made our weary way up to our room. It was sparsely furnished and had two wooden bunk beds. At least the room was clean. We unpacked and fell into bed. Soon asleep, we were rudely awakened by a siren. I looked out of the window. Next door was a large, brightly lit building. The neon sign disclosed that it was the Kwong Wah Hospital. The siren was an ambulance delivering a customer. Back to bed. Awakened by another siren, this time on the other side, though I could not see any building. What I did see was a fire truck pulling out onto the roadway. The Y was located directly between the hospital and a fire station. Our sleep was regularly interrupted by the noise of traffic from these two institutions.

I finally awoke at six in the morning, my sleep confused by jet lag. Gill was still fast asleep, so I got up, dressed, and decided to go for a walk. The first thing I discovered, from a street sign, was that the Y where we were staying was on Waterloo Road. The harbour was nowhere in sight. I looked at my map of Hong Kong. Waterloo Road was not anywhere near the Peninsula Hotel. We were one block off Nathan road, a good mile from where we were supposed to be.

I continued on my walk, crossing Nathan Road, the main thoroughfare in Kowloon, already busy with traffic and pedestrians hustling off to work. I strolled into some back streets and at an intersection came across a couple of dozen young men standing around in groups, and moving from one group to another. They were all dressed in light grey suits. They had some objects in their hands and were showing these to each other. Money was passing between them, as were the small objects. I sidled up to one group and realized that they were trading gems. I asked one of the men what was going on, and he informed me that this was the morning gem exchange. Each day, the local jewellers send out representatives to buy precious and semi-precious stones for their daily needs. I was a little surprised that there were no guards, as I had noticed that all the jewellery stores had at least one heavily armed guard standing at their entrances.

I walked on. The next block was confined to shops selling coffins. Each shop had a wide-open entrance at the side where men were busy at work, sawing and planing and hammering as they constructed coffins—cheap deal coffins as well as expensive varnished coffins with silver fittings. It was only six o'clock in the morning, and they were all hard at work, with wood shavings all over the sidewalk. I reached Tsim-Sha-Tsui park. On the sidewalk at the corner was a barber's chair, occupied by a patron having his hair cut. But not everybody was hard at work. I came across four elderly Chinese men playing mahjong. There were a great deal of Hong Kong dollar bills on the table, changing hands at the end of each round.

People everywhere seemed to be in a hurry—all going at ninety miles an hour and bent on making money. All the shops were open, packed with merchandise, and staffed by assistants who importuned one to come in and purchase something, if you so much as hesitated by their store. The streets were thronging with people. The shops were colourful and the whole town was plentifully supplied with restaurants—all exuding the distinct smell of Chinese food. Garishly neon-lit nightclubs, which seemed to offer twenty-four-hour service, each had a beautiful Chinese girl wearing a *cheongsam*, standing at the door and holding out the promise of a sinful frolic inside.

Hong Kong seemed full of noise—vibrant, cheerful noise, with gongs predominating—and the Cantonese (of course) don't just talk, they shout. I have never come across a race with such consistently loud voices. Kowloon gave the impression of being coloured in scarlet and gold, with flags, bunting, and shop signs competing with each other for the most colourful advertising. The narrower streets were crisscrossed with ropes, from which hung a variety of coloured trappings and a great deal of washing. Washing does not go into dryers. It gets hung out over the street to dry.

That night, the mystery of our accommodation was solved. The Canadian High Commissioner in Hong Kong was an old friend of mine, Maurice Copithorne. We had been articled students together in 1953 in Vancouver. He had opted to join the Canadian Foreign Service and this was his next posting after serving as Canadian Ambassador to Austria. He invited us to dinner at the Canadian Commissioner's residence halfway up Victoria Peak. We told him our sorry tale about our accommodation.

He chuckled. "There are two YMCAs in Hong Kong," he said. "You seem to be staying at the Chinese Y." We decide that it would be too much trouble to hunt for alternative accommodation, so we stayed where we were. We learned much from Maurice about the economy of Hong Kong. It is the ultimate *laissez faire* capitalist society. At that time, it was a British Crown colony governed by the governor and a legislature, which ran the colony with a very light hand. Income tax was sixteen per cent, and imposed only on earned income, not on income from investments. The legal profession, like the English system, was divided between barristers and solicitors. Maurice said that a moderately competent barrister would earn the equivalent of $400,000 Canadian a year. It is a very inexpensive colony to run. Over six million people are crammed into 426 square miles. Kowloon is the most densely populated area in the world, with 520,000 people per square mile. The population is 98 per cent Chinese. We could not walk one block without encountering a construction project. Transportation consists of buses, the efficient little underground railway, the Star ferries—for passage between Kowloon and Hong Kong Island—and the taxis. All the taxis are red, and all are of Japanese make. The taxi companies buy all their cabs from Tokyo. When the Tokyo taxi companies deem it time to sell their old taxis, they sell them to the Hong Kong taxi companies. There are about the same number of cabs in Hong Kong as there are private cars. To avoid traffic congestion, the Hong Kong government imposes a vicious tax on private cars, and forces the taxis to charge very low fares. If you want to take a taxi, you simply raise one arm and a cab will draw up to serve you within the space of a very few minutes. Apart from the red taxi cabs, you only ever see Mercedes Benzes, Rolls Royces, Bentleys, and (for the less well off) BMWs. Traffic drives on the left.

The border between Hong Kong and communist China was heavily guarded—when we were there—by a regiment of Gurkhas. An impassable fence, which runs from the Pearl River in the west to where the New Territories come down to the sea to the east, keeps refugees at bay. Almost daily, someone is caught trying to gain entry to Hong Kong, usually by swimming down the Pearl River and creeping ashore in the harbour at night. However, the administration had a policy that, if a refugee succeeded in slipping past the guards, they were considered to be home free and would not be sent back to the communists. The British, who largely influenced the governmental policies of Hong Kong, thought that if refugees were clever enough to outwit the border guards, then it simply wasn't cricket to send them back. They were allowed to stay, unlike the Vietnamese boat people who were held in miserable confinement on Lantau Island.

The new territories were mainly agricultural, and populated by the Hakka. It was also the main source of Hong Kong's water supply. Without the new territories, Hong Kong could not survive. The new territories had originally been leased from China and the lease terminated in 1965. It was the termination of this lease that caused Britain to hand Hong Kong back to China. Margaret Thatcher, the then Prime Minister, must have been monumentally ill advised, for the British government seemed to make no effort to negotiate a new lease with China. It simply ironed out the terms of the communist take-over. Those who know about these things maintain that the Hong Kong and Shanghai Bank alone had enough money to tempt the Chinese to renew the lease. With all the fabulously wealthy companies operating in Hong Kong at the time, it remains a mystery why the government did not tap this source of wealth, with which to approach the Chinese and bargain for a new lease.

After breakfast in the Y cafeteria, I set off in search of a briefcase. At the corner of Cameron Road and Carnarvon, I spied a store: The Part Luggage Supply. It offered suitcases, wheeled and otherwise, duffel bags, backpacks, cabin trunks, handbags, shopping bags, hat boxes, golf club cases, musical instrument cases. In fact, it had every conceivable receptacle for the carriage of goods that one could imagine. It displayed specialty cases that I did not know existed. Most of the merchandise seemed to have spilled out onto the sidewalk, and there was a narrow alleyway between all this luggage, by which customers gained entrance to the shop. Inside, luggage was piled up to the ceiling. I had the impression that if I pulled one bag out at the bottom, I would be buried under a Niagara of baggage. In the window was exactly the briefcase I was seeking, except that it was black. I wanted brown. I entered the shop to be met by the beaming Cantonese proprietor. Upon enquiry, he said the case cost was $750 HK. I realized this was less than I would pay in Vancouver, but remembering the advice of Hong Kong ex-patriots, I decided to bargain. I told the proprietor that $750 was too much. He saw me hesitating, and guessed I was just wavering about the price. He assured me it was a fair price. I turned to make as if to leave.

"Oh well, sir. Perhaps, just for you, I can make a special price." This went on for a while, until I decided to see what other shops could do for me. I politely excused myself, with the usual excuse that I would think about it.

I noticed a shop just around the corner. In the window I saw a brown brief case—just what I wanted. In I went. $700 HK. Ten minutes of haggling got this shopkeeper down to $650 HK. But I left in search of an even better bargain. The next day, I returned to Part Luggage. We commenced negotiations where I had left off the previous day, but I got the impression that he knew I was determined to have the brief case, so I played my ace. "The shop next door will sell me one for $650 HK," I announced. He held up both arm, palms extended inward and reduced his price to $600 HK. I shook my head and went next door. There I succeeded in getting an offer at the same price. The next day, I plodded back to Part Luggage, to be greeted as if I were an old friend. In Hong Kong, the old principle that the customer is always right seems still to be at the forefront of all shopkeepers' thinking. We were now down to $575 HK. A visit next door resulted in an offer of $450HK. I trudged back to Part Luggage.

"Look," I said, "the shop around the corner will sell me one for $450 HK. I can really only pay you $300 HK." After a little more haggling, we settled on $375 HK. He held out his hand. Am earnest gesture. We shook on it. "But," I said, "I really wanted a brown case. This one is black."

"Ah, sir, that is easily arranged. In our shop around the corner, we have brown one. I go fetch." And with a flash of his brilliant smile, he bustled out of the shop. I followed and peered around the corner. Sure enough, in less than a couple of seconds, he emerged from what I had thought was a rival shop, carrying the brown briefcase I had been bargaining about over the last two days. Back in Part Luggage, I paid the $375 HK and left with my prize.

I had been bargaining against myself for the better part of three days, and had come up against an insider. However, I had bought the case I had been coveting, and it had only cost me the equivalent of $62 Canadian. I carried documents in it, always overfilling it, for the best part of a quarter of a century. It is now seriously battered, and one lock no longer works, but it is still serviceable and I have grown attached to it.

THE PARAKEETS OF VICTORIA PEAK

There must have been upwards of a hundred of them: pure white birds with feathered crests, which were reminiscent of the fore and aft hats British naval officers wore during the time of the Napoleonic wars. They were parakeets—the size of a large crow. I suspected that they were not native to Hong Kong, but must have been transported from the jungles of central Africa. They had established their home in a thickly wooded area of Victoria peak, on the western side of Hong Kong Island—a small oasis amongst the proliferation of shiny new apartment blocks that had mushroomed since the end of the war. Housing a multitude of the more heavy-pursed folk who toiled in the money-driven offices (all going at ninety miles an hour, making money), Hong Kong Island was a Star Ferry ride across the harbour from Kowloon. And the parakeets flew about this snuggery with noisy arrogance.

This woody haven seemed an anomaly in a society where every square inch of land had been bartered to some enterprising developer. Out of curiosity, I wandered down to explore this leafy phenomenon. Scattered about the copse was a series of old, abandoned, brick buildings that had evidently once housed a regiment or so of British soldiers. Each building had a name inscribed above its door—names that were the *dramatis personae* of the British High Command of the Victorian age. Field Marshall Lord Kitchener, Lord Roberts, Field Marshal Buller, Lord Gort, and so on. This relic of the Crown Colony's distant past was in a state of serious disrepair, neglected by a government for whom it no longer served a purpose, but who had not yet summoned up the wit do anything creative with it.

Intrigued, I set about making enquiries about the birds. This did not take long. My enquiries soon revealed that the entire population of Hong Kong was familiar with the history of the parakeets. They were the centre of a current and ferocious controversy. One of their striking assets was a vicious, little, curved beak that would have done credit to any bird of prey. Among the many things for which they used these beaks, the most important was chipping away at the bark on the trees in their small woods. This they did in order to turn up the insects that lived in the interstices of the bark—insects which were a feast they seemed to enjoy above all else. The local bureaucracy that had charge of the woods had concluded that, if the birds continued to gorge themselves on these insects, the bark would all be strewn about the floor of the woods, and the trees would be doomed to a premature death. Thus the bureaucrats decided that the birds had to go. Poison was determined to be the procedure of choice to rid the wood of its feathery inhabitants.

As soon as this edict became public knowledge, a hue and cry went up. Not just because people liked the birds, but because they were part of Hong Kong's interesting and tragic history. In 1941, there lived on Victoria Peak a white family. For the amusement of their children, they had acquired a pair of white African parakeets, which they kept in a small aviary just off their kitchen.

Now 1941 was a year of increasing anxiety for anyone who lived in Hong Kong, or anywhere in Southeast Asia, for that matter. The Japanese had been at war with China since 1937. Reports of the behaviour of the predatory Japanese Army spread apprehension and horror amongst their enemies, and all those who began to realize that they were in the path of Emperor Hirohito's modern samurai, and their turn was approaching fast. Their comfortable lives were threatened with invasion by vicious and brutal troops, to whom other people's lives were so cheap as to be of no consequence. Oppression, rape, torture, and murder were considered to be this army's standard of behaviour. All armies behave badly, but the Japanese had escalated pillage and rapine to a height unknown since the days of Genghis Kahn.

Everyone in Hong Kong knew what the Japanese had done in Nanking. In December 1937, the Imperial Army marched into China's capital. There followed six weeks of uninhibited carnage. The Japanese captured some 90,000 Chinese soldiers, who had surrendered. In the Japanese culture, surrender was the ultimate violation of the regal code of military honour, a code which had been drilled into the troops since their enlistment. They looked upon prisoners with contempt—viewing them as despicable cowards. The entire group of Chinese prisoners was forcibly marched to the outskirts of Nanking and systematically butchered. Many were used for bayonet practice. Many were beheaded. Some were soaked in gasoline and set on fire. In the city, the depredation was, if anything, worse. Thousands of women were gang raped and then bayoneted to death. Whole families were shot out of hand. Shopkeepers were murdered and their stores looted. Citizens were herded into buildings, which were then set on fire. This vicious rampage went on for six weeks. Soldiers shot people on a whim. Corpses littered the city streets. Thousands of women were forcibly enlisted into the infamous "comfort women" system for the pleasure of the Japanese soldiers.

This was all widely reported in the American newspapers, and of course, in Hong Kong. The death toll could only be estimated, but it is believed to have been well in excess of 300,000 in a city of 600,000—over half the population.

It was this conduct that gave the Japanese the reputation that marched ahead of its advance into Southeast Asia. The citizens of Hong Kong understandably viewed the possibility of an invasion by the Japanese as an indescribable disaster. Many of the white people began to leave—not an easy endeavour, as it was impossible to get to the British Isles, which was under siege by the Germans. Many left for Australia. Some were trapped. Most of the Chinese had nowhere to go.

The Japanese attacked Hong Kong the day after Pearl Harbour, December 8, 1941.The Commonwealth troops put up a stiff resistance for over two weeks, but were eventually overwhelmed. On Christmas day, the Governor surrendered the Colony to the Japanese. The date went down in history as "Black Christmas". The Japanese treated those left in Hong Kong little better than the Nankingese. Drunken soldiers attacked the hospital in Repulse Bay. They shot the two doctors who tried to deny them entry. The troops rampaged through the wards, bayoneting all the wounded soldiers in their beds. The nurses were raped and shot as a matter of routine.

The white civilian population and all the Commonwealth soldiers were imprisoned in Stanley Internment Camp, starved and mistreated over the ensuing three and a half years. The Japanese deported to the mainland any Chinese they found unemployed. Many people went into hiding. Two English nuns were taken in by the Chinese fishing fleet. They lived on the Chinese sampans moored in the typhoon shelter in Causeway Bay. For three and a half years, they never set foot on shore, living aboard the fishing boats and running a school for the children of the fisher folk.

No one now knew who the family was that owned the parakeets. It was not known if they got away before the Japanese arrived. What was well known was that, before the surrender, the family set the parakeets free, as it must have been obvious to them that they would not be able to tend them during the occupation. The birds flew down and proliferated in the copse where the British soldiers had lived. They grew to become the flock that the people of Hong Kong were now defending from elimination by an unfeeling and blinkered bureaucracy—a bureaucracy that did not seem to comprehend that the birds were a mute and enduring symbol of Hong Kong's defiance of the Japanese.

THE SPELL OF THE DRAGON

The Chinese are a singularly superstitious race. Many of their endeavours are intertwined with efforts to invoke good fortune. Feng Shui is a classic example. Feng Shui, which literally means wind water, is an ancient Chinese system of aesthetics believed to use the laws of both heaven (astronomy) and earth (geography) to help improve life by receiving positive Qi. Qi is a movable positive life force, which plays an essential role in Feng Shui. It provides a philosophical approach to building construction and has been an influence in Chinese life since about 4000 B.C.. It governs the architecture and construction of Chinese homes, and dictates the layout of office buildings and factories.

Gill and I have made several trips to Hong Kong and one to mainland China. It only takes a day or two in mainland China before it becomes evident that it is a communist, totalitarian state, and that if you step out of line you can be arrested simply because the police choose to do so. During the Cultural Revolution, the practice of Feng Shui was rendered illegal and suppressed. As soon as Mao Tse-Tung died, and the revolution ended, it took no time at all for it to return to rule Chinese life.

You cannot sell a green tractor to a Chinese farmer. John Deere is the world's leading manufacturer of tractors. Their products are famous for their bright green hoods, but Massey Ferguson tractors have red hoods. Red is the colour of luck in China, so Masseys outsell Deeres by an overwhelming margin. Green is not a favourable colour to the Chinese, and is specifically associated with adultery. No Chinese farmer is going to be taken for a cuckold by being seen driving a green tractor.

But it is in Hong Kong that the Chinese obsession with good fortune manifests itself most obviously. Hong Kong is a bustling, modern metropolis and a major financial centre. With over six million people crammed into 426 square miles, the city is lively, garish, noisy, and prosperous. Seven million people all rushing about making money.

The Hong Kongese go to startling lengths to bring good luck upon themselves. This does not seem to have a religious base. It appears to be a purely secular superstition harking back through the mists of history to an era of unrecorded time. The number eight is important and a great bringer of good fortune. The Chinese will go to endless trouble to have as many eights as possible in their telephone numbers and street addresses. The number four is to be avoided, like the number thirteen in western cultures. The sound of the number four, in Cantonese, is much like the sound of the word for death. Thus it is that in highrise buildings there is often no floor numbered four.

Feng Shui flourishes in Hong Kong. There are those seers who make a good living by consulting on the architecture and layout of buildings so that they conform to Feng Shui, and rare is the architect or engineer who will dare to design a building without paying close attention to Feng Shui.

On our first trip to Hong Kong we found ourselves in need of some Hong Kong dollars. The Hong Kong and Shanghai Bank seemed the obvious institution to minister to our financial needs, so we waved down one of the bright red taxis that serve the transportation needs of the populace, and journeyed down to number one Queen's Road, where the main branch of the bank is located. The bank is housed in what was then a brand new building, having been finished only that year. The taxi deposited us outside the bank. We paid the driver a sum that was little more than a bus fare in Vancouver. He gestured in the direction of the bank. We found ourselves outside a fifty-three storey glass and steel tower with a glassed-in atrium (which was, itself, eleven storeys high) on the ground floor. We entered the atrium, which was thronging with people, not all of whom were evidently there on bank business. It seemed to be a common meeting place—a location for lunch and informal gatherings.

Access to the bank above was facilitated by two escalators. They seemed to be placed at odd angles to each other. Ordinarily, one would have expected that they would be positioned so as to service customers at each end of the atrium. Not so these escalators. The building contractors seemed to have placed them randomly. Both were of unusual length. We later made enquiries about the building and were told that the escalators were the longest free-standing escalators in the world. They had been placed with infinite care on the advice of a Feng Shui master who had worked out their positioning so as to be most advantageous in invoking good fortune. The Hong Kong and Shanghai bank is one of the largest and wealthiest banks in the world, so it was evident to us that Feng Shui worked.

It was, however, the spell of the dragon that most impressed us. One day, we thought that we should take the bus and visit Repulse Bay, which is a wealthy settlement on the south side of Hong Kong Island, facing the South China Sea. Upon arrival, we ate an expensive lunch at an upscale restaurant on the waterfront, and then wandered about the town. Needing some exercise to counteract the effect of our over indulgence, we wandered into the back country, climbing up a steep hill to look at the view. We rambled along a ridge and began to descend into a long valley, at the foot of which we saw a large, imposing apartment block—obviously of recent construction and equally obviously an expensive place to live. To our astonishment, we observed that, though the whole edifice was some twelve storeys high, and must have had ten or twelve apartments on each floor, there was a huge hole in the building. At least six, and maybe as many as eight apartments had been completely left out of the construction. The hole was two storeys high, and each floor would have accommodated three of four apartments. This seemed odd, to put it mildly. The value of the ten or twelve missing apartments must have represented a significant financial devaluation.

We wandered back to the town, past this strange apartment block, and bent on finding out what this quaint architectural phenomenon was all about, stepped into a bar and each ordered a beer—Tsing Tao, of course. We enquired diffidently of the barman as to the meaning of the hole in the apartment block.

"Ah," he said, as if we really ought to have known. "There is a dragon. He lives farther up the valley, near the top. The construction of the apartment block would have spoiled his view, so the owners decided that they must leave a gap so that the dragon could still see out to the ocean and live in peace with his view. Otherwise it would have brought terrible bad luck and misfortune on the owners." He served us our beers with politeness that was only slightly marred by his mild disdain for the naive ignorance of these foreigners.

Hiroshima

I had experienced some minor culture shock when I arrived in Montreal, in 1953—a naive and innocent immigrant from England. It took about a year, and relocation to Vancouver, to assimilate adequately,

Real culture shock requires experiencing the habits, customs, and practices of a completely alien culture. In 1986, Gill and I visited Japan at the invitation of some old friends, the Foremans, who were then living in Tokyo.

We flew Japan Airlines, and for some reason that was never explained to us, were upgraded to business class. It was like staying at a flying luxury hotel. The immaculately attired Japanese air-hostesses were exquisitely polite and unfailingly attentive, and the food was what you would expect from a high-class sushi bar.

We took a cab to the Foremans' apartment. The driver spoke no English. This, we discovered, was standard in Japan, except in cabs connected to the more expensive hotels and facilities that catered specifically to tourists. The car was spectacularly clean. It even had little antimacassars upon which to rest your head—sparkling white and edged with lace. At the end of our journey, after the driver helped us with our luggage, we tried to give him a tip. He politely shook his head, bowed, and got back into his taxi.

David Foreman gave us a short rundown on Japanese culture. He explained that we did not need to worry, ever, about having our pockets picked or being mugged. Japan was virtually free of violent crime and theft, especially where foreigners were involved. No citizen of Japan would ever assault or steal from a foreigner. Doing so would cause the Japanese nation to lose face. We had noted that the English language newspaper had, that day, reported a series of criminal offences and questioned his premise.

"That," he said, "is the total extent of the crime committed in the whole of Japan, today. A half a dozen infractions of the law, this day, in a population of 127 million. You can go anywhere in Tokyo. You will not be in any danger. You can leave a bicycle leaned against a lamp post and it will still be there the next day. There are lots of white-collar crimes, and a few gangs that deal in drugs, but you won't ever be in danger. Oh, and don't bother to add up a bill in a restaurant. They will never rip you off, and if they see you checking the bill you will only offend them. I hope you didn't try to tip the taxi driver. There is no tipping in Japan. They find it offensive."

We soon learned that Japan was *not* the efficient country that produced those marvellous motor vehicles that never break down. We also learned that the highest denomination bill in Japan is ten thousand yen—roughly a hundred and twenty dollars. The Japanese paid for everything in cash. David told us that any Japanese businessman will run a tab at the restaurants and shops he uses, and once a week, will take a fistful of cash out of his bank account and personally go around and pay off his accumulated debts.

The numbering of houses and apartments on Tokyo streets does not lend to finding an address in a hurry. The street numbers are not consecutive, with odd numbers on one side and even on the other. The houses are numbered in the order in which they are built. The Japanese carry business cards, on the back of which they print a map of the location of their homes and offices. If you take a taxi, you simply hand the driver the card to show him where you want to go.

David told us that he ran into considerable trouble when he first arrived in Tokyo. He was running Continental Grain's Tokyo office, in which he was the only westerner. He discovered that, at the end of each week, the office manager would go to the bank and draw out enough cash to pay the wages of the thirty employees in the office. David decided to put an end to this inefficiency and asked the manager to use cheques to pay the wages in future. The manager said, "Yes, Mr. Foreman."

"Yes, Mr. Foreman," he soon discovered, did not mean that the person he was talking to was going to do what he had been asked. Instead, it was the polite Japanese way of indicating that he had heard what you had said. The next week, the staff were paid in cash, as had been the custom since the office opened, and as was the custom all over Japan. It took David six weeks of diligent persuasion to get his manager to use cheques.

He discovered that the reason for this initial intransigence was that all Japanese men always take their pay package home and hand it over to their wives. In Japan, the wives manage the family finances—despite the way Japanese men treat their wives, which puts them somewhere between a servant and a concubine. The wives hand the husband enough cash to get him through the week, and use the rest for household expenses—banking any surplus. The manager's reluctance to use cheques to pay the staff was because the men could not bring themselves to explain to their wives what the cheque, this funny piece of paper, was to be used for. They were used to giving their wives cash—bank notes, not meaningless bits of paper.

We took a trip out to the Yasakuni Shrine—a park honouring the dead. It was a serene and beautifully laid out garden of seemingly endless dimensions. It was populated by a herd of small deer. The deer expected to be fed, and came up to us in search of offerings. We had bought some food for them and were startled to discover that, when you offer the deer food, they will bow to you, just like the Japanese themselves—who spend a significant amount of their waking hours bowing to each other. We were warned not to try a Japanese bow, which is a strict ritual. We would inevitably get it wrong, which (for reasons unexplained) the Japanese would find to be a social faux pas. The movement is quickly executed. Hands by the side, the head moves forward first and the torso inclines strictly from the hips.

Close by the park was a small shopping centre, which we visited in search of lunch and out of curiosity to see what fare was for sale in Japanese shops. I needed to go to the washroom, and since I could not read Kanji, had to ask directions. Of course the shop assistant I chose for this purpose spoke no English. I managed to convey my desire and the man pointed down the corridor, inclining his hand to the left. He beamed and bowed. I marched off and found the washroom without difficulty. As I passed through the doorway, I was startled to see a Japanese woman washing her hands at a sink. I fled in a panic. I did not relish the prospect of being caught, a foreigner, in a woman's washroom. I began to wonder about the Japanese police, and if I were arrested, how I would be dealt with by the Japanese criminal justice system. My thoughts wandered to the possibility of imprisonment. My only knowledge of the Japanese prison system was gathered from movies about the war in the Pacific, *The Bridge on the River Kwai*, and the infamous prison camp at Aberdeen on Hong Kong Island. I furtively looked about me to make sure there were no security guards about to take me into Japanese custody.

Loitering about in the corridor, wondering what to do next, and casting about for the men's washroom, I saw the woman emerge from the washroom I had just vacated in such a hurry. She walked to the end of the corridor. As she did so, a man strode briskly past her, down to the washroom she had just left, and entered it. Puzzled, I slunk back to the door and peered round it. There he was, boldly pissing into a urinal that I had not noticed in my earlier confusion. Encouraged by his example, I took up station close by him. We both finished and washed our hands. As I left the washroom, another woman entered, and I felt a wave of relief that I had got out in time.

Of course, I made enquiries about this disturbing experience and discovered that all public washrooms in Japan are unisex. There are no men's and no women's—just washrooms. Everybody uses them.

I needed to cash a traveller's cheque, so I journeyed to a bank close by the apartment. Yes, they could cash the cheque. Would I please be seated while they processed it? Twenty minutes later, as I was getting restive at the delay, a charming young Japanese teller marched briskly up to me, bowed, and handed me a small tray with a teapot and a cup. Would I like some tea while I waited, and oh yes, they were sorry about the delay, but my money would be ready soon. I drank the tea. Twenty-five more minutes went by. I got up and went over to the teller's cage, ready to complain about the delay. The teller stood up, and of course, bowed and greeted me with a brilliant smile. Ah! I shouldn't have to wait very much longer. So sorry. Please sit down. Very soon now. Well, it had been three quarter's of an hour. At last, I received my money for my traveller's cheque. This time two tellers approached me, and both bowed. One bore in her hands, as if she were making an offering at an altar, a china saucer. On the saucer, arranged in a neat pile, was my money. On top of the pile of money was a little brass token inscribed in Kanji and attached to a red ribbon. The teller proffered the money with outstretched hands, managing another bow as she did so. Her apologies at the delay were profuse, but they were not accompanied by any explanation. I thanked her, took the money and the token, and left. I attached the token to the inside of the big briefcase I had bought in Hong Kong a year earlier. It is still there, a charming reminder of the inefficiency of the Japanese banking system.

We decided to visit Hiroshima and spend a week visiting various places on the way back. I borrowed a railway timetable and wrote out an itinerary, armed with which I went down to Tokyo Central Station. The clerk spoke no English, but took my itinerary, nodded, and disappeared into a back office. Fifteen minutes later he returned with a fistful of tickets. He laid them out on the desk and took me, ticket by ticket, through our journey, beginning at Hiroshima and then calling at various towns on the way back. Two days in Kyoto, two more on the Island of Miyajima, and a night in Takayama, which was an ancient town up in the mountains to the south of Tokyo. The journey to Hiroshima would be 800 kilometres, and the Shinkansen (the bullet train), on which we were booked, made it in four hours, with several stops on the way.

Our tickets told us the number of the carriage and the seat numbers. The train was drawn up on the platform, which had signs hanging from the roof telling passengers where each numbered carriage was to be found. I noticed that, at each station, the train drew up carefully so that the carriages stopped exactly at the correct number. A sign painted on the platform indicated where the door giving access to your carriage would be found. The train always stopped precisely so that the doors were exactly opposite the appropriate door. We also noticed that the train stopped when it was scheduled to do so—not a second early and not a second late. Passengers had two minutes to get on, or off, the train. No more, no less. If you weren't paying attention, the train would leave without you.

We settled into our comfortable seats. The train was travelling fast. There was no vibration and the carriages were not rocking at all. It was as if it were progressing on a cushion of air. I cast a glance out of the window and calculated that it must be doing seventy or seventy-five miles an hour. There was a clock on the end wall of the carriage, which also indicated the speed of the train. When I glanced at it, I learned that it was, in fact, travelling twice that fast, at 240 Kilometres an hour.

After a while, we decided to walk down to the restaurant car for some lunch. We had a fair number of possessions and our bags were stowed in a rack above our seats. We decided to leave everything where it was. The restaurant served only Japanese food. But it was a high quality repast and filled our needs. We returned to our seats. All our belongings were exactly where we had left them, including my camera.

The train arrived in Hiroshima on schedule, to the very second. I was amazed at this efficiency. However, it was not confined to the Shinkansen. On our way back, we had arranged to stay at Takayama. This meant changing trains and travelling up into the mountains on a two-carriage train, which was obviously the local milk run. This little train was as precisely on time as the Shinkansen had been, and yes, you still had two minutes exactly to get on and off.

Takayama is a logging town, many centuries old, with a number of medieval buildings and houses. It was a quaint, old town meticulously preserved. It was moderately interesting and looked and smelled like Kamloops. We disembarked from our train and walked the two blocks to the hotel we had booked into. We left our luggage at the train station, asking the ticket clerk to keep an eye on it. By this time, we were used to the fact that the Japanese would not steal our possessions. Unsurprisingly, it was still there when we returned for it. It was noon when we checked at the front desk of the hotel. Check-in time, the genial clerk told us, was 3.00 p.m. and we could not go to our room before that. Since the hotel looked about one-third full, we remonstrated with the clerk.

"No. Thee o'clock." He smiled, bowed, and was exquisitely polite, but we could not check in early. We asked him why not. Check in time, he told us, was 3.00 p.m.. He gave no other explanation. Nothing would persuade him to let us into our room early. There was no reason why we shouldn't, except that we were three hours early. That, it seemed, was enough reason. Yes, he would guard our luggage while we went for lunch. It was an example of the strange Japanese stubbornness that we had come across before.

I made enquiries, when we returned to Tokyo, about the efficiency of the Japanese railway system and discovered that the efficiency came at a cost. The Japanese railway system was then running a deficit the same size as the American national debt, which in those days was 200 billion dollars. We realized that the Japanese were not good at keeping costs under control. As an example, when we were on the Shinkansen, a ticket collector came round to check our tickets, but not just one ticket collector. There was one who actually asked us for our tickets and scrutinized and clipped them, and another who accompanied him and bowed. That was his function: to bow to the passengers. Two salaries for two ticket collectors, when one would have managed nicely.

Arriving in Hiroshima, we took a taxi to where we were to stay. This time we offered no tip. We had booked in to a ryokan, which is a sort of

Japanese bed and breakfast. Our rooms were spotlessly clean but we had no bed. We were to sleep on tatami mats on the floor. They turned out to be surprisingly comfortable and we soon got used to them. The ryokan was run by three Japanese sisters and catered to westerners, so we encountered no difficulty talking to them. Breakfast was provided and we could choose bacon and eggs, or pancakes.

The next morning, we journeyed down to Hiroshima Peace Memorial Park, which was the memorial to the detonation of the atomic bomb at 8.15 a.m. on August 6, 1945. We took the tram to the wrong end of the park, misunderstanding the tram conductor who spoke no English. At the gate stood a large granite block with a big brass plate inscribed with Japanese writing. A young Japanese man stood reading the inscription. He smiled at us and wished us good morning in meticulously articulated English.

"What does the inscription say," we asked.

"Oh, it's about the bomb."

"Yes, but what does it say?"

"It's about the dropping of the bomb."

"Yes. Can you tell us what it says?"

"Well, it's about the Americans."

"But what does it say?"

"I am very sorry. It is not very polite."

"We aren't Americans. We're Canadian."

"Oh. How nice."

"Now, can you tell us what it says."

This exchange went on for some time, but we never did get him to translate the inscription. It was one of the experiences that led us to discovering that the Japanese are uncommonly stubborn. This young man was exquisitely polite, but there was no way he was going to embarrass himself by telling us what message the brass plate held for its readers. So we thanked him and walked on down towards the museum. We passed the ruins of the Hiroshima Chamber of Commerce, immediately above which the atomic bomb had exploded that sunny August morning in 1945. The concrete in the great dome had melted in the blast, leaving the iron frame open to the sky: an eerie sight, deliberately left as a stark, mute memorial.

The museum was graphic, informative, and exquisitely depressing. It contained many photographs of the devastation and of maimed citizens. A brick wall had been transported into the museum. It had been blackened by the blast, except for a small portion that had been shielded from the intense heat by a human body. The shadow of the body was quite evident on the wall, as if a shroud had been nailed to it. Some sixty or seventy thousand people had been killed on the day of the blast. Many more died later of radiation poisoning. The total toll was never known.

Sadly the city had been full of students that day: teenagers. They had been brought to Hiroshima to help build fire breaks, in case the Americans set fire to the city as they had done to Tokyo a couple of months earlier.

The message born by the artifacts in the museum was clear. Japan had been done wrong and the dropping of the bomb was a war crime. We wondered about that. Japan's invasion of China had caused the death of fifteen million men, women, and children. Fifteen million. Many of these had been raped, tortured, and enslaved. 350,000 American, British and Commonwealth military personnel had been mistreated as prisoners of war, a significant proportion died of starvation. The Japanese routinely beheaded captured allied airmen. Pearl Harbour was bombed without a declaration of war—a completely unprovoked attack.

There are closely argued reasons both to support and to condemn Harry Truman's decision, made at the Potsdam Conference, to drop the bomb. It is true that, for several weeks before Hiroshima, the Japanese had been trying to interest Joseph Stalin in helping to negotiate a peace treaty. Stalin ignored the approach. Two thirds of the Japanese navy was at the bottom of the ocean. The population of the Japanese islands was short of food. Japan's industrial base was virtually destroyed and the American blockade had cut off oil supplies. Sixteen square miles of Tokyo had been burned to the ground in the American incendiary raids, killing more people than died at Hiroshima. The Soviet Union declared war on Japan in August 1945 and attacked the Japanese army in Manchuria. Wasn't it obvious, those critical of Truman argue, that Japan was incapable of holding out much longer and would collapse within weeks.

The Americans were preparing to invade Kyushu in November 1945 and when that island was subdued, an assault on Honshu was to follow. The American high command calculated that anywhere from 20,000 to 50,000 American casualties would be sustained in such an invasion.

By contrast, the Japanese high command calculated that to withstand successfully an American invasion, some twenty-two million lives would have to be sacrificed, American and Japanese soldiers, and Japanese civilians. The high command was prepared to suffer those losses rather than endure the humiliation of surrender.

Before Hiroshima, Japan was interested in negotiating a peace treaty and it was to this end that it approached the Soviet Union and advanced diplomatic enquiries via the Swedish government. But it was not prepared to surrender. Japan had never lost any war it had ever been involved in. The Japanese believed that surrender was dishonourable. It was one of the reasons that they treated their prisoners with such contempt and cruelty. The only decent alternative to victory was death. The Japanese cabinet contained a number of generals and admirals as well as the chief of the Imperial General Staff. When the American, Chinese, and British broadcast their proclamation calling for the unconditional surrender of Japan, the cabinet considered it and decided to ignore it. Suzuki, the Prime Minister, announced to the cabinet that they would "*mokusatsu*" the proclamation—that is to say, to kill it with silence.

Hearing nothing, the Americans dropped the first bomb. The Japanese Cabinet met once, decided to inform the Emperor what had happened, and (at the Emperor's urging) began its deliberations about what to do. Hearing no response from the Japanese, the Americans dropped the second bomb on Nagasaki. The Japanese cabinet was deeply divided. The military members were determined to fight on. The civilians felt that surrender was the only option. General Korechika Anami, the Minister of War, summed up the army's position.

"We cannot pretend," he said, "to claim that victory is certain, but it is too early to say that the war is lost. That we will inflict severe losses on the enemy when he invades Japan is certain, and it is by no means impossible that we may be able to reverse the situation in our favour, pulling victory out of defeat. Furthermore, our army will not submit to demobilization. Our men will simply not lay down their arms. And since they know that they are not permitted to surrender, since they know that a fighting man who surrenders is liable to extremely heavy punishment, there is really no alternative for us but to continue the war."

The cabinet remained divided. Normally, the Emperor was only ever presented with a decision of the cabinet if it had been arrived at unanimously. The Emperor himself never took sides or stated his own opinion. His august mind was not to be disturbed by such party strife. The responsibility for decisions was not his. Normally if a cabinet could not decide, it resigned. But in this situation, they decided that they had to perform the unthinkable: to ask the Emperor to break the impasse. And so he eventually did, deciding that Japan had to accept the terms of unconditional surrender. It took the Japanese seven days and two atomic bombs to respond to the proclamation seeking its surrender.

This, then, was the mindset of the Japanese rulers, when Truman decided to use the atomic bomb. It is probable that had it not been used, the war would have had to be pursued with appalling casualties on both sides. And after all, Truman's duty was to his own country, and to his own soldiers. What answer, one wonders, would he have made to the soldier's widow, confronting him on the White House steps, who asked, "President Truman, why did you continue this war and make my children orphans, when you knew you could have terminated it by using the atomic bomb?"

Years later I met a Dutch engineer at a dinner party. He had been born in Java. When he was six years old, he and his family had been caught by the Japanese and interned in a hell hole of a prison camp. Four years later, the Americans rescued the survivors. Inmates were dying daily of disease and starvation. Right at the end of the war, the Japanese guards had been ordered to try and eliminate all the prisoners. 'No witnesses.' We fell to talking about whether Harry Truman had done the right thing to drop the atomic bombs. "Well," said my Dutch friend, "if he hadn't, there is no doubt that I wouldn't be here today."

General Korechika Anami was one of the Japanese dignitaries who signed the document of surrender on August 14th. The next morning he committed suicide, as did a number of the senior officers in the Japanese army. It was the only honourable course for them to take in the event of this unthinkable surrender.

We wandered round the Peace Park, with its formal flower beds and patches of sand carefully and elegantly combed with big bamboo rakes to create intricate patterns. The time came to return to our ryokan. We had lost our bearings and could not find the tram that had taken us to the park in the morning. There was a little pagoda near the museum that sported a sign in English: Tourist Information. So we entered and told the polite, young Japanese lad, who was manning the counter, that we needed to find the tram to return us to our ryokan. Surprisingly, for an information bureau that was supposed to cater to tourists, he spoke almost no English. After five minutes of struggling to make ourselves understood, he suddenly leapt over the counter. "Wait, please!" He called over his shoulder as he ran out of the pagoda. So, we waited. In five minutes he was back, accompanied by a half a dozen giggling schoolgirls around fifteen or sixteen years of age. "Speak English," he said, with a note of triumph in his voice, gesturing to the girls. They did speak English. It was very rudimentary English, but they were anxious to try out what English they had learned at school. They understood what we wanted and where we needed to go. They gave us careful directions on how to find the tram we needed.

One of them said, "When you find the tram station, you take the wrong tram." The wrong tram? We puzzled over this for a while and cross-examined them about their description of the tram. "Yes, the wrong tram," they insisted. After a minute's more struggle with this, and with their pigeon English, we decided to follow their directions to the tram station. At least we would be at the beginning of our journey. Perhaps someone would find us the *right* tram. At the tram station, we came upon a collection of trams, some loading passengers and leaving, and more arriving and disgorging passengers. Then we espied what we were looking for. It was a double tram—two tram cars joined together. Of course, this was the "Wrong tram." The Japanese have trouble pronouncing the letter "L" in English. The girls had been trying to tell us to take the "Long tram," the two-car tram.

On the way down to Hiroshima, the train stopped at Himeji. This is a town that dates back to medieval times. The railway runs through a wide valley, and Himeji is spread out up a steep hillside. Looking out of the carriage window, we spied a great pagoda at the top of the hill. It was, we were told, an old fortress perched at the top of a long, wide boulevard that stretched from the railway station all the way up to the pagoda fortress. It looked intriguing enough that we decided that, on the way back, we would get off the train and have a look at it. This we did, even though our train tickets did not cater for this unscheduled stopover.

It was worth the effort. We walked up the long avenue and explored this immense pagoda, built of huge, interlocking logs with some six or seven storeys. It was a tourist attraction and an English-speaking guide took a number of us round the edifice. The view from the top floor was spectacular. You could see for thirty or forty miles all round. No hostile army could approach this castle without being detected hours before it reached the place. Because it had been fortified, it was blessed with many embrasures and in consequence was drafty. It must have been bitterly cold in winter.

We left the castle and walked back down to the station in time for the next train to Tokyo. On the way, we ran into a gaggle of some dozen twelve-year-old schoolgirls, all in immaculate school uniforms with imitation Scottish plaid skirts. They saw that we were westerners, asked our nationality, and when we revealed that we were Canadian, began chattering to us in very broken English. This troop followed us all the way to the train station, like a flock of geese on the lookout for food. They engaged us in conversation, though it was a pretty primitive exchange as their English was quite rudimentary. They all waved and cheered us goodbye as we entered the station.

I walked up to the clerk at the ticket counter, who unlike our schoolgirl friends, spoke no English at all. I handed him our tickets for the train we had just abandoned, tapped my watch, pointed at the castle with extended my hands sideways, palm upward, and managed to get across to him that we needed tickets to get us back to Tokyo on the next train. He smiled, nodded, bowed, and then disappeared into his back office. In a few minutes, he returned with two tickets for the next train to Tokyo. We all bowed to each other. I said, "Arigato gozaimasu da," which I had learned meant, "Thank you very much for what you have done for us." He looked surprised, said something in reply, which I assumed meant, "You're welcome." We all bowed once more and then we retrieved our luggage from the little room where we had left it, just in time to catch the next train home.

Just south of Yokohama, we were treated to the extraordinary sight of Mount Fujiyama. Fuji-san—the extinct volcano, sacred to the Japanese— is 12, 389 feet high, and some one hundred and seventy miles in circumference at its base. We had seen dozens of mountains higher than this in Canada, but what makes Fujiyama so impressive and beautiful is its unblemished symmetry, the cap of snow at the summit and the fact that you look at it from sea level. It is a long climb to the top, but the climb offers no challenge. You just walk up a twelve-thousand-foot mountain to the shrine at the top.

Our train journey back to Tokyo was interrupted when the train slammed to a stop, from the two hundred and forty kilometres per hour it was doing after it left Yokohama. It stopped on a long curve. Because of the trains' speed, this curve was heavily banked, and though you don't notice it while the train was at that speed, when stopped, it tilted the train sideways, making for considerable discomfort. An announcement came over the PA system, in Japanese, so we couldn't understand what had happened. Sitting next to us was a young Chinese man. He spoke good English as he was a Cantonese (from Hong Kong), and travelling on business. He spoke no Japanese, and had not understood the announcement either. The written language, Kanji, is common to Japan and China, so he wrote an enquiring note and handed it to the Japanese person seated across the aisle. A note came back, informing us that there had been an earthquake. In Japan, when an earthquake strikes, the entire Japanese railway system shuts down—everything stops. They make no attempt to get going until all danger is past. Then they slowly get the trains to their destinations. There is no point in trying to make up lost time. They simply get all the trains destined for Tokyo back to Tokyo, and start all over again the next day. Passengers are used to this. It is preferable to having the turbulence derail the Shinkansen at over two hundred Kilometres an hour. We arrived at Tokyo Central Station several hours late and took a taxi back to the Foremans'. We refrained from tipping the driver.

DOWN THE MACKENZIE RIVER

The Mackenzie River flows out of the west end of Great Slave Lake at Fort Providence, a former North West Company trading post. Depending on where you start to measure it and where you finish, the river is 1738 kilometres long. It is the longest river in Canada, and with its headstreams, second only to the Mississippi-Missouri in all of North America. It and its tributaries drain 1,895,200 square kilometres of northwestern Canada. It is said to be one of only four major rivers in the northern hemisphere to flow north. All the others flow south. The Mackenzie, at full flood, discharges 9,700 cubic metres of water per second into the Arctic Ocean.

So much for the impressive statistics. We flew from Edmonton on a Canadian North Boeing 737. Canadian North is a really outstanding airline. The service is cheerful, the food is as good as that served in business class in most other airlines, and the flights were on time. The emblem on the tail of the aircraft is the midnight sun with a polar bear silhouetted in front of it.

Landing at Yellowknife Airport, we walked into the lobby of the little terminal to be confronted by a startlingly lifelike display of a stuffed polar bear hunting a seal. There is also a display of old mining equipment lined up outside the terminal, and a little mining museum inside. One is tempted to linger and inspect it. In the North, it takes very little time to discover that the people are friendly and helpful. We needed a luggage cart. A woman was standing at the edge of a knot of people all joyfully greeting each other. She had two carts, the one inserted into the other as airport carts are designed to be. I pointed to her carts and asked where I could find one. She grinned and said, "Right here. This one is for you. Every visitor to Yellowknife is entitled to a luggage cart." With that she disengaged her surplus cart and handed it over to me. It seems that it has to do with living in a community that faces constant challenge. The weather is a challenge. In summer, there is no night, as the sun never sets. In winter, daylight is only a few very short hours and is bitterly cold. If you do not exercise constant caution, you can freeze to death in a few minutes. People have

223

to hang together to survive. There is a strong undercurrent of humour everywhere. For instance, in Norman Wells the street signs are shaped to resemble ravens: a raven flying, a raven standing, two ravens kissing, and a raven picking up food. The effect is delightful.

Yellowknife is by far the largest town in the Northern Territories. It has a population of 20,000 and is home to the Territorial Legislature, housed in an impressive modern structure on the edge of town. It has a superb museum, with rooms dedicated to the history of aviation in the North—the only means of transportation to many communities—medicine in the North, water transportation, Dene art, clothing, and culture, and paintings. One set of about twenty oil paintings was done by Mary Harrington, a young teacher who painted northern scenes in the late 1940s. They are brilliant and could pass for something by Tom Thomson.

We had booked passage on the *Norweta*, a twenty-passenger riverboat (out of Yellowknife), that takes people on an eight-day trip down the Mackenzie to Inuvik. The boat ties up each night, either at one of the hamlets on the river, or one of the storage sites where the Canadian Coast Guard stores its buoys. The Coast Guard lays down these buoys immediately after the ice goes out in June and takes them out before the ice forms in October. Except for Norman Wells, which owes its existence to the oil and gas industry, all the towns on the river are old Hudson Bay or North West Company trading posts (or factories), established to promote the fur trade.

Anyone with an ounce of romance in their veins should make this trip. If you go, a copy of Alexander Mackenzie's journal of his voyage to the Arctic Ocean is a must. Starting at Fort Chipewyan on Lake Athabasca, on June 3, 1789, he canoed down the Slave River with a dozen men, some with their wives, and encountered ice clogging Great Slave Lake. By June 29th, he reached what is now Fort Providence and the entrance to the river. He was seeking a passage to the Pacific Ocean and did not know that the river, which now bears his name, emptied into the Arctic Ocean. We left Fort Providence on July 8th—218 years and nine days after Mackenzie. What was significant was the difference in what we experienced and what was described by Mackenzie: "*5*[th] *July. A quantity of ice along the banks of ye river.*" We encountered no ice at all.

We stopped at Fort Simpson, the old HBC trading post at the confluence of the Liard and Mackenzie rivers. This used to be the capital of the North in the days when the HBC was the government.

Two of our fellow passengers were Peter Jackson and his wife, a Scottish couple. Both were in their late sixties. Peter Jackson had grown up in the Outer Hebrides. When he was in his second last year of high school, the Hudson Bay Company recruiting officers came to his school on the hunt for young men to work for the company, as factors in the fur trade. Peter Jackson signed up, did his last year of high school, and sailed for Canada. He was sent to Fort Smith. After a year there, he sailed for home to marry his high-school sweetheart and brought her out to Fort Smith. Apart from the RCMP officer, they were the only white people in town.

When we disembarked at Fort Good Hope, Peter set off to find his old house. It was gone, but he did find his old HBC warehouse. More impressive, he encountered the Dene man who had taught Peter how to harness and run his sled-dog team. It was an emotional encounter, as the two old men renewed their acquaintanceship from half a century before.

The Dempster Highway crosses the river at Tsiigehtchic. A ferry takes traffic across en route to Inuvik. The highway is named after Corporal W. J. D. Dempster who traversed the route by dog sled in 1911, in a vain search for a lost North-West Mounted Police patrol.

Inuvik, a town of 3,300, is far north of the Arctic Circle. It is quite disorienting to experience the sun simply going round and round the sky without setting. One of the pleasant attributes of the North is the friendliness and humour of the people. It is hardscrabble country and people are forced to rely on each other. Tourists are beneficiaries of this attitude.

There is a Roman Catholic church built in the shape of an igloo. Some of the buildings in Yellowknife have had to be abandoned. They are sinking. The reason for this is that it was once possible to immerse the foundations in the permafrost. As its name implies, permafrost is permanently frozen ground. You dig into the permafrost, lay the foundations, and the ice will hold the foundations rigid in its frozen grip. Global warming has interfered with this hitherto cunning architectural artifice. The permafrost has begun to melt, and the buildings, their foundations now unstable, are in danger of collapse.

Behind the church, there is an old disused ice rink. The inhabitants have converted this into a vast community greenhouse. Inside we found seventy-two plots of ground, each held in place by squared logs. A wonderful miscellany of vegetables were growing in these little allotments. Several had signs which bore the following legend: My owner is away. Please water me. Two had scarecrows guarding them, though there was no bird in sight. The greenhouse functions year round. In winter it is heated by the town's gas heating system. Inuvik owns its own gas well, so it can use this inexhaustible and inexpensive fuel to heat the entire town.

Visiting the North impresses one with the importance of hunting and trapping to northerners. Those not working in the oil or gas industry live off the land. The alternative is welfare. The caribou are the prime source of subsistence, providing food and clothing, which is why it is vital to prevent any incursion into the caribou's territory. Every spring and every fall, the 125,000 strong "Porcupine Caribou Herd" crosses the Dempster Highway to (and back from) the calving grounds on the Beaufort Sea. The Dene and the Inuvaliut still run trap lines and subsist by using the furs both for their own use and for sale to the HBC, still a fur-trading company.

The Menin Gate

F landers, also known as the killing fields of Europe, is the blood-soaked farmland cemetery of the First World War. Kiffa, Gill, and I decided that we would visit Flanders. My father and Gill's had both fought in the First World War. Her father, John Bostock, was in the Royal Horse Artillery, which historically was the artillery that protected the cavalry. My father was in the infantry, specifically the 2nd Battalion of the Monmouthshire Regiment. We wanted to see the country where they had served. Neither of them would willingly talk about their experiences in that war, so it was difficult to know where they had been. I knew that my dad had been wounded at the beginning the Battle of Passchendaele. The whereabouts of the Royal Horse Artillery's activities remained unknown to us.

We visited my uncle's grave in the little military cemetery at Hermies, just a few miles northwest of Cambrai. He had been a signaller in the Royal Fusiliers. In July 1917, at the age of nineteen, a shell tore open his stomach. He died within minutes, near where he is buried. We left flowers.

Then we journeyed to Ypres, the old Flemish town, which in the middle ages was the centre of the textile trade. Its jewel is the Lakenhalle, the thirteenth-century cloth hall. It took a hundred years to build what was, in effect, a covered market, where ships moored and loaded and unloaded cargoes into a covered quay alongside the banks of the Yperlee. The town certainly looked as though it had been built in the middle ages, but we discovered that the entire town, and its ancient and beautiful cloth hall, had been totally destroyed during the three battles of Ypres. As it now stands, it is only some sixty to eighty years old. The Belgians rebuilt the entire town, with scrupulous attention to its old design. In truth, you cannot tell that it isn't the original thirteenth-century town. The cloth hall, with its great tower, and the large church behind it were the first buildings to be demolished by shell fire. Church towers were used extensively for spotting the drop of artillery shells, so if the enemy held a town with a church, your shell fire was instantly directed to bring down this observation post. This was standard procedure for both sides. Ypres is now a bustling town, which seemed to have more shops selling Belgian chocolates per capita than any I have encountered anywhere else.

Meensestraat is a short street that leads from the enormous and elegant old main square to the Menin gate. Halfway down it is a shop, called "The British Grenadier", which is run by a couple of old British ex-servicemen. It will sell you books, artifacts and relics (mostly shell casings), and runs tours. We took a tour. It was November and the bitterly cold wind, with nothing between us and the North Sea to interrupt its driving force, was intermittently spattering us with rain. We were taken to an old field-dressing station housed in the arches of an aqueduct, and shown the remains of some trenches and concrete pillboxes. As we stood at an intersection that was surrounded by dead-flat farm land, we heard an explosion off in the distance. Upon enquiry, we learned that this explosion was the weekly demolition exercise. To this day, the farmers plough up unexploded shells. They pile them at the intersections, and once a week, a truck comes by to pick them up and take them away to be exploded. The farmers also still dig up bones, skeletons, and weapons. The authorities try to identify the human remains, a usually impossible task.

The village of Passchendaele was obviously newly built, as was its church, whose tower suffered the inevitable fate of all church towers at the hands of the artillery. The country was uniformly flat, with only occasional rises of ground. Though the weather we encountered was wet, we saw nothing of the mud that figures so prominently in histories of the war in Flanders. Our guide explained that the reason the battlefields and trenches became so muddy was because the artillery destroyed the drainage systems, meticulously laid out by a millennium of farmers. This caused the rain to lay where it fell, turning the fields into quagmires of mud, blood-soaked slime, and rat shit. The reason they are still disinterring unexploded shells is that fully one third of the millions of shells fired during the war did not explode. This was mainly because the ground was so soft and many shells did not encounter anything hard enough to trigger the detonating mechanism.

Returning to The British Grenadier, I enquired of one of the proprietors if he sold regimental histories, and if so, did he have one of my father's old regiment. He didn't, but looked it up on the internet. To my astonishment, he told me something my father had never mentioned. I had always thought Dad was an ordinary infantry lieutenant. What little he told us about his experiences certainly led me to believe his recounting of life in the trenches and of leading a platoon of men on night patrol. But the British Grenadier told me that the 2nd Battalion of the Monmouthshire Regiment had been a pioneer regiment. A pioneer regiment's function was to dig the trenches, and (more importantly) the mines that travelled under the enemy lines. These mines were filled with explosives and then detonated just before an attack. This made sense, because the Monmouthshire regiment was a Welsh regiment and it would have been populated by

Welsh coal miners, who earned their keep by digging underground in the coal mines of South Wales.

That evening we attended the ceremony at the Menin Gate. This is a huge brick gate, which replaced one of the old town gates that was destroyed in the course of the three battles. It is a monument to those British and Commonwealth soldiers whose bodies were never found, or not able to be identified. The gate is inscribed with the names of sixty-two thousand soldiers whose fate was never known: the unknown soldiers.

The ceremony takes place at 8:00 pm, and this has occurred every evening for ninety years now, since very shortly after the end of the First World War. Three members of the Ypres fire department, sharply at eight o'clock, parade at the gate and play the "Last Post" on their three bugles. The evening we were there, as the last echoes of the "Last Post" died away, a man with a thick Flemish accent stepped forward and recited the famous verse from Laurence Binyon's poem.

> They shall grow not old as we that are left grow old,
> Age shall not weary them, nor the years condemn,
> At the going down of the sun and in the morning
> We will remember them.

There must have been about fifty tourists in attendance at this ceremony, and I do not believe there was a dry eye amongst the lot of us.

GLACIER BAY

W e picked up the boat in Juneau—the old gold rush town struggling
for elbow room between the harbour and the steep mountains to the
east. The streets were narrow and winding; hastily fashioned by the mining
community, it followed the contours of this sparse strip of land a century
earlier. The buildings in the old town certainly bore the architectural
imprint of 1890's frontier construction. The farther from the old town you
wander, the newer the buildings become, until when you walk across the
bridge over the Gastineau Channel, you could be forgiven for thinking that
you had stumbled into any nondescript town in the American mid-west.

Juneau is the capital of Alaska, which has been a state of the union
since 1959. The capital used to be Sitka, a relic of Russian sovereignty until
Czar Alexander sold Alaska to the Americans in 1867. Russia had run short
of funds at the end of the Crimean war, a disaster for Russia, and offered
Alaska to the Americans for seven million two hundred thousand dollars.
William H. Seward, the American Secretary of State, feared that the British
would likely seize the land, as the Hudson's Bay Company already had a
lease of some of the southern part. So he leapt at the opportunity. It was
known for many years as Seward's Folly. It worked out at a cost of 2.5
cents per acre. This was a better deal than the Louisiana purchase, which
cost fifteen million dollars, or 2.9 cents per acre. Napoleon Bonaparte,
though equally strapped for cash, managed to drive a better bargain.

The state capital is housed in a quaint little seven-storey Art Deco brick
building on the edge of the old town. It was opened in 1931. Before that,
the territory's affairs had been run out of the Elks' Hall, when the Elks
weren't stabled there. The harbour is entirely given over to a huge fleet of
fishing boats. There were so many that it was impossible to count them.
Their masts were massed across the water like a field of harvested corn
stalks. It is no wonder the salmon stocks are running low.

Our cruise ship was small by cruise-ship standards, with only two
hundred and ten passengers. Its size facilitated easier navigation of narrow
passages and shallow bays. The ship visited Sitka, which could well have
been perched on the banks of the Volga, with the onion domes of the

Cathedral of St. Michael dominating the town. The Cathedral is Russian Orthodox. There are no pews. You stand during the service—tough on the old knees and the lower backs of the faithful.

We also put in at Skagway. Not an hour after we arrived, two normal-sized cruise ships docked. Each vomited forth two thousand passengers, four thousand energetic, souvenir-hunting Americans, pouring through the streets, clogging the shops and elbowing each other (and us) off the sidewalks. Of course, the shops were there exactly for the purpose of selling Chinese-made souvenirs to these mobs of ill-disciplined, garrulous, marauding shoppers. We discovered that most of the shops are owned and operated by one or other of the cruise lines. As soon as the tourist season is over, the shops shutter down and the shopkeepers return to their homes in Milwaukee, Los Angeles, and other mundane American towns.

We fled, and walked inland along the White Pass &Yukon Railroad, and soon came across the old cemetery. No gravestone bore a date of death later than the First World War. Almost all the gravestones memorialized men, and the majority had met violent deaths in their twenties—either shot or the victims of mining accidents. Not a few died of diseases that could be cured in a trice today. The cemetery constituted a mute history of Skagway and the Chilkoot Trail. A further attempt to escape the legions of foraging tourists led us to book a return passage on the ancient railway line up to Lake Bennett. A four-car train, pulled by a venerable steam engine, bumped and rattled up a steep valley that gave onto the plain that was home to Lake Bennett. We stopped, wandered around the old station, and then returned to Skagway. It would have been fun to take the train all the way to Whitehorse, not that much farther along the line, but we did not have the time, and in any event the White Pass & Yukon Railroad had ceased journeys to Whitehorse many years back. Though the track was still in place, the onslaught of winter ice would have rendered it hopelessly unsafe without major repairs.

The ship put into a tiny bay, home to a village of perhaps fifty inhabitants, fisher families all. The ship had not been anchored ten minutes when there occurred a huge splash alongside. Every one rushed to the railings to watch a grey whale, the size of a double decker bus, fly out of the water and land on its side creating a monumental upheaval of water. It repeated this exercise several times to the delight and amazement of the passengers. It was driving a school of herring towards the shore, herding them into a small pod before feasting on them.

Glacier Bay provided a stunning sight. Ninety miles long, this fiord is home to a series of great glaciers, which run down the valleys debouching into Glacier Bay on each side of the main fiord. At the head of the fiord stood the face of the main glacier. We dared not edge too close to it, as the face, many hundred feet high, was constantly calving. Chunks of ice, many thousand tons each, kept falling off the glacier face. Despite this, hundreds of seals lay on the ice, floating at its foot in the bitterly cold water, tending their calves and fishing.

Upon our return to Juneau, I telephoned an acquaintance, Jim Bradley. Jim and I had met on a number of occasions at meetings of the American College of Trial Lawyers, to which both of us had been elected. He had practised law in Juneau for many years. Surprised to hear we were in Juneau, he offered to show us round the town, proposed a time to meet, and gave us an address where he assured us we would find him. The address turned out to be a coffee shop in the old town. Gill and I walked down to look for him and found him playing poker with a group of friends, who all looked as if they had only just broken off moiling for gold that morning. Jim swept up his winnings. The fist full of change did not give the appearance of amounting to much. I think they were playing penny-ante poker, though from the strained concentration on their faces it might as well have had them wrestling with Mississippi steamboat-sized stakes.

Jim took us to the recreation centre—a startlingly luxurious sports facility that would have done credit to any Vancouver suburb. It housed some squash courts. Jim said he occasionally played. I had trouble believing this. At any rate I didn't think he should be playing at all, and occasionally would have been dangerous. Jim was an inch shorter than I was, and must have weighed little short of 250 pounds. He could have been described as bulky. A short step away, he parked and walked us up to the local glacier. An enormous serpent of ice, its crevasse-ridden path snaked up into the mountains and disappeared behind a bank of cumulus clouds.

We told him about our tour of Glacier Bay. "Ah yes," he said, "a couple of years ago the Tlingit brought a land claim to trial. They claimed the whole of Glacier Bay. They asserted that their ancestors had fished in the bay 'since the time whereof the mind of man runneth not to the contrary'— since time immemorial. Well, someone dug up Captain Vancouver's log for July 1794. Vancouver recorded that the bay was a glacier right down to its mouth, all ninety miles of what is now open water was impenetrable ice. That was the end of their land claim. Jim told us that a hundred years later, in 1879, John Muir reported that the glacier had retreated sixty miles inland. The glacier had been created during the little ice age. Now it had reached ninety miles inland and it and the glaciers that fed it were melting at an accelerating rate.

We bade Jim goodbye and repaired to the ship. Sadly Jim died not long afterwards—a victim, I suspect, of his occasional game of squash.

Intrigued, I conducted some research. The tale Jim had told us was true. Glacier Bay was not a fiord two hundred years ago. It was a glacier. Captain Vancouver's journal relates how his ship, HMS Discovery, could not safely negotiate the ice, so he sent a cutter under the command of Lt. Joseph Whidbey to explore the ice that was cluttering up what he thought might be an inlet. Whidbey reported that he had found a bay, some five miles wide with "a compact sheet of ice as far as the eye can distinguish."

The bay was home to a wall of ice, the face of a great glacier. The glacier stretched inland towards the St. Elias Mountains.

Vancouver's journal is written in the stilted matter-of-fact language of an eighteenth-century British naval officer. The letter "s" is always written as an "f". He recounts frequent meetings with natives, Tlingit and Kodiak, with whom the sailors traded, and occasionally Russian merchant ships— though Vancouver's journal discloses little commerce with the Russians. Reading Vancouver's description of his voyage, one wonders at the endurance of the crew of a man-o'-war, spending several years aboard with no means of heating the ship, drafty and wet beyond belief, and with the crew sleeping in hammocks slung wherever their occupants could find space to hang them.

NEW ORLEANS

Two dollars will admit you. The generally accepted procedure is to go next door to Pat O'Brien's pub and buy a beer. Then you pay your two dollars at the door of Preservation Hall and take a seat wherever you can find one. Staff of Pat O'Brien's will collect up their empties the next day. We surrendered our admission fee at the door into the hands of a cheerful lady who bore a resemblance to Scarlet O'Hara's nanny. She was at pains to inform us that the band would play any tune you asked for if you gave them two dollars, and for five dollars, they would play "The Saints Come Marching In".

"Hall'" is a grand name for what, in fact, is the bare (if spacious) cavern at 726 St. Peter's Street, in the heart of the French Quarter of New Orleans, which we discovered had been converted from a shop in 1961. Since the band was already playing, we stood and waited before searching for a seat. Someone must have slipped the band a fiver, because what they were playing was, indeed, "The Saints Come Marching In". We stood in awe as the joyful noise rose. It filled the room. A spirited rendition of the old tune, it was a flood of sound, full of exhilaration and gaiety. Oh, and the energy, bouncing off the walls! I turned to look at the band. To my astonishment, it only had four members. No percussion. No Bass. How could such a small group conjure up so much compelling music from just four instruments? The rhythm was hypnotic and the whole piece lifted your spirits. The audience was bouncing about to the beat of the band.

The Saints eventually finished marching, to enthusiastic applause from the audience—whom we could now see were ranged on plain wooden benches scattered about a bare wooden floor that raked up to the back of the hall. We located a bench and sat down on it. The benches were loose, so you could pull them around if you needed a better view.

The band leader, on clarinet, was a grey-haired white man. Three black musicians were playing a cornet, trombone, and a sousaphone respectively, though there were other instruments spread out at their feet. At the behest of an audience member, the band played "Stompin' at the Savoy", which was lively, though without the riotous exuberance of "The Saints

Come Marching In." There was a short pause and then the leader took the opportunity to introduce the band. He told us his name and then introduced the other band members. Each stood, waved a hand as his name was called, and grinned, each showing pure white teeth against a black face. The sousaphone player was the largest human being I have ever seen, closer to seven feet than six, with a girth beyond measure. Each of his hands would easily have concealed a large soup plate. I wondered that he was able to wriggle between the coils of his sousaphone. The band leader waved his clarinet in the direction of this amiable giant. "And on sousaphone is Algernon Lacey." Lacey beamed at us through the curving sweep of his instrument. Algernon Lacey, indeed. This was a name that belonged to the formal elegance of the court of Elizabeth I, not this massive exponent of Dixieland jazz.

From chatting with other members of the audience, we learned that each night there was a pick up band selected by those who ran Preservation Hall, from the musicians who played each day and night in the bars, brothels, restaurants, and on the street corners of the Mecca of jazz that is New Orleans. Preservation Hall was established for the specific purpose of preserving and promoting this gorgeous music. There is a permanent group of about a dozen players from which is drawn a number of bands that go on tours of North America. You can purchase their discs at the Hall and we did, but I found that listening to a disc simply does not give you the same drama and excitement as listening to these superb musicians—many untrained and some who cannot even read music.

They played "Jeep's Blues", with which I was unfamiliar. It demonstrated where this music originated: an amalgam of western, and southern States, and influences straight out of the jungles and plains of Africa, with its poly-rhythms, syncopation, swung notes, and (above all) improvisation.

Gill decided that she wanted them to play her favourite piece of jazz, "The World Is Waiting for the Sunrise," so she went down to speak to the leader. I saw her talking to him, holding out her two one dollar bills. He was looking puzzled and shaking his head. She said that she thought it was a Sydney Bechet tune. (In fact she was wrong. It was written by a Canadian called Ernest Seitz, whose father had invented the Olivetti typewriter.) The conversation went on for a while, with Gill doing the talking and the leader gently shaking his head with the corners of his mouth pulled down. Gill thrust the money into his hand. He held up a finger and made one of those gestures that means something between "I'll try" and "I just don't know." She returned to the seat beside me. "He doesn't know it. He doesn't think he's ever heard it." She was disappointed. The leader turned and spoke to the rest of the band. Each of them smiled and shook his head. They gathered up their instruments and played "Muskrat Ramble." The leader didn't join in. He sat, elbows on knees, with his head in one hand and his clarinet in the other. He sat like that until the band had almost finished. Then he sat up, looked over at Gill, and shook his clarinet in a gesture of success. The band Finished "Muskrat Ramble" and he turned and spoke to them. Nods of agreement. He shuffled himself into a comfortable position, raised the clarinet to his lips, flung a glance at Gill and started to play, slowly at first. I recognized "The World Is Waiting for the Sunrise". I'd heard Benny Goodman play it, but not like our leader played it. There was an air of joyful triumph in the notes. As he warmed to the tune, he sped up and began improvising. As he played, the other members of the band listened, and each slowly took up his instrument and began to play along until, at last, the band was going at it pell-mell, as if it was something they did every day. Then each member, individually and without any apparent signal from the leader, began to improvise, with the rest of the band supporting him. At the conclusion of the individual interpretations, the band played the tune together—a wonderful rendition that sounded as if it had been rehearsed for weeks.

It was a brilliant piece of musicianship. Three of them had never heard the tune before and the leader had only remembered it while cudgelling his brain over the strains of "Muskrat Ramble".

Gill and I stood and applauded loudly, attracting stares from the rest of the audience. But then, they didn't know what the band had just achieved.

KALAUPAPA

D rawn up in a line of impatient traffic, waiting for the relief of the green light, one's jaded eye sometimes drifts down to a bumper sticker on the vehicle ahead. Some carry pious warnings, "*If you drink, don't drive.*" Others express a wistful complaint, "*I'd rather be fishing.*" But drivers are occasionally puzzled by a bumper sticker bearing this curious legend: "*Wouldn't You Rather Be Riding a Mule on Molokai?*" To most people, this message will be a complete mystery. Mules? Molokai? This article reveals the secret behind this odd communication.

First, Molokai. It is one of the smaller and least developed of the Hawaiian islands, lying eight miles northwest of Maui and twenty-three miles east of Oahu. I use miles as the unit of measure, because that is how the Americans measure distance. The island is roughly rectangular, thirty-eight miles from east to west and eight to ten miles from north to south, depending on where you measure it. It has a single twelve-square-mile peninsula jutting into the constantly rough ocean on the north shore. This is the Kalaupapa Peninsula, also (and more properly) known as Makanalua Peninsula, and is deserted except for the few remaining inhabitants of the leper colony.

Until a few years ago, Molakai had a population of about six thousand all told. The western end was largely owned by the Dole pineapple people, but they closed down their huge pineapple operation in 1975 and moved it to the Philippines, where labour costs were lower. Now the old pine-apple fields lie fallow, the acres of red earth growing only luxuriant grass. The population of the old company town, Maunaloa, is smaller now, with an under-used hotel and a few shops. One of those shops is a wonderful establishment called the Big Wind Kite Factory, run by a dear, eccentric couple whose tubby three-legged dog greets customers at the door. They manufacture every conceivable kind of kite, from huge box kites to some that resemble birds of prey, which must strike terror into the heart of any passing seagull. This shop sells local history books, artifacts from all around the South Pacific, sweetmeats, incense, and an eclectic collection of merchandise.

Since the defection of Dole, the population of the island has shrunk to about twenty-seven hundred. Molokai's main town is Kaunakakai. Its shops fill the main street for all of two blocks, and it boasts the only traffic light on the island. There are two food stores. One could hardly call them supermarkets, because neither is large enough to warrant that description. Tuesday is the day to shop, when supplies come in from Maui. Over the next seven days they tend to run short of goods. There is a bakery that sells beautiful bread and cookies of all descriptions, but it closes as soon as the bread supply runs out, usually by mid-afternoon. There is a well-stocked liquor store, but do not expect to be able to buy Dubonnet or Pernod. A request for either provokes a mystified stare from the cheerful, robust Hawaiian lady who runs it. There is a small police force that is not much in evidence. Only recently has it owned its own police cars. Before that, each member of the force used their own private vehicle to fulfil constabulary duties.

It is said that Molokai is at the same stage of development now as Maui was forty years ago. Recently there was a proposal to have cruise ships dock at Kaunakakai's little harbour. The islanders were incensed, and festooned the south shore with signs bearing the legend, "No Cruise Ships". The project was shelved and the island returned to its sleepy muddle. The airport exercises no security measures. It was issued one of those gates that squeal when you walk through them with any metal on you, but the cheerful islanders who run the airport have pushed the gate into a corner where it stands idle. It caused them too much trouble to no purpose that they could see.

We decided that we could not leave the Island without visiting the leper colony. Now there are only four ways to do this and taking a car is not one of them. There is no road into the colony, which nestles on the peninsula of Kalaupapa at the foot of a sixteen-hundred-foot cliff that extends for miles on each side of the peninsula. The cliff is virtually perpendicular, but there is a tortuous path cut into it, with twenty-three switch backs that will take you down to the rocky beach below. You can walk down this path, and back up. Climbing up takes over two hours for someone in really good shape. There are small aircraft that will fly you in, to land on a bumpy grass airstrip. Boats can berth at the battered dock, but berthing is dangerous because of the constant and vicious south-bound surf that pounds the north shore. Very few people are rash enough ever to try it. One barge a year brings annual supplies, and it is quite a performance to get the barge docked and unloaded.

The adventurous way to access the colony is by mule. There is a stable with some thirty mules about a half mile back from the top of the cliff. The mules belong to a company by the name of Ali'i Mule Skinners of Molokai, run by one E. Buzzy Sproat. You book a ride and show up at about eight in the morning. The muleskinners give you a short talk about the ride. They assure you that the mules know what they are doing and that you should leave them to find their own way. They are saddled and equipped with a halter, but no bit, so it is quite difficult to steer the animal in any other direction than the one it is bent on following. It is also quite a task to pull it to a halt. Mules are amazingly stubborn and this lot is no exception. They know that their job is to get their passengers to the bottom, where they also know they will be fed, and they will countenance no delay.

When we took the mule train, there were about fifteen of us and two muleskinners to shepherd us along—a large silent Hawaiian boy and an engaging roustabout in a huge dirty cowboy hat. He looked like someone whose carousing had aged him prematurely, with his mouthful of missing teeth like a failed hockey player who had been gravitated down into the minor leagues. One of the guests on this journey with us was a pretty, if well-built, Hawaiian girl in her early twenties. Big Hat had discovered that she was the daughter of a famous Hawaiian singer, and pursued an endless attempt to ingratiate himself with her—an attempt that met with little but a stony reaction from her. I fell into conversation with her while we were going round the colony, and she turned out to be very informative about the history of the islands. She said that the first Polynesians had reached Hawaii by canoe in about 400 A.D.. It is believed that the bulk of the immigrants came at first from the Marquesas Islands and a second wave from Tahiti some 500 years later. The early settlers lacked a written language, so their culture was entirely oral and rich in myth and legend. Clans with chiefs and priests evolved and frequent wars occurred in the struggles for power, not unlike the feudal strife that ravaged Europe in the middle ages. The Polynesians were accomplished navigators and their outrigger canoes were of marvellous construction, and highly serviceable. She said that virtually all the birds and animals now found in the islands came from elsewhere. Very few were indigenous, as was the case with much of the vegetation and trees. This seemed logical to me, since the islands are entirely volcanic in origin. Once they erupted from the sea, all life had to come from somewhere else, including the humans.

The leper colony has a terrible history. Leprosy is a disease of very ancient lineage. It is referred to in the Old Testament, (Leviticus13-14). It is commonly thought to have originated in India, where reference to it has been found in documents dating as far back as 600 B.C.. Travellers seem to have distributed the disease. Crusaders, Spanish conquistadors, Asian seafarers, and Arabian, African, and American slave traders were the main vehicles for its spread into Europe and the Americas. Medical historians believe that Alexander the Great's soldiers carried it from India to Europe. It is a tropical disease and does not flourish in cold climates. Leprosy peaked in Western Europe between 1100 to 1300 A.D. and then declined as living conditions improved. The World Health Organization reports that 95 per cent of cases now occur in just eleven countries, with India and Brazil having the largest proportion.

Mycobacterium leprae was first identified as the cause of the disease by a Norwegian physician, G.H.A. Hansen, in 1874. Leprosy is also known as Hansen's disease. There are two forms of leprosy, tuberculoid and lepromatous. In tuberculoid, the lesions are few and small. Lepromatous leprosy is the more severe form, with widespread lesions containing more bacteria, which form hard nodules and folds of skin on the face, which often cause the nose to collapse, giving the victims a lion-like appearance. The lesions result in a loss of sensation and enlarged peripheral nerves, particularly in the joints. This anaesthetic effect causes patients not to notice injuries to the skin, so that they remain untreated and become infected with other bacteria, causing tissue damage and stiffened and mal-formed joints, ultimately crippling the victims. Both forms of the disease can cause blindness.

Historically, leprosy was widely believed to be highly contagious, hence the widespread fear that it created, causing people to shun and banish lepers. In Europe in the middle ages (5th to 15th centuries), lepers were declared dead and banished after being made to witness their own funerals. They were then either forced to wander about begging in order to survive or were confined to leprosaria, some two thousand of which were built by monks who called them "Lazar Houses", after Lazarus, the poor leper who features in Luke16:19-31. Those outcasts who wandered abroad were required to warn others of their approach by ringing bells or banging clappers.

In fact, the disease is not easily transmitted. Research has not estab-lished the precise way in which it can be spread, but it is thought that nasal droplets may contain the bacteria which could infect someone who inhales them. Another theory is that the bacteria may enter the body via cuts and lesions. Scientists believe that fewer than five percent of those infected actually contract the disease, because the body's immune system easily fights off the infection. It is not known why some people succumb to the ailment while most do not. The leprosy bacterium multiplies very slowly, once every two weeks, compared to once every twenty four hours for the related bacterium that causes tuberculosis and once every twenty minutes for some other bacteria. An infected person can live for as long as ten years before developing symptoms.

In the 1940s sulfone antibiotics were developed, which can halt the progress of the disease, although they cannot reverse the deformities or nerve damage that may have already been caused. The drugs also prevent it from being passed on to others.

The world Health Organization reports that in 1985 there were 5.4 million registered cases and estimated that there were probably 10 to 12 million worldwide. By 2000, there were only 680,000 registered cases and an estimated 1.6 million worldwide.

The first white men to see the Hawaiian Islands were Captain James Cook and his crew, amongst whom was William Bligh, Cook's sailing master. They landed at Waimea on Kauai in 1778. Cook named the Islands the Sandwich Islands, after the Earl of Sandwich, then First Lord of the Admiralty—a sly way to curry favour with the boss. European settlers followed in due course, finding the islands populated by about three hundred thousand Polynesians. During later immigration, the Europeans brought their diseases with them, including leprosy. The population of indigenous peoples withered to about fifty thousand within a hundred years of the arrival of the white man. Many of the Chinese immigrants intermarried with the Hawaiians and contracted the disease, which became known as "Mai Pake"—the Chinese sickness.

The first recorded case of leprosy on the Islands was in 1840, and over the next thirty years it became an epidemic. In 1866, the authorities (terrified of the disease and unable to treat it) decided to round up all the lepers and consign them to a settlement on the peninsula of Kalaupapa. This forcible resettlement was authorized by the Act to Prevent the Spread of Leprosy, passed by the Hawaiian legislature. Victims of the disease were identified, tracked down, torn from their families, and forcible deported. Kalaupapa was chosen because of its remoteness and inaccessibility. The first group of lepers was forcibly loaded on board a sailing ship on January 26, 1866 at a dock in Honolulu. The ship set off for the north shore of Molokai, intending to put the lepers ashore on the east side of the peninsula at a spot now known as Kalawao. There was, of course, no harbour. The surf was wild. There was no way that the ship could dock, and it was dangerous for it to get too close to the lee shore. The crew were, accordingly, ordered to fling the lepers overboard. Many drowned in the surf. The survivors dragged themselves ashore, where many died on the cold, inhospitable, and windswept shore. They had been given two days worth of food. More shiploads of lepers followed, so that by the end of 1866 there were 141 lepers living on the peninsula. Between then and 1873, 797 lepers were sent to Kalawao, of whom about half died. The little community was ill provisioned and lawless. The strong preyed upon the weak. There was no medical aid, no hospital, and only intermittent supplies of food. In the main, the lepers were left to fend for themselves. They made liquor from tree roots and drunkenness became common. Parts of the peninsula are actually very fertile and they were able, slowly, to provide for themselves from the fruit and berries they gathered, and what they began to grow for themselves. Public indignation at the conditions in the colony forced the Board of Health, known to the natives as the Board of Death, to make some effort to improve the lot of the lepers. A superintendent was appointed and consignments of food and clothing increased. Doctors were occasionally commissioned to visit the colony, but they were afraid of contracting the disease and their ministrations to the lepers were quick and superficial. One physician used to examine the lepers' wounds by lifting the bandages with his cane.

Then, in 1873, a young Belgian priest, Father Damien De Veuster, volunteered to serve as the colony's pastor. A tiny chapel, St. Philomena's, had already been built at Kalawao by the Brothers of the Sacred Heart, to which Father Damien belonged. Upon his arrival, he found a colony of victims whose bodies were in ruins. They coughed incessantly, their breath was fetid, and their poor, infected bodies exuded foul odours. Father Damien resorted to smoking a pipe in order to counteract this smell.

Father Damien did wonders for the lepers, immediately striving to restore some sense of personal worth in each one. He fenced off the little cemetery he found beside the chapel, thus protecting it from marauding pigs and dogs, and instituted dignified burial ceremonies for those who died, for death was a frequent occurrence. He supervised the construction of cottages, a rectory, and built a home for the lepers' orphaned children. The colony slowly expanded over to Kalaupapa on the west side of the peninsula, where he directed the construction of a serviceable dock, still used (with minor modifications) today. He taught his flock to farm and raise animals so that they gradually became self sufficient. He constantly pestered the government for help, and gradually converted an unruly rabble of physical wreckage into a devout, hard-working, cheerful flock. In the place of the small collection of miserable huts he had found at Kalawao, there now arose the two villages, consisting of neat white cottages with flower gardens and vegetable patches.

Father Damien and his colony became quite famous, to the embarrassment of the local government, for he was constantly, and quite successfully, begging for funds for his leper colony, which the government felt was giving it a bad image.

Father Damien eventually contracted leprosy himself and died in 1889. By this time a number of nuns, priests, nurses, and one Civil War veteran had come to help him run the colony, and it has been able to survive in a state of civilization to this day. The population of the colony peaked at about 1400 in the early 1900s. By 1966, twenty years after therapeutic relief was available to treat the disease, the population had declined to about 162. Many patients, when their disease had been arrested, elected to stay in the colony, and so it eventually consisted mostly of cured lepers who preferred to stay in the colony that had been their home, rather than risk the uncertain reception that might await them in the outside world. Kalaupapa has for many years been administered by the Federal government, which is obliged to keep the colony going until the last leper leaves it, or dies. When we visited it, Richard Marks, a cured leper himself, told us that the population had dwindled, with the death of an old inhabitant the previous night, to 36.

Marks ran a tour company that took visitors around the colony. He calls it Damien Tours and its only physical asset is a very old, yellow and black rattletrap of a school bus, in which he drives his tourists around the colony. The disease had claimed the sight of one of his eyes, but he seemed to us to be otherwise unaffected by the disease. There is a handful of extremely old cars, used by the residents. We saw several of these antiques—mostly Model A Fords and cars of that nature. Marks warned us to get out of the way of any car we saw, because none of the drivers had licenses and they tended to run down pedestrians. This, he explained, was not because of any innate discourtesy to visitors, but because the eyesight of most of the drivers had been sufficiently impaired by the disease that they were often unable to detect the presence of pedestrians on the road.

Marks met us at the airstrip as we parted company from our mules. He gave us a short description of the colony and warned us not to offend the remaining inmates by taking their photographs. There is a company store, an attractive large shop in the middle of the village, but he asked us not to go into it, as the lepers guard their privacy and don't like being gawked at by tourists. He then went off to feed the cats. The peninsula has, he explained, 140 or so resident cats—wild feral cats descended from pets brought by some of the lepers years ago. The cat population is a problem, as it is constantly increasing. Fairly recently they had managed to persuade a veterinary surgeon to pay a visit and spay as many females as they could catch. He pointed out that the spayed cats were recognizable by their clipped ears.

Marks showed us around the neat little village of Kalaupapa and took us into the surprisingly large church built by Father Damien, where we met the resident priest. It had a big, bright interior decorated with Hawaiian motifs and art. He walked us down to the dock—a long, battered concrete and rock wharf. We could see why few ships ever visited. The surf pounded against the windward side, flinging spray over the whole edifice. To navigate anything into the lee of this wharf would require a skilled effort of seamanship. After he had shown us the church, Marks left us to wander round the village of Kalaupapa. He ensconced himself comfortably on a bench in the shade of the church porch, and held forth on the subject of his colony to those of us who chose to stay and listen. The village is a spacious collection of cottages scattered around well kept and extensive lawns. There is a small hospital, a sizable assembly hall, and sundry buildings for storage, to house the village's generator and other communal equipment. Most of the cottages are painted white and all were in good repair. They all seemed to be of one uniform design that indicated that they were government issue, the product of some bureaucratic architect with no imagination. However, the occupants of these little homes had made up for this lack of inspiration by planting beautifully kept gardens around them and decorating them, mostly with flower boxes full of exotic plants. Some had repainted the houses in startling colours and others had added shutters and architectural extras that bespoke the affection and respect the occupants had for their homes. One had been turned into a museum, full of artifacts and photographs of the colony and its inmates, some dating back almost to its inception. A Hawaiian lady, presumably herself a leper, presided over this small museum and was at pains to tell us inquisitive visitors as much as we wanted to know about the colony.

Scattered about the village are a number of statues and memorials to those, mostly nuns and priests, who had served the colony in the past. We came across an old disused 1930's pickup truck. It had been filled with earth and was overflowing with bougainvillea—an eccentric adornment to a collection of sheds holding gardening equipment.

Marks finally roused himself from his porch and chivied us back into the bus. He drove us past a neat cottage adorned with a mass of colourful flowers. This was his own home, tucked away from the main village amongst a group of homesteads and up on the side of a little hill, so that he had a view of the village and its inadequate harbour. He drew our attention to an old car, a Ford Model T, in a lean-to beside the house, which served as its garage. He said that it was not just then in service, as he was waiting for a part from Seattle (ordered some six months previously) to get it going again. One of the problems, he grumbled, with living in the colony was the time it took to requisition anything out of the ordinary. It all had to come from the continental United States and either had to come in on one of the visiting aircraft or on the annual boat, which was how those few who owned vehicles had ferried them to the colony.

Marks then drove us the two and a half miles over to Kalawao on the east side of the peninsula. It was much less hospitable than the fertile, lush environs of Kalaupapa. Open to a strong north wind, it offered little shelter and the shoreline was rocky and spectacularly inhospitable. It was surprisingly cold compared to Kalaupapa. The shoreline was intimidatingly magnificent. Huge cliffs, all covered with trees and bushes and none less than a thousand feet high, ran as far as the eye could see—like a series of monstrous buttresses. It was easy to see why so many of the lepers, cast ashore from their prison ship, had perished a century and a half earlier.

We were fed a spartan lunch, attended by more of the colony cats in search of food from indulgent visitors, and then shown St. Philomena's chapel, a small austere building somewhat ravaged over the years by the elements. The graveyard stands adjacent to the chapel. We were shown Father Damien's grave, fenced in with wooden palings. He had apparently died while effecting repairs to this little church. There were many traces of the old village: a reservoir, which Father Damien had built; the foundations of an old assembly hall; and the remains of a number of the old habitations. Nobody has lived in this village for years, even though services are regularly held in the chapel. Kalaupapa is by far the preferable location, more sheltered, warmer, and with more fertile soil. The inhabitants of Kalawao had gradually drifted over to the western side, attracted by the equable climate there.

Marks was very critical of the Federal administration of the colony. He sounded like a western Canadian talking about Ottawa, and we began to realize that western alienation was not a phenomenon unique to Canada. His references to the Federal civil service consisted of calling those charged with the administration of the colony "some dumb cluck in Washington." He was highly critical of clerks, ignorant of the colony's needs, trying to conduct supervision from six thousand miles away and across half an ocean. He cited a litany of mistakes, some quite costly, that the Washington administration had made. He showed us a six-foot-high, wire-mesh fence that had been built around Kalaupapa to keep the deer out of the gardens and orchards. The problem was that it had been built just below the top of a little slope so that the deer could easily jump over into the village, but because of the slope, could not leap back out. In consequence the villagers were repeatedly opening the gates and shooing the deer out, in order to preserve their fruit and vegetables.

In due course, we were taken back to the corral where our mules, now well fed and rested, were waiting to take us back up the path to the relative civilization of Molokai. We bade goodbye to Richard Marks, of whom we had grown quite fond while he shepherded us around his tiny homeland. We mounted our mules and sorted ourselves into single file. The ascent was not as nerve wracking as the descent had been, partly because we had become used to the precipitous route, and partly because we were looking up rather than down. But halfway back up I saw something that had escaped my notice on the way down. Cut into the face of the cliff was a small cave, two feet high and about ten inches deep. On the floor of this little cavity was a foot-high statue of the Virgin Mary. Fresh flowers were strewn about her feet. I turned to look back at the muleskinner who was riding immediately behind me—the burly, taciturn Hawaiian lad. "What is that for?" I demanded to know. "It's nothing," he hastily replied. I realized from his hurried, over-loud tone of voice that I was not going to wring any further information from him. I strongly suspect that this statue was a memorial to someone who had gone over the edge, but no one was about to confirm my suspicions. We all arrived safely back at the stables, dismounted, and were each of us given a little testimonial that certified that we had, indeed, accessed the leper colony by mule train. It gave the date of this feat and the name of our mule. Mine was called Maikai. I was disappointed not to be able to acquire a bumper sticker for my car.

OMNIUM GATHERUM

BOTTLE SIZES

My curiosity about wine-bottle sizes was triggered by the spectacle of five wine bottles, all of different sizes, in the window of a delicatessen in Ashland, Oregon.

Ashland lies a half a dozen miles north of the California border, a hundred miles inland in the Rogue River valley. At 2,000 feet, the altitude assures a wonderful climate. It is an attractive town of some twenty thousand souls, home to South Oregon University and The Oregon Shakespeare Festival, which is arguably the best repertory theatre in the English-speaking world. The Festival was founded in 1935 and its season each year lasts from February to November. About half its plays are Shakespearean, while the rest are an eclectic selection of classics, musicals, and modern pieces. Occasionally, it produces a world premier. It has three theatres—one an open-air theatre, fashioned like London's famous Globe Theatre—and thus the Festival is able to produce thirty or so performances a week. We have been attending the Festival these last fourteen years. Last fall we saw eight plays in seven days. The company, of some seventy-two actors, is highly professional. The sets are magical and the productions skilled. Two years ago we saw *Pericles, Prince of Tyre*. Without doubt, it contains Shakespeare's silliest plot, but the production was so masterly that when Pericles is reunited in the last scene with his wife, whom he thought he had lost at sea years earlier, I had a tear in my eye. Now, nobody can enjoy a play more than that.

Ashland is populated by academics, students, retired people, theatre folk, and working hippies with dogs. On one occasion, while browsing the window of a bookstore, I encountered a young girl walking a ferret on a lead. Second-hand bookshops abound. The restaurants are first rate, and there are dozens of cottages and B & Bs for the accommodation of visiting theatre buffs. One rarely sees a police car. I can only surmise that there is an underemployed police department tucked away in some back street of the town. Five miles south is Mt. Ashland, which is host to a little ski resort that we were assured never had line ups longer than five minutes.

Adding to the enjoyment of one's visit to this theatrical Mecca is the availability of unending quantities of superb wine. The Rogue Valley is just south of the Willamette Valley, which runs a hundred miles south from Portland. That valley produces, though I say it ever so softly, the finest Burgundy in the world. The French get upset if you call wine Burgundy when it is not produced in the country to the west of the Swiss Alps, so the Oregonian vintners call it Pinot Noir, and Pinot Gris. Oregon is host to just over two hundred wineries. All produce good wine and some bring forth quite exquisite vintages. All the wineries welcome visitors and encourage the tasting of their wares. A trip through a few wineries is an enjoyable experience, if a little tough on the liver. If you plan a wine tour, first buy a copy of the Oregon Winery Guide published by the Oregon Wine Advisory Board and available in any wine shop in Oregon. It is a barrel of information, lists almost every winery in Oregon, and demystifies the etiquette of labelling.

Close by the Festival's three theatres nestles the neat, little, well-stocked delicatessen, the Chateaulin, which is attached to a French restaurant of the same name. The first time I walked past it, I noticed the five wine bottles in the window. They were all different sizes. Four had labels: 375mls, Magnum, Rehoboam, and Methuselah. I was intrigued by the absence of a label on the middle bottle. I entered the shop and accosted the owner. "Why don't you have a label on the middle bottle in your window?"

He smiled sweetly, and said, "Ah, that's a ruse to entice people like you to come into my shop and ask what you just asked. The middle bottle is a Jeroboam." His ruse worked. I bought some paté, two feet of French bread, and several bottles of wine.

The names of the different-sized bottles intrigued me, and embarking on some research, I discovered that there seem to be fifteen sizes of wine bottle: split (also called a piccolo, but only for champagne), Chopine, (but only for Bordeaux), Fillette or Demi bottle (375 ml), Magnum, Marie Jeanne, Double Magnum, Jeroboam, Rehoboam, Methuselah, Imperial, Balthazar, Salmanazar, Nebuchadnezzar and the mighty Melchior. I say "seem to be", because I soon discovered that the size of a particular bottle depended to some extent on what wine the bottle contains. There is a different hierarchy of sizes for Champagne and Burgundy than for Claret, and the amount that a particularly named bottle holds sometimes seems to depend on who is selling the wine.

The custom of storing wine in glass bottles dates back to the fifteenth century. Before that, wine was kept in ceramic or metal pots and jugs. Leather bottles were used by travellers. These were known as *boutilles*, from which the modern English word "bottle" is derived. Towards the twelfth century, glass containers came into use, known variously as flagons, decanters, carafes, and flasks. In Greek and Roman times, wine was stored in Amphorae—the two-handled ceramic jugs that were also used to hold grapes and olive oil. But the modern bottle, with its recessed bottom, is only six hundred years old. The recessed bottom we know today was developed as a means of minimizing the effect of sediment on the wine. Sediment lying in the recess is in contact with less of the wine than it would be if spread across a flat bottom. Different-shaped bottles were developed for different wines: the tall slim-shouldered bottles for hock, square-shouldered for claret, something between the two for Burgundy, and of course, the well-known shape of the Champagne bottle.

My research disclosed the following confusing situation:

According to Liberty Wine Merchants, Champagne and Burgundy have a fixed hierarchy of wine bottle sizes:

> A split is a quarter of a bottle, 7 oz.
> A pint is half a bottle, 14 oz.
> A standard bottle, 750 mL., is one quart or one pint, 11 oz.
> (Yes, I know a quart is two pints, but not in bottle-ese).
> A magnum holds as much as two bottles, is also referred
> to as two quarts.
> A Jeroboam, four bottles.
> A Rehoboam, six bottles.
> A Methuselah, eight bottles.
> A Salmanazar, twelve bottles (a case).
> A Balthazar, sixteen bottles.
> A Nebuchadnezzar, twenty bottles.

But Liberty says that for claret six bottles is a Jeroboam, and eight bottles is an Imperial—just a different name for a Methuselah.

Schott's Food and Drink Miscellany, by Ben Schott, claims that, in addition to Liberty's list, the following exist:

> A Chopine, for Bordeaux only, a third of a bottle,
> A Fillette or Demi, half a bottle, for all kinds of wine,
> A Marie Jeanne, for Bordeaux only, is three bottles,
> A Double Magnum, for Bordeaux only, four bottles,
> An Imperial, eight bottles, for Bordeaux only,
> A Melchior, twenty-four bottles, for all kinds
> of wine. And that's two whole cases!

When the fifteenth-century wine makers settled on the various sizes of bottles to contain their wine, they consulted the Old Testament and chose the names of biblical kings and captains.

Jeroboam, son of Nebat, was a mighty man of valour. Solomon made him ruler of all the charge of the house of Joseph. 1 Kings: 28,16. He founded the Northern Kingdom of Israel when it broke away from the original twelve tribes. Jeroboam had been previously in charge of Solomon's taxes and slave labour.

Nebuchadnezzar was the ruler of Babylon (what is mostly now Iraq), from 630 B.C. to 562 B.C.. He built the hanging gardens of Babylon. In his old age, he went mad and fell to eating grass.

Methuselah (in Genesis 4, called Methushael) was an antediluvian patriarch, said to have lived for 969 years. He was Noah's grandfather.

Balthazar was one of the three Magi. He brought a gift of Myrrh (a symbol of mortality) for the baby Jesus.

Rehoboam was the son of King Solomon and the last king of the united kingdom of Israel. 1 Kings: 11-14. It was his stupidity in increasing taxation that lost him the ten northern tribes to Jeroboam. He reigned for seventeen years and Jeroboam for twenty-two, and there was war between them all their days.

The derivation of a Salmanazar was not easy to trace and this is partly because it is spelt in several ways. The Canadian Oxford English dictionary links it to Shalmaneser V, king of Assyria. There were five kings of that name, but he who figures in 2 Kings: 17-18 conducted ceaseless campaigns against Assyria's neighbours and particularly Israel. This part of the Old Testament makes gruesome reading and confirms the opinion that the near east is in no more turmoil today than it has been, on and off, for six thousand years. The king referred to in Ch. 17-18 is probably the donor of the name to the wine bottle. He ruled Assyria from 726 to 721 B.C.. In Assyrian, the name is Shulmanuasharidu. I have also seen it spelt Salamanazar. Five of the Kings of Assyria, from 1274 to 721 B.C., bore the same name, though there were other kings interspersed throughout that period.

Melchior was another of the magi. He brought Jesus frankincense—a symbol of divinity. The third Magus was Gaspar. There is no known explanation as to why he didn't rate a bottle size. Gaspar brought the gift of gold.

Different sources give different sizes for some of the bottles. Bottle sizing seems not to be an exact science. *Alexis Lichine's Encyclopedia of Wines & Spirits* holds that a Nebuchadnezzar is only ten bottles and a Balthazar "sixteen reputed quarts or 12.8 litres."

The Oxford English Dictionary claims that a Jeroboam can be either ten or twelve bottles.

Buying a Melchior of wine would surely be an intimidating experience. One would leave the liquor store carrying a bottle that weighs, by my calculation, about sixty-five pounds. Drop it and several hundred dollars worth of wine would spill into the gutter. Better to send the butler to fetch it.

Further research disclosed that beer also has its hierarchy of bottle sizes, as follows:

A nip is a quarter of a pint,
A small is half a pint,
A large is a pint,
A flagon is a quart, (two pints),

An anker is ten gallons, and,
A tun is two hundred and sixteen gallons.

The latter two quantities would come in barrels, rather than bottles.

Then we must remember that there is the schooner. This is a measure used mainly in Australia. Not unexpectedly, schooners are not all of a uniform size. In Adelaide, a schooner holds 9 oz., and in New South Wales, 15 oz., so the schooner's size depends on where, in Australia, you happen to be on walkabout when you order one.

I remembered that the Royal Navy used to issue (and perhaps still does) a daily tot of rum to each member of the crew of its ships. So I turned my research to spirits and discovered that a tot can be a sixth, fifth, quarter, or a third of a pint, and a noggin is a gill, which is a quarter of a pint. In Elizabethan times, a quarter of a pint was called a gyll. I was surprised that the stout trenchermen of the sixteenth century would have had a name for so small a quantity of spirits.

There are other receptacles that hold liquor, demijohns, pipes, butts, and hogsheads. *The Oxford English Dictionary* (OED) supplies the information, but of course, none of these containers is a uniform size.

A demijohn is a large bottle with a bulging body and a narrow neck, holding anything from two to fifteen gallons, though the most usual size is five gallons. It is encased in a wicker or rush basket with two handles, by which to carry it around. This is the favourite container for home-brewed beer. There is some argument about the etymology of this word. Some scholars claim it derives from Persian, or Farsi, but the better theory is that its origin is French—Dame Jeanne, corrupted (in translation) into demijohn.

A pipe of port is a consignment of one hundred and twenty bottles, enough to start an epidemic of gout. The OED, however, has it that a pipe is "a large cask of wine" and tells us that it is variously a half a tun, or two hogsheads, or four barrels, usually one hundred and five imperial gallons. Naturally, the OED concedes that the size varies with the contents.

A hogshead, the OED tells us, is simply a large cask for liquids, which varies in capacity according to not only the contents but also the locality. In London, a hogshead of beer is fifty-four gallons, and of ale, forty-eight. Elsewhere it holds fifty-one gallons of beer.

A butt is a cask varying from one hundred and eight to one hundred and forty gallons. But the OED maintains that, when it contains ale, it equals two hogsheads, for beer, one hundred and eight gallons, and for ale one hundred and twenty-six, but it concedes that these standards are not always adhered to. Shakespeare has George, Duke of Clarence (a younger son of Edward IV), murdered in the Tower by being drowned in a butt of Malmsey wine. This incident is corroborated elsewhere than in Richard III, so we do not have to rely on Shakespeare's politically adaptable imagination for its veracity. A butt of one hundred and twenty-six gallons would certainly accommodate quite a sizable Duke, put to death in a cask about three times the size of today's standard forty-gallon barrel.

The following year, we made another of our annual pilgrimages to Ashland; we saw eight plays in six days. But when I went to the Chateaulin to buy some cheese and French bread, I noticed that all the five bottles in the window were labelled. I entered the shop only to find that it had fallen into new hands—hands that obviously were not privy to the sly bait of the absent label.

THE GREAT DEBATE

The question before the special general meeting was whether or not the club should admit women as members. It was the only question to be discussed and the meeting had been called specifically to deal with it. The vote required an amendment to the constitution of the club, and this could only be achieved by a vote of 75 per cent in favour.

Soon after the great fire of 1886, a group of Vancouver business men, envious of Victoria's Union Club, which had been established in 1879, decided to form a club in their own city. Naturally it was to be a gentlemen's club. The old country had dozens of gentlemen's clubs, and this one was to be modelled on those bulwarks of male superiority. In fact, the English clubs had not started out as gentleman's clubs. Originally their membership included women. However, in the early nineteenth century, they encountered trouble with the young Regency bucks bringing streetwalkers into the clubs. It was difficult to distinguish between some member's wife and a lady of the night, so they were driven to resort to excluding women altogether.

Money was raised and the first Vancouver Club premises were opened in 1894, on land purchased from the CPR, on Hastings Street. There were 175 members, and all were men—well, actually, all gentlemen. Ladies were not permitted entry to the premises, except as guests of a member when the club gave a ball. In that case, ladies, an essential ingredient for any ball, were welcomed. In 1905, there was a petition by a small group to permit members to bring their wives or lady friends to dine at the club. The club's legal counsel, E.P. Davis, gave an opinion that, since the constitution of the club referred to members and guests with the masculine personal pronoun, he, him etc., it would take an amendment to the constitution before ladies could come as guests of members. He charged a $5.00 fee for the opinion.

In 1915, a resolution was passed that "members wishing to entertain guests at dinner in the private dining room shall be permitted to have ladies among the guests." Then, in 1918, the wives and unmarried sisters of members were allowed to use the ladies' dining room for luncheon, afternoon tea, and dinner. Ladies under the age of eighteen were not to be admitted.

The old building had been replaced in 1931, by the one that now stands at 915 West Hastings Street. It was built with two front doors: the main door, up an elegant flight of stairs, and another door discretely off to the side. Any lady entering the club had to use the side door. It opened into a small lobby and cloak room. Later on, an elevator was installed that took ladies up to the ladies' dining room and lounge. Beyond these confines, ladies were not supposed to venture. In 1944, ladies were finally admitted to dinner in the main dining room. It took two world wars to have members change their attitude towards having ladies dine in the club.

I never joined the Vancouver Club. I viewed it as moribund and stuffy and I had had a run in with its secretary manager, John P. Chutter, when I had an office in the Bank of Canada building across the street from the club. I was annoyed by the daily emission of thick black smoke from the club's chimney as it burnt the daily garbage. I complained, to Chutter, who didn't seem to care, and then to the City of Vancouver. The City took steps to stop the club polluting the atmosphere and Chutter had disliked me ever since. The feeling was mutual.

However, ladies were still not permitted in the main premises of the club during the day. Sometime in the 1970s, I was invited to a reception in the club for the Law Reform Commission of Canada. The reception had been organized by E. Davie Fulton, PC, QC, MP., then Minister of Justice and Attorney General of Canada. The commission had one lady member, a French Canadian Judge. The reception was in full swing when the odious Chutter discovered that a lady was present in the off limits part of the club. He confronted Davie Fulton and demanded that she leave. A number of us discovered what was going on and determined that if she were thrown out, we would leave too. The Judge also learned what was afoot and offered to leave of her own accord, rather than spoil the party. It was all very embarrassing. Fulton took Chutter by the elbow and gently ushered him out of the room. He must have exercised all his tact and charm, for he managed to persuade Chutter to go about his business and leave us all alone.

The annals of the club record one instance when a member, lunching in the bar, suffered a heart attack. An ambulance was called and a cardiologist accompanied it to the club. The problem was that the cardiologist was a woman. The staff insisted that she use the side door and tried to prevent her from entering the bar, which was (of course) off limits for ladies.

As a result of all this, I joined the University Club instead. Even that club was not immune from institutional misogyny. It had been formed by a number of academics and businessmen, who were offended by the Vancouver Club's anti-Semitic tendencies, but even this liberal-minded club did not admit women members. The University Club was in the habit of bestowing honorary memberships on the presidents of the Universities in British Columbia. In 1975, Dr. Pauline Jewitt was installed as president of Simon Fraser University. She was nominated for membership in the University Club. This required a change in the club's bylaws, which when it came to a vote, was turned down by a vote of two to one. Dr. Jewitt was indignant at being excluded because of her sex. She issued a memorandum asking staff and faculty at Simon Fraser to boycott the University Club.

In 1988, both clubs were in some financial distress and membership in both was dwindling. After lengthy negotiations, both clubs determined to amalgamate. It was a condition of the University club's decision that the humiliating side entrance, reserved for ladies, be closed and that ladies be admitted through the front door. So despite my original dislike of the club, and caught up in the march of progress, I became a member of the Vancouver Club.

But the members were growing restive. There was pressure to admit women. Other clubs were doing so. The Naval and Military Club in London had been forced, at the end of the Second World War, to admit women members of the armed forces. After all, women had served with distinction in the armed forces and it was illogical, if not actually churlish, not to admit them to an armed forces' club.

In 1994, a formal motion was brought before the membership of the Vancouver Club for this purpose. The special general meeting took place in the graceful main dining room. It was packed to overflowing for the occasion. Those proponents of the admission of women had dragooned as many like-minded members as possible to attend. There were lengthy and eloquent speeches made, for and against. Older members reminded the assembled multitude that the Vancouver Club was and had originally been intended to be a "gentlemen's club". It was argued that the increased membership would improve the club's finances.

One member could not understand what the other members had against women. He liked women. Didn't the other members also like them, or was there something about the members that he had not been told? He resumed his seat in stony and unappreciated silence.

The debate rumbled on. Members began repeating what others had already said. It was getting late. We were all growing tired. Surely we should vote on it and then we could all go home. It was not obvious which side was going to win this divisive wrangle.

It was at this point that Allan Williams rose to his feet. Allan was a respected lawyer. He had recently been Attorney General of British Columbia, a member of Premier Bill Bennett's cabinet. He looked around and waited till the room grew silent—the orator's old trick. "When I was working in Victoria," he said, "I lived at the Union Club during the week and came home on weekends. I often dined at the club. There were three old British ex-army officers who lived at the club, and they always dined together every evening. Their conversation was usually delivered at parade square volume and it was impossible not to overhear what they were saying. One evening, one of them said to the others, 'Ye know, it's a pity, but you never see ladies riding sidesaddle these days, do you?'"

The vote in favour of admitting women to membership passed by the required majority.

THE DOG BOOTS

Everyone was talking about the events of the previous day. There was no laughter. The crash of two airliners into the World Trade Centre and one into the Pentagon had taken all joy out of what otherwise would have been a beautiful summer's day. We had all watched, on television, the horror of the second aircraft hitting the building. We had seen the sickening sight of people jumping and falling from floors so high up that they stood no chance of survival, presumably a choice between a clean swift death and a slower, agonizing incineration. The television showed us scenes of police and firefighters and rescue crews desperately combing through the huge piles of rubble in search of survivors. Heavy equipment was gingerly removing debris into trucks to be taken away. Heavy rain was impeding the search for any who might have survived the terrible collapse of the buildings. There were scenes of dogs, mostly German shepherds, sniffing around the wreckage, searching for live bodies under the rubble.

The blood banks in Vancouver had suddenly become very busy as people donated blood for the victims in New York. Money was being accepted by the banks. A rescue team was readied to fly to New York, although ultimately it did not leave, as there seemed so little prospect of finding anyone. No one in the top floors above where the aircraft had struck could have survived, and those at the bottom who might have done so would be buried so deep under one hundred floors of disintegrated building that it would take too long to reach them before they died. Most disheartening was the news that there were, in fact, people alive in the rubble. Cell phone calls had been received from several survivors from under the debris, but of course, it was impossible to tell where they were. The rescue dogs were working through the carnage in vain, their tails wagging with the excitement of being on the job.

On Wednesday September 12, 2001, I drove up to the local shopping centre in search of some items for the weekend, including some dog crumbles for our German shepherd, Guinness. After visiting the bank, the grocery, and the post office, I walked into the pet store. It was unusually busy. Two women were at the cash desk counter. I could see the green bag

257

of crumbles on the floor behind the cash desk. It had been put aside for me to pick up.

I waited while the first woman was served by René, the manager of the pet store. The second woman, short, middle aged, and fair haired, began a long conversation with the manager. Irritated at the delay, I turned and examined the pet-oriented merchandise behind me: squeaky toys, a cat scratching post, a doghouse in the shape of an igloo. That last one was labelled, "Dogloo". It crossed my mind that that could denote a dog out-house, as well as a kennel. I turned back to the counter to find the manager still in conversation with his customer. On the counter was a packet of dog biscuits, and a large plastic bag containing four boots. Dog boots. The feet were black and the shafts to cover the dog's legs were blue, with Velcro straps to hold them in place. The manager and the customer were discussing the boot sizes and usage. Eventually he put the boots and dog biscuits in a bag and ran up the price on the cash register. "I'll give you a thirty-one percent discount on the boots," he said. "Oh, thank you," said his customer. She picked up her bag and hustled out.

At last, my turn had come. I told the manager what I wanted. He bent and picked up the bag of dog crumbles and put it on the counter. As he was processing my credit card, I asked him what on earth the woman had wanted dog boots for. I fortunately did not say so, but thought boots for dogs a foolish extravagance, like dog raincoats—only for the most pampered of canines.

Afterwards I was glad that I had not expressed this sentiment, for the manager then explained why his customer had bought these items. "She's been watching the news on television," he said. "There was a news item about the rescue dogs. Apparently the rubble is full of glass and sharp, twisted metal. It cuts their feet and interferes with their work looking for bodies. That lady wanted to send the boots to the rescue teams to protect their dogs' feet."

THE PRINCIPLES OF TRAVEL

John Welson is a stockbroker of our acquaintance. An American, he enjoys travelling and tends to journey to places that most people would not normally visit. One day he hit upon the idea of visiting Buenos Aires. Argentina in the year two thousand would not be most travellers' destination of choice. Its economy was in chaos. There had been a run on the banks. Riots had broken out and been suppressed, and the peso was in a free fall against the dollar. John reasoned that, since he possessed dollars to spend, none of this would matter. He was right. Argentina turned out to be extremely inexpensive, and he said that its capital was a grand old city—sophisticated, elegant, and cosmopolitan. He found the people to be kind and accommodating.

Just before he left on this foray, he was bent over in his back garden disinterring some weeds. He heard a voice behind him summoning his attention. He turned to find his neighbour leaning over the fence. She is a tall, gaunt, forthright English woman of indeterminate age, but likely closer to eighty than sixty. She engaged John in conversation and eventually learned that he was about to leave on holiday for foreign parts. "Oh," she barked, "well, you know the rule for travellers, don't you? Always take half the luggage and twice the money." And with that admonition she disappeared, leaving John to his weeds and his travel plans.

But the precept, delivered at him over his fence, lodged in his mind. For the Argentina trip he packed less than was his habit—not half, but significantly less. He admits that he wanted for nothing on the journey and still carried with him clothes he never wore. Half, he thinks, probably brings one to the bare essentials, while reducing the burden of luggage to a minimum. Since Argentina was so inexpensive he was unable to test the second half of his neighbour's principle, but from his past experience in Europe, he believes it to be sound. The problem is that, though it is easy enough to reduce a load of luggage, it is not so easy to find the money to double a travel allowance.

An Assurance of Competence

It was July 1988. They were celebrating the fiftieth anniversary of the establishment of Tweedsmuir Park, named after Canada's fifteenth Governor General. The festivities took place in the village on the Bella Coola Highway. At the same time, the Alexander Mackenzie Society was sponsoring a celebration of Alexander Mackenzie's trek from Lake Athabaska to the Dean Channel, where he inscribed upon a rock Canada's most famous memorial, "Alexander Mackenzie, from Canada, by land, the twenty second of July 1793".

We had been invited to join an expedition on horseback from the Mackenzie Valley, in central Tweedsmuir Park, down the old grease trail to the Bella Coola Valley, following in Mackenzie's footsteps exactly 195 years earlier. There were about a dozen of us on this trip, which was scheduled to take two weeks. It was led by Dave Dorsey, the grandson of the famous American guide of the same name. Dave had a small ranch at Anahim Lake, functioned as a hunting guide, and ran horseback tours in summer. His mother was a member of the Chilcotin band, and he was married to Joyce, who was ten years older than he. We discovered later that she had an arts degree from the University of Washington. Now she was a rancher's wife, a cook for the expedition, and the engine at the administrative heart of the venture.

We had been invited on this trip by our neighbour, Ainslie Manson, a member of the Alexander Mackenzie Society. She and her husband, a urologist and head of surgery at St. Paul's Hospital, in Vancouver, were to be joined by a group of local Mackenzie enthusiasts, who made up the rest of the guests. Joyce had told us to rendezvous at a point on the Bella Coola Highway thirty miles west of Anahim Lake. "You can't miss the camp," she said. So, at the appointed hour, we drove west on the highway in search of our hosts. Thirty miles went by and we were still driving through brush and lodge-pole pine. No camp.

Some way past the thirty-mile point, as we were beginning to fear we had missed the Dorseys' camp, we saw a couple of battered old pickup trucks beside the road, and some people in the woods. I decided to stop to ask for directions. As I walked across the road, I could see a half dozen snotty-nosed children playing with a dog. There were some women in the trees who had a fire going. A man with a broken leg in a cast was gamely trying to chop wood. A canvas sheet was strung between the trees, and beneath it I could see a pile of cardboard boxes. There was one horse munching at leisure from the grass beside the road—its front legs hobbled to stop it wandering off. As I approached, several men ambled over to the trucks and hefted goods out of them, several saddles, more cardboard boxes, and a quantity of tarps and rope. The whole scene looked like a troop of gypsies making camp for the night.

I walked over to this raggle-taggle band to be confronted by one of the largest men I have ever encountered. His dirty, brown, ten-gallon hat gave him the appearance of being taller than he actually was, but he still looked as wide as he was tall, and I judged his weight to be little short of three hundred pounds. I guessed him to be a member of the local Chilcotin band. I addressed this somewhat intimidating apparition. "I think we're lost. We are supposed to meet Dave Dorsey somewhere along this road. Do you know where we would be likely to find him?" There was a short silence as he surveyed me closely. He pursed his lips, "Yup. That's us." My heart fell. What had we got ourselves into? Were we going to consign our safety, on a two-week trip into the uninhabited wilderness, to this troop of disordered and grubby misfits? I introduced myself. He held out his hand. "Dave Dorsey," he said, as I winced in the grasp of his huge fist. He invited me to get our kit and join them for supper. I returned to our Volkswagen van and diffidently told Gill that these were the people we were going with into Tweedsmuir Park. We briefly discussed the option of bailing out of the venture there and then. We decided that we could not do that. We would be letting the Mansons down, and anyway how would we explain our sudden defection to Dave Dorsey? It would be distinctly unseemly, if not actually cowardly, to do a fast U-turn and leave without any explanation. It was while we were mulling over our options that the Mansons drove up. We expressed our misgivings to them, but they had met the Dorseys before and assured us that we were in good hands. At least Ainslie did. I noticed a certain hesitant reluctance on the part of David.

At this point we heard the sound of horse's hooves in the distance. Out of a cloud of dust, rising beside the road, about thirty horses trotted up, shepherded by three women in cowboy hats—obligatory wear amongst the Chilcotin ranchers. We eventually settled in for the night after a supper of T-bone steaks, baked potatoes, and assorted vegetables. We were surprised at the quality of the fare produced by Joyce Dorsey.

We found out over supper that most of the people in the camp were not coming on the trip with us. The children, the man with the broken leg (an injury he had sustained a month earlier at a stag party when Dave Dorsey fell on him), and all the extra men were staying behind. Some were to drive our cars, to be left for us at Tweedsmuir Lodge where our excursion was to terminate. Dave and Joyce were to go with us, as well as their eight-year-old daughter, Leslie. Leslie turned out to be a superb horsewoman. She rode her pony bareback for the whole trip. Sometime into the second week, I watched as she rode up to a wild hedge beside a stream. She needed to get across it. She surveyed the obstacle from her seat on the pony, turned it round, trotted back fifty yards, and then set it at the hedge at full gallop, clearing it without difficulty. Several of us complimented her on this feat. She had no idea why we were so impressed.

The Dorseys had hired three wranglers to help on the ride. These were the three women who had shown up with all the horses, only half of which were for us to ride. The rest were pack horses. All three women were ranchers' wives, pleased to have a couple of weeks off from helping run their ranches, and to earn a little pocket money. Ginger was a big, strong, handsome woman wearing an Australian Akubra hat. Wanda was married to Dave's cousin. She and her husband had a big spread near Kleena Kleene. The third was Françoise. She looked about eighteen, but was in fact nearer to thirty. A pretty kid with long, black, curly hair, she was married to a man much older than herself. That was what Wanda and Ginger told us, with knowing nods of their heads that bespoke some disapproval and doubts about this liaison. Françoise had a master's degree in psychology from UBC and her father was, or had been, the Dean of Arts at the same university. She looked completely out of place. Small and dainty, she would have been more at home at a faculty tea.

David Manson expressed serious misgivings about Françoise's ability to perform the heavy work expected of a wrangler on our expedition. What if there was a crisis? Would she be able to cope?

The next morning we were all assigned our horses. David was given Slats. Slats was a white horse with black blotches all over him. He had weak eyes, it was said, so they had painted an indigo substance around his eyes to cut down the glare of the sun. At fifteen and a half hands, David wondered if Slats wasn't too big for him. Françoise led Slats, by a halter, over to where David was surveying the collection of horses. She had a western saddle on her shoulder. "Here. Hold this while I get his bridle on," she said, as she handed David the saddle. She inserted the bit into Slat's mouth and buckled up the bridle. David decided to put the saddle on to save Françoise having to do it. He lifted the saddle up, but forgot that he should put the saddle blanket in place first. Françoise took the blanket and put it in place. She took the saddle from David and heaved it up onto the horse, jiggling it into place. Then she bent and grasped the girth to bring it under the horse and buckle it to the other side of the saddle. She had her back to a large tree, so she was between the tree and Slats. Slats took against the prospect of having to carry someone on his back all day, so he sidled over and began to press Françoise into the tree—an old trick that horses have used ever since the first man ever rode one. David was aghast. She would be crushed. He stood in anxiety as he wondered what he should do.

As soon as she realized what Slats was up to, Françoise brought her knee up into the horse's ribs, a sharp movement that instantly caused Slats to step sideways away from her. Then she swore at him, "Goddamn you! You stupid fucking son of a bitch. You do that again, I'll beat the shit out of you." Then she kneed him again sharply in the ribs.

David listened in awe to the abuse Françoise hurled at the horse. He later told us that it was this tirade that persuaded him that, yes, he was in good hands, and need never have harboured doubts about Françoise's capability.

ERNIE WINSTANLEY

The voice on the telephone was immediately recognizable as that of David Purvis. He was an old friend, one of a group of amiable roustabouts with whom I shared a ski cabin at Mt. Baker in the winters. "How would you like to go shooting grouse on Galiano Island next weekend," he asked, without any further introduction. The idea was appealing, although I had never shot a grouse, nor any other bird for that matter, and I owned no shotgun. We discussed the project for a while and formed a plan. David arranged the ferry trip and somewhere to stay. I set about laying my hands on a shotgun and eventually borrowed a 12 gauge from Jimmy Lawrence, another old friend and fellow lawyer. David brought his own gun. Thus armed, literally, we set out by ferry on the Friday evening.

David had booked us in at the only hotel he knew, the Bellhouse Inn, which turned out to be a lovely old farmhouse at the neck of Mary Anne Point, which juts into the eastern entrance of Active Pass. Then it was surrounded by acres of farmland, which are now, alas, littered with summer cottages. There was a huge lawn that sloped down to the sea, dotted with fruit trees, under which sheep were grazing. I don't think the Bellhouses ever mowed this lawn. The sheep acted as lawn mowers *and* fertilizer spreaders. The Bellhouse family, in addition to farming their land, ran a bed and breakfast, though Mrs. Bellhouse, if pressed, would provide other meals as well, served with her family and odd farmhands. The family included two remarkably pretty daughters in their late teens, whom David and I attempted to woo with startling lack of success. In retrospect, their aloof lack of interest in us was probably due to shyness, though at the time I assumed that they were so attractive that they were used to young men paying court to them and thus treated such approaches as ours with disdain.

On Saturday, furnished with lunches packed by Mrs. Bellhouse, we set out to bag our quota of grouse. We thought the local mountain, which dominates the western entrance to Active Pass, would be the likely lair of our prey, so we walked for hours around its base and halfway up its steep slopes. No grouse. Not one. A bird of indeterminate species flew through the trees. Frustrated by our lack of a better quarry, we both fired at it. We both missed. It may have been a crow.

We returned to the Bellhouse Farm, hot, dusty, tired, and embarrassed at our completely unsuccessful hunting expedition. Mr. Bellhouse listened to our description of the mysterious absence of grouse with a slightly cynical grin and said nothing. He did, however, invite us to take part in the annual Galiano turkey shoot to be held that Sunday afternoon and offered to give us a ride to it.

On Saturday night, the locals put on a dance in the village hall. This event was dry, as was the custom in those days. People entered the village hall furtively clutching plain brown paper bags, which contained bottles of liquor, mostly rye, the drink of choice for most people then. Purvis had a bottle of rye, but no bag in which to conceal it, so we hid it behind a stump outside the hall. We tried to interest the Bellhouse girls in sharing it, but they seemed mildly offended at the suggestion and only consented to dance with us out of an apparent sense of obligation to their parents' guests. It was with no small sense of humiliation that we observed the gaiety and verve with which they danced with the local youths.

I had never been to a turkey shoot. This one consisted of a clay pigeon contest and a .22 calibre rifle competition along with a farmers' market. At that time, I was a member of the Canadian militia and had twice been to Camp Wainwright, east of Edmonton, on officers' training courses, where I had been taught how to fire a rifle. Army rifles in that era were the old, trusty, Lee Enfield 303's and I got quite good at target practice. I once scored 93 out of 100, which I was told, would have been a respectable score, even at Bisley.

The clay pigeon shoot was the first event. Purvis and I paid our entry fees and our names were entered in the list of shooters. Each contestant fired once, followed by the next. If you missed you were defaulted. If you hit the pigeon you entered the next round and so on until only one shooter was left: the winner of the turkey. I was by no means sure what I would do with a turkey, but at that point I had no hope of getting past the first few rounds, so the turkey and its fate in my hands was academic. Perhaps I could sell it. I was then an impecunious lawyer earning about $250 a month and a prize of any sort would have been a bonanza.

Now, I had only rarely fired a shotgun before, including the day before at the crow, and again that Sunday morning, just before the turkey shoot. However, as a teenager in England I had heard about clay pigeon shoots. I remembered being told by a local farmer about a technique for hitting these flying objects. The pigeon, a small clay version of the Greek discus, is projected into the air at speed by a spring-loaded arm, which is released by its operator on the command from the shooter. "PULL!" The clay projectile rockets upwards very fast, slows down as it traces a parabola, gliding to the ground, unless broken up in the air by the shot from the shooter's gun. There is a point in the pigeon's flight when it ceases to climb and begins to descend. For a split second the bird hangs as if stationary, motionless, moving neither to right or left. That, my farmer friend told me, was the instant to fire, when it was stationary in the sights of the shooter. Thus it was not necessary to judge the speed of the brute and estimate how far ahead of it to aim, as you would if you were aiming at some poor partridge. Armed with the memory of my farmer friend's advice, I watched the early contestants and noted the flight of the Galiano pigeons. I realized that, standing where the shooters were stationed, there was indeed a split second when the bird hung, as if stationary, in mid-air, just before it slowed and fell to earth. I was sixth in the line of shooters. I watched the first five raise their shotguns. Each cried "PULL!" and the pigeon shot up at a 60 degree angle. Each shooter swept his gun around until he thought he was aiming sufficiently ahead of the fast-moving target and then fired. It seemed to me that each man was trying to hit his bird as soon as possible and before it flew out of range. This was clearly quite an art. The pigeon must have been travelling at 100 miles an hour, and though it decelerated quickly, it was still travelling very fast when they all fired at it.

My name was called. I stepped forward and raised my gun. I shouted "PULL!" with some authority and followed the bird in my sights. I waited and waited and heard a murmur from the crowd of accomplished shots standing behind me, clearly wondering why I had not fired. The bird reached its apogee and hung there, motionless from my perspective. I pulled the trigger. The bird disintegrated in a most satisfactory manner. There was a slightly surprised buzz from the crowd, which clearly thought I had waited too long to fire.

About half the original shooters entered the second round. I was now the third shooter. The first two fired as soon as they could. One missed. I followed my previous procedure and fired as the bird hung in the air, poised to fall to the ground. It disintegrated, though not quite as decisively as the first had. Half the bird continued its flight and the rest fell to the ground in three or four small pieces. I realized that waiting this long to fire had its disadvantages. Shot from a shotgun spreads out and slows down before petering out. Thus, at the distance I was firing, fewer shot will hit the target and at a slower velocity.

The contest continued. Most of the duffers had been eliminated by the third round. Those who were left were good shots, so as the event wore on fewer shooters dropped out. By the tenth round there followed several rounds when everybody got his bird. By the fifteenth round there were three of us left. I began to wonder what I should do with my turkey. I decided that I would give it to Mrs. Bellhouse, partly to encourage her to ingratiate us with her daughters.

There was a pause in the proceedings for tea and soft drinks. I welcomed the respite. My ears were ringing with the noise of the firing and my right shoulder was becoming sore from the unaccustomed recoil of the shotgun.

During the tea interval, several amiable know-it-alls came up to me, asking to see my gun and marvelling at the distance it seemed to be able to reach. Several asked why I waited so long to fire. I decided not to explain. After ten minutes, the contest resumed. The next round saw the elimination of one of us three. The thought of the prize made me nervous and my heart rate accelerated. I began to tremble with excitement. Two rounds went by in which I was firing first. Then in the next round, my bird fell to earth unharmed. I had missed, or perhaps the shot had scattered sufficiently that it passed around the bird. My opponent, a gruff uncommunicative and self-assured countryman wearing an Andy Capp hat, still needed to down his last bird. If he missed we would go another round. He seemed to fire almost as the bird left the trap. It exploded into a thousand pieces and the prospect of my turkey exploded with it. I turned and congratulated my opponent who responded with a grunt that indicated some contempt for a young city interloper.

Earlier that day, just after breakfast, I had strolled down Mary Anne Point, taking Jimmy Lawrence's shotgun with me. It was a lovely, soft fall morning. There were birds everywhere and a loon fishing off the point. I was joined by a tall old man who had been staying at the Bellhouse B & B. We fell into conversation. He asked what I did for a living, and when I told him that I was a lawyer, he asked if I knew his nephew, Allan Billsland. I knew him well. He was a friend of mine. He had articled at the firm where I worked, just one year after me. When he was called to the bar, he went to practise in Kelowna, where he has lived ever since. The old man told me that his name was Ernie Winstanley and reminded me that Allan Bilsland's second name was Winstanley—Allan Winstanley Bilsland.

He then fell to reminiscing about his life and told me that he had been involved in the Yukon gold rush. He had been on board a steamer that had exploded and sunk. He said that he was the only survivor and that the authorities could not find out what had caused the wreck, though he knew, because he had been standing on the fore-deck, which had as part of its cargo a pile of boxes of dynamite secured by rope at the bow. A cabin boy was standing close to him, shooting birds with a rifle. A bird flew across the bow of the boat. The boy followed the bird, keeping it in the sights of his rifle. Just as the bird disappeared behind the piled boxes of dynamite, he fired, hitting the dynamite, which exploded in a huge fireball. Ernie was blown overboard and swam to shore. The boat foundered very quickly, taking all the crew and passengers with it, except Ernie. He swore that the reason he survived was because he had been wearing a set of Stanfield long johns, thick and covering him from ankle to neck and wrists. He made a claim against the owners of the ship for loss of all his possessions, but he could not produce his ticket as it had gone down with the ship. The owners claimed that he was a stowaway. Ernie says that was the reason that all the accounts of the wreck hold that there were no survivors. Pierre Berton mentions the wreck in his book *The Klondyke*, (page 140). He says,

"The Clara Nevada, ignoring the laws against booking passengers when the cargo contained dynamite, blew sky high between Skagway and Juneau with the loss of all sixty-five souls, except for the inevitable dog, who survived." Ernie never mentioned a dog.

I later did some research into the sinking of this ship. It is a well-known disaster in the annals of the gold rush. The sinking occurred on February 5, 1898. Some accounts claim that 104 people were lost. Another maintains that there were four survivors. This demonstrates how careful one must be, if it matters, when relying on newspaper accounts. What is certain is that the ship went down, and that there was no explanation for the explosion. It was owned by the Pacific and Alaska Transportation Company and was southbound out of Skagway and went down off Eldred Rock. I was surprised that a ship going south out of Skagway would be carrying dynamite. I was also surprised at the date, in the middle of winter. No wonder Ernie owed his survival to his Stanfields long johns.

We stood chatting for a while at the end of Mary Anne Point. I remarked on the loon swimming just off the beach. Ernie observed that it was not possible to shoot a loon on the water. I didn't believe him and said so. He said that loons will dive so fast that no shot can kill them. He challenged me to shoot the loon. I did not want to as I had no wish to kill it. He was very insistent and after a prolonged argument, I relented, aimed at the loon and fired. I saw the pattern of shot hitting the water all around the loon, which had dived as soon as I fired. There was a long pause. "There," I said, "Look what you've made me go and do. I've killed it."

"Wait, wait," said Ernie. Sure enough, after about a minute, which seemed like an hour, the loon surfaced, some distance away, shook his head and swam off.

THE HEFFEL GALLERY

We had time to kill before our appointment. Hard by where we had parked the car was an old bank building. It had once been a branch of the Bank of Montreal. Some new broom of a president had embarked on a program of rationalization, the word now in vogue for what used to be called scrapping something. The branch had closed and all its customers had to move their accounts elsewhere. That left the bank with an old building of limited use. Under the Bank Act of Canada, banks are not permitted to own real estate, except for their own immediate use. Thus the Bank of Montreal put its venerable old building up for sale. It had been purchased by an art dealer and turned into an art gallery where one could view and buy all kinds of art, sculptures, tapestries, modern paintings by BC artists, and some by minor old masters.

The gallery was holding a show of Joe Plaskett pastels and this attracted us inside. Plaskett was then living in Paris, so most of the paintings were from Europe, though there were a few he had done in the Queen Charlotte Islands some years earlier. The gallery was spacious. The Heffels had renovated it with some skill and had created a tranquil environment, ideal for the unhurried examination of what they had on offer. I wandered around looking at this and that. We had no intention of buying anything. The Plasketts were a temptation, but we already had one—a pastel of Santa Maria della Salute in Venice, given to me by the Vancouver Bar Association as a reward for editing the Advocate, but it was fun to browse around. I wandered off and found myself in a room that was completely bare except for an easel facing away from me. The old building's thick walls successfully kept out the sounds of the street, and this bright, airy room had about it the stillness of a chapel. Such ecclesiastical calm promotes concentration on one's devotions. The stillness and silence in this room forced one's attention on the picture that the easel displayed. I walked round the easel and saw a quite small pencil sketch perhaps eight inches square. As I scrutinized it I became fascinated. It was a sketch of Salome dancing before Herod. The seventh veil had fallen and she was completely naked. Her back was to the artist. Herod sat facing her, a fat old man in Arabian robes with a very strange cushion-shaped fez on his head. The expression on his face was that of a man with a problem he could not solve, which indeed Herod had on that occasion. The King always bedded the girls who danced for him, but Salome was his stepdaughter and she wanted something he was not willing to give. His expression was a combination of lust, anxiety, and embarrassment. What attracted me was the force and energy of the sketch. Salome had worked up to a frenzy of activity. One leg was flung forward towards the King, her arms curved above her head, she seemed poised to pirouette. The whole picture was magically overlaid with understated overtones of lust, sin, cruelty, and a thousand generations of cunning, all concentrated in Salome's gestures.

I stared at the sketch for a long while. I was mesmerized by its simple brilliance and energy. There was not one line too many, no curve out of place. Yet the artist had laid bare this whole brutal, legendary story in this simple startling sketch.

I would dearly have liked to buy it. I looked down at the price. $10,000. Out of the question. Reading the price brought me back to reality with a start, and I began to wonder why the gallery was asking so much for it. After all it was only a pencil sketch, and quite small. I looked at the card pinned to the edge of the easel to see who had drawn this little master-piece. The name on the card explained everything. It was a Picasso.

FAREWELL DUTHIE BOOKS

Bill Duthie was once employed by the Macmillan Company of Canada as a bookseller and agent. He was sent to Vancouver to represent Macmillan's. In 1957, he tired of peddling Macmillan's wares and decided to establish his own retail book store. So he mortgaged his house and opened up shop at the corner of Robson and Howe. The shop was round the corner from the Vancouver Public Library. Duthie always maintained that the ideal location for a book shop was as close to a library as one could locate it. His book shop prospered and it became the preferred place for the bookworms of Vancouver to buy and browse. Bill Duthie decided to open a paper-back department in the cellar of the shop. It was accessed by a spiral staircase and was run by an amiable communist called Binkie Marx. Binkie was a member of the Arts Club, which was where I met him. It was said, by those who knew him well, that he maintained the largest collection of pornographic literature in Vancouver, not in the shop, but at his home.

Sometime in the 1970s, Duthie's landlord decided to tear down the building and replace it with a highrise office tower, or what passed for a tower in those days. It was to be eight stories high, and be called the "Avord Building". Duthie's duly received notice to vacate the premises. But Bill had a lease that had several more years to run. So he retained a lawyer, an old friend, Bill McConnell, himself an author and busybody amongst the literati of Vancouver. McConnell gently apprised the landlord of the terms of the lease and informed them that Duthie's was disinclined to move. The landlord offered a small, then a larger sum to get the bookstore out. Duthie was adamant. No, he would not move. The landlord was desperate. Money had been spent on plans. A mortgage was in place. Interest rates were rising. After a longish standoff, the landlord agreed to move Duthie's temporarily into another shop and to grant a lease on the ground floor of the new building with a favourable rent and a nice long term, as soon as the building became occupied.

Duthie had never been squeamish about the books he sold. He maintained a special table for what was euphemistically billed as "esoterica".

271

Everyone who knew him suspected that Binkie was in charge of its contents. Then, in 1969, Duthie's was charged with obscenity. He had been
selling *Last Exit to Brooklyn*, by Hubert Selby Jr.. Duthie's was convicted,
and appealed the decision. The Court of Appeal dismissed his appeal, a
predictable result as the court was composed of three straight-laced, if not
actually stuffy judges, who were revolted by tales about homosexuality.
Duthie's was no more successful in the Supreme Court of Canada. Most of
the costs of this litigation were born by the publisher of the book.

Duthie went to great lengths to promote local authors. He was their
champion. For many years Duthie's published a monthly book entitled
The Reader. It was a literary review containing reviews of recent books
that Duthie's stocked. You could pick it up free off the counter. Duthie's
managed to persuade the most amazing people to write the reviews.
I remember a particularly funny and literate review of a book about
Newfoundland called *The History of the Cod*. The review was written by
Senator Royce Frith, later Canadian High Commissioner in London.

Duthie's always handed out entrancing bookmarks with any purchase.
One sported a list of "Readers Rights" and these included:

> The right to choose,
> The right to re-read,
> The right to skip,
> The right not to have to defend your judgement,
> The right to dog ear and mark up books,
> The right to quit,
> The right to read more than one book at a time,

> ... and so on.

Bill Duthie expanded his business over the years until he eventually
ran eight separate stores: one in the new library complex; the old store on
Robson; a store that sold technical books; Manhattan Books on the ground
floor of the Manhattan apartment block, which sold magazines, remain-
ders, and French books; Arbutus Village; a store on Seymour Street where
Bollum's books used to be (and that was opened by Celia Duthie to try to
repel the effect of Chapter's buccaneering descent upon Vancouver, which
it didn't); one on 10th Avenue; and (the store that eventually survived the
foredoomed bankruptcy caused by over-expansion) Duthie's 4th Avenue.
Some of the stores were a financial disaster. About ten years before Bill
died, his daughter Celia took over the stores. She opened a restaurant
behind The Manhattan Bookstore and called it Binkie's Oyster Bar, in
memory of Binkie Marx, who had by then, as the Salvation Army puts it,
been promoted to glory. It was not a money maker and closed within a
couple of years. One day I was browsing in the Robson Street store and fell
into conversation with Celia. She pointed to the ceiling and said that she

was going to replace it with something more attractive. Now, this ceiling consisted of a set of hangings that had been designed for Bill Duthie by Ned Pratt. It was lovely, if a little dusty. I was appalled. "Celia," I said, "you can't do that! Anyway, how many more books will a new ceiling sell?" She gave me a withering look and stalked off behind the counter. The ceiling was duly replaced a few months ahead of the bankruptcy.

The 4th Avenue store was rescued, phoenix-like from the ashes, by Cathy Duthie, who ran it for ten years. Perched between Capers and the Magic Flute, it was in an ideal location. Then Capers was bought by Whole Foods, and the Magic Flute went out of business. The rent went up to $16,000 a month, and the red ink months increased in frequency until eventually December was the only month in which Duthie's on 4th was in the black. The parity of the Canadian and US Dollars, the advent of predatory box stores like Chapters, The Book Warehouse, and Indigo—ruthlessly offering discounts by forcing the publishers to sell in bulk at a discount that Duthie's couldn't obtain—Amazon.com, and finally Kindle, all drove Duthie's out of business.

Cathy preferred not to wait and see if she could withstand this perfect financial storm until she was forced into bankruptcy. She decided to close while she could still pay off all the creditors, and pay the seven staff members the severance they deserved for years of loyal service.

It has been like the death of a beloved relative. All the customers were in a kind of mourning. Where were we going to buy our books? Is Munro Books in Victoria to be the next victim of all this new technology and piracy by discount bookstores?

Worst of all, we ask, what is going to happen to all the authors? Canada has been blessed for several decades, with an Aladdin's cave of truly talented writers. Will they be driven to accept discount fees for their writing, for the privilege of being read on a portable screen?

Well, one supposes that such gloomy thoughts went through the minds of the readers and scribes when Johannes Gutenberg invented his printing press in the fifteenth century. No doubt life and literature will go on in some way, but it won't be the same without Duthie's.

Jimmy Watson's Wedding Night

Jimmy Watson was married in Glasgow. Jimmy himself had been born and raised in Dublin, where he would have preferred that the ceremony take place, but Glasgow was the hometown of his wife, Rosemary, so that was where they had decided to be wed. The reception was held at a hall close to the little church where the ceremony was held. At the end of the festivities, changed out of their formal wedding attire, they both bade their farewells to the assembled crowd of convivial friends and relations, picked up their baggage, and took a taxi to the hotel where they were to stay before embarking on their honeymoon.

The London, Midland, and Scottish Railway Hotel is an imposing, Victorian edifice with a spacious hall, at the side of which stood the reception counter. They booked in. A bellhop picked up their bags and made for the grand staircase that led up to the first floor rooms. Jimmy and Rosemary preceded the boy up the stairs to the room that had been allotted to them. The boy put down the bags, produced a key, opened the bedroom door and struggled into the room with the bags. It was at this point that Jimmy turned and, glancing backwards, noticed that one of the bags had been leaking a profusion of confetti in its wake. Some mischievous friend had stuffed the bag with confetti, so arranged that it was scattering the little round pieces of coloured paper all over the floor as the bag progressed up the stairs and down the hallway to their room. Jimmy hastily tipped the boy and dismissed him. He guessed that some of his roistering friends were likely to journey to the hotel, follow the trail of confetti up the stairs, and embark on some unlovely prank to the discomfort of Mr. and Mrs. Watson. As soon as the boy had retreated back down the stairs, Jimmy opened the door and peered furtively about. None of their friends were in sight. There was no time to be lost.

Rosemary had walked over to where the bellhop had placed her suitcase on one of those strange bag holders that look like a truncated sideways deck chair. She bent down and unlatched the case, a gift from her bridesmaid. She had packed it with care. The clothes she expected to use on her wedding night were disclosed to view as she raised the lid.

She picked up her dressing gown and laid it on the bed. Next came the nightdress—a thoughtful gift from her mother with a lace collar, and cuffs to match at the end of long sleeves. She held it up. It was a delicate pink, its diaphanous quality not in keeping with its otherwise chaste design. She noted that it would disclose more of her than it would shield, which brought a faint blush to her cheeks. She began to wonder about this night-gown, and the occasion that called for its initial use. Should she put it on? But what then? She fully expected that she would soon end up naked and debated the purpose of putting it on at all. *Oh, well,* she thought, w*hy don't I put it on and then just let Jimmy take it off? I suppose that's what he'll do. I wonder what he'll do about his pyjamas?*

She turned to see what Jimmy was unpacking, but he was nowhere in sight. She checked the bathroom. No Jimmy. Then she noticed the trail of confetti leading from the door to Jimmy's suitcase. The door was open, which she thought was odd. She walked over to it and peered out into the wide hotel corridor. The trail of tell-tale confetti stopped just inside their bedroom door. She looked down the corridor. She was startled to observe her new husband, halfway to the top of the stairs on his hands and knees, diligently collecting up hundreds of pieces of confetti, little coloured piece by little coloured piece, until he reached the top of the stairs—picking each piece up as he shuffled along on all fours. Then he stood up and labo-riously laid the whole collection of confetti back down again in a trail to some other guest's door, far away from their own room.

THE TRANS-ATLANTIC COXSWAIN

Miles observed that it was not the most appropriate gift for an uncle to bestow on his niece just as they were departing Southampton on their trans-Atlantic voyage. The ship's overall length was forty-six feet. The *Tzu Hung* had a beam of eleven and a half feet, which was roomy enough for a ketch, but they expected to take anything up to two months before reaching the American seaboard and every available space had been stocked with food and equipment. Clio, then aged ten, accepted her uncle's gift, thrust into her arms on the dock, the day they set sail down the Solent and into the swell of the English Channel.

It was a teddy bear, but not just an ordinary teddy bear that you pick off a shelf at Hamleys. This bear was the same size as Clio herself. It was a big, beautiful, brown teddy bear, with a sweet expression and big, black, button eyes. They waited till the *Tzu Hung* was well out of range of uncle's binoculars. Then the Smeetons and their daughter held a conference in the ship's cockpit. What to do with this incubus? Clio's tears backed up her veto of Beryl's vote that it be cast overboard. They could stow it in the bilge, or hang it in the rigging. Neither of these courses bode well for the welfare of the bear. Tired of the argument, Miles finally picked it up, walked forward, and stowed it under the ship's dinghy, which was lashed to the deck just aft the mainmast. They never gave it a name. It was always referred to as "the bear" and it stayed in its refuge under the dinghy, tucked above the seat, to shelter it from the rain and most of the spray, until they reached the Doldrums.

They had progressed more or less on schedule, stopping in at Madeira to replenish their water supply and provision the ship's larder. Against his better judgement, Miles gave in to his wife's pleas and bought two cases of Portuguese wine. These they did stow in the bilge.

Partly to stretch their legs after two weeks at sea, and partly out of curiosity, they wandered down to the harbour in Funchal. It was crammed with fishing boats. They had bought sandwiches at a delicatessen and settled down on the dock to eat them for lunch. They watched the fishermen, drying nets, landing their catch, effecting repairs, and simply sitting around drinking coffee, smoking, and gossiping. A game of boules was underway, accompanied by shouts of triumph as some contestant edged his opponents off track. Noticeably there was not one woman in sight.

A thin wiry man with a patch over one eye walked past, carrying a sack and followed by a small dog, whose lineage was in serious doubt. It bore no resemblance to any known breed, was brindle and white and wore no collar. It was painfully thin, and obviously in need of a square meal. The man stopped by a fishing smack and flung the sack onto its deck. He turned and shouted at the dog, which was cowering behind him. He kicked it, extracting a yelp of pain. He pointed at the fish boat and yelled again at the dog, which slunk aboard, keeping a wary eye on his master. The man jumped aboard, picked up his sack, and pointing at the stern, shouted, "*A poopa!*" The dog slunk off to the stern and lay down. The man continued to swear at the dog in Portuguese, as he set about dealing with shipboard chores.

He went below. The dog lay at the stern with his chin on the deck. Some time later, the fisherman reappeared with a bowl, which he put down on the deck. He yelled to the dog, which crept nervously towards him. He bellowed at it and pointed to the bowl. The dog sniffed the bowl, and keeping a watchful eye on his master, ate his meal. There didn't seem to be much of it as the dog finished it off in under a minute. The fisherman was busy coiling rope and the dog was now in his way. With a swift kick, which the dog adroitly evaded, the man shouted, "*A Poopa!*" and pointed once again to the stern. The dog obediently slunk off to his preprandial perch. The man continued his work, grumping his way around the boat and swearing at the dog whenever he came close to it.

Clio watched this ugly performance, close to tears. "Daddy, can't we take the dog and look after it? He's being so cruel to it." Miles knew they didn't have accommodation for a Portuguese mongrel. On an ocean voyage, a full-sized teddy bear was bad enough. At least it was stationary and didn't have to be fed. But a dog? Even a small dog would have to be fed, entailing more stores. How do dogs crap and pee at sea? They would have to make a box with some kind of kitty litter or doggy litter and then set about training it to use it. No. This was not feasible. Then he looked at his daughter. The tears were now in full flood. Somehow the dog sensed an ally. It had stood up and was looking at Clio, wagging its stringy little tail. Miles knew he was beaten. This dog was beseeching them to adopt him, and his daughter would be heartbroken if they didn't. He looked sideways at his wife. She raised an eyebrow and nodded imperceptibly.

Miles approached the fish boat and called to the fisherman. Of course, he could not speak Portuguese and the fisherman knew no English. Miles gestured to the dog and made pantomime signs trying to say he would buy the dog. At first the fisherman was confused. Miles whistled to the dog and beckoned to it. He pulled out a five Escudo note and held it out to the man pointing at the dog. The man shook his head. Miles insisted, holding out the note and gesturing all the while at the dog. The man pulled down the corners of his mouth and shook his head. Miles pulled out a second note. Ten escudos. Holding them out, he noticed a spark of interest kindling in the man's eyes. He'd better be careful or the man would go on refusing until Miles ran out of escudos. He finally pulled out a third note. The interest was now evident, but he continued to shake his head. Miles shrugged and thrust the money back in his pocket, turning away as he did so. "Oh Daddy," Clio whimpered, only to be shushed by her father. The fisherman said something in Portuguese, waved his arms about, gestured to the dog and pointed at Miles' pocket where the money was secreted. It appeared that they had reached a bargain.

The fisherman roughly shoved the dog ashore, taking the money with ill grace. He returned back on board. The Smeetons now owned this scrawny, underfed cur. No collar, no lead, no name. Clio sat down and stroked it. She gave him the uneaten half of her sandwich, which he wolfed down in an instant. That secured its immediate and undying devotion. They walked into town, followed by the dog, who clearly regarded this strange trio of humans as a heaven-sent meal ticket. They bought it a collar and a lead. They encountered difficulty kitting the dog out with these and it became apparent the dog had never worn a collar before. They bought a box at a junk shop. Enquiries at the tourist information bureau directed them to a pet shop where they bought the biggest bag of kitty litter available. There was no such thing as doggie litter, they were told, but were assured that dogs would use it if trained to do so.

Back on board, they fell to choosing a name for their new crew-member. Beryl suggested, "Funchal ... where we got him." Miles suggested, "Scruffy, because that's what he looks like." Clio shook her head. "No. No ... Let's call him Poopa! That's what the man called him." Beryl explained, "No, that's where he was ordered to go. The poop of the fish boat." But Poopa stuck. He stayed with them until he died some years later at their house at Musgrave Landing on Salt Spring Island. None of them really liked the dog, with his ugly habits, but they had saved his life and were necessarily obligated to look after him. He remained devoted to them, they suspected because they were his unfailing source of food—a pure case of cupboard love.

Leaving Funchal, they sailed west, making good time until they reached the doldrums. They had encountered this area of the Atlantic at a time when there was no wind at all. They could not use up valuable diesel, but were forced to wait for a wind. It took a week. The *Tzu Hung* rolled in the light swell with its boom gently passing to and fro across the boat. Miles pulled out his anthology of poems and read to them from the Rime of the Ancient Mariner:

> *Day after day, day after day,*
> *We stuck, nor breath nor motion;*

As idle as a painted ship
Upon a painted ocean.

They invented ways of warding off boredom, especially for Clio. There was only so much home schooling one could impose on a child in a day before provoking a scholar's revolt. They taught her to play chess and indulged in endless rounds of Monopoly. One morning Miles extracted the bear from its lair under the dinghy and stood it up at the ship's wheel, fastening its paws to the spokes. The rocking of the ship in the light swell gently turned the rudder from side to side, causing the wheel to turn so that it looked as if the bear was steering the ship.

The next morning at breakfast, they heard the sound of engines through the water . From the porthole they could see a freighter hull, down on the horizon. A quick look through the binoculars revealed that it was Japanese. They returned to breakfast. Minutes went by and the sound grew louder, and then much louder. Eventually the noise of engines was so loud that they looked again. The freighter had changed course and was making towards them, obviously coming over to have a look. Now the noise was right upon them. All three climbed up the companionway. They were confronted by the sight of a large Japanese freighter sailing past, at half speed, a hundred yards away. Its rail was lined with two-dozen Japanese crewmen, most with binoculars, staring down at the sight of a big brown teddy bear sailing a ketch across the Atlantic. The Smeetons waved. The Japanese lowered their binoculars and waved back, grinning, some bowing (the Japanese bow, from the hips). The freighter gained speed and disappeared over the horizon leaving *Tzu Hung* wallowing in its wake, still under the command of the big brown bear.

CHIVALRY AT SEA

W arfare is a thuggish occupation. Rules of civilized conduct are the first victims in any conflict. The Geneva Convention has done much to alleviate the suffering of the victims of war. 196 countries have ratified it. There remain some which have not and some which ignore its provisions in the heat of battle. Civil wars are particularly notorious for grossly uncivil behaviour.

In fact there is more than one Geneva Convention. The first was a treaty promulgated in 1865. There are four treaties and three updating protocols, the last was made in 2005. They create international standards for the treatment of the victims of war, including prisoners of war.

The Convention was inspired by a book written by Henri Dunant in 1862, describing his experience at having watched the Battle of Solferino. In the book, he proposed the establishment of a permanent relief agency for humanitarian aid in time of war, government treaties recognizing the neutrality of the agency, and allowing it to provide aid in time of war. Out of these two proposals grew firstly The Red Cross, and then the Geneva Conventions. Dunant was awarded the very first Nobel Peace Prize in 1902.

Until these treaties, armies could commit endless crimes with little fear of punishment. The unfortunate prey of marauding soldiery are so often the innocent civilians caught up in the maelstrom of battle and the indiscriminate plunder of armies in the midst of campaigns. Mealy-mouthed politicians responsible for such hostilities butter over the carnage and misery they cause by designating it as "collateral damage".

There were, however, some ancient rules of conduct that some armies adhered to some of the time. Chivalry was a medieval concept that had to do with the institution of knighthood and encompassed all the knightly virtues, especially courtly love. It was a moral, religious, and social code of conduct. Chivalry thinned away into oblivion with the disappearance of the mounted knight. As Benjamin Disraeli once observed, "The age of chivalry is dead. Bores have succeeded to dragons."

Nonetheless, before the Geneva Conventions formalized civilized conduct in time of war, there did exist unwritten codes of conduct that sometimes alleviated suffering. The Duke of Wellington tried his best to prevent the battalions under his command from looting. The Navies of Great Britain, France, and Spain never deliberately set out to kill the crews of enemy ships. Their objective was to destroy or capture the enemy's ships. Though their crews inevitably suffered casualties in the course of a sea battle, the killing of sailors was not the prime objective. During the Battle of Trafalgar, HMS Bellerophon actually hove to for a few minutes, in order to pick up a couple of dozen French sailors who were clinging to the wreckage of their sunken man-o'-war.

Some twenty years ago, I discovered an obscure example of the fact that the officers and men of the British, French, and Spanish Navies did not take the war they fought personally. While staying with my mother-in-law near Winchester, I decided to fill a few idle hours by driving down to Portsmouth to look at HMS Victory. It was a cold, wet, blustery day. In consequence, there was only a smattering of tourists. I paid the admission fee and assembled with five other sightseers. An ex-Royal Navy Petty Officer showed us round the ship. Because there were so few of us, he was able to spend more time with us and he became very informative.

The Victory is surprisingly small—only 227 feet overall, with a beam of 51 feet ten inches. The gun deck is 185 feet long. The ship had a crew of 850 men. Only 67 of these were needed to sail the ship. The remainder—gun crew, marines with muskets, and powder monkeys—were needed only when the ship went into action. The Victory was a "first rater", which means that it carried at least 100 guns. The Victory mustered 104, along with some carronades.

The Napoleonic era was a brutal age. Nations were constantly at war with each other, struggling for power, wealth, and land and striving to take all three away from each other. Life aboard a man-o'-war, at least on the lower decks, was appalling. Boredom was a serious problem, so the occupants of the lower decks were kept busy at useless tasks, like the daily holystoning of the decks, which entailed scouring them with a piece of sandstone. Most of the crew were illiterate. At least half chose to serve as an alternative to prison. Many were taken from the jails by the press gangs, which also kidnapped drunks from the local waterfront taverns when there was a shortage of manpower aboard. The crew slept in hammocks, and each man had 14 inches for his hammock. Anyone who took an inch more space was disciplined. Discipline was savage. Flogging was the standard punishment, and the yardarm had other uses than just to sustain the spanker at the stern. The officers were only marginally better housed. Senior officers were provided with appreciably better accommodation. Admiral Nelson's cabin ran the entire width of the Victory at the stern on the second poop deck, and was equipped with the most elegant Georgian furniture, including a long table that could seat 75 officers for dinner. It was constructed in two-foot sections, for fast disassembly when the ship had to be cleared for action.

The ship could be cleared for action in six minutes. Personal possessions found lying about the deck were instantly heaved overboard. The furniture in the admiral's cabin was disassembled and stored in the ship's barge, which along with the pinnace and the three cutters, was towed astern to get them out of the way of cannon fire. Any boat left on deck was likely to be struck by cannon balls, and its flying splinters would cause savage wounds to any crewman struck by such missiles. Some ships stored their officer's furniture in the bilge (not good for the patina), or even strung it up in the rigging to be out of the way, though furniture thus stored tended to be destroyed by chain shot aimed at the masts and spars. The barge towed behind was the preferred and safest location for all furniture.

There was an unwritten protocol amongst the French, Spanish, and British captains that they never fired at each other's furniture. It was in any case a waste of valuable shot. It only succeeded in causing inconvenience and in the long run was ineffective in achieving victory. It was counterproductive, because it tended to encourage retaliatory gunfire at your own furniture. Firing at your opponent's furniture was not an offence against naval regulations and would not result in a court marshal, but anyone who did it was looked upon as a cad. It was ungentlemanly conduct and frowned upon. It was not done. Such incidents were remembered by the Lords of the Admiralty when promotion was under consideration.

THE CALCULATED RISK

The advice was not what I wanted to hear. My cardiologist leant over his desk, and looking me firmly in the eye, raised a warning finger. "You know, you really ought to give up playing squash. I used to play, but I gave it up when I was much younger than you are now. And I hadn't had a heart attack. It's the sudden surge when you're trying to reach a ball dropped at the front wall when you're in the back corner."

I had played this delicate game since I was sixteen. I was no better at it than I was at any of the other games, never progressing beyond the bottom of class "C". But it was high-pressure fun and good exercise. I slowly became reconciled to belonging to class "C", which was the class that encompassed all the advanced duffers. I realized, after some serious thought on the matter, that this was of no real consequence. If I did begin to take it seriously, take lessons from the coach and advance into the "B" class, I would only end up playing against different people—same game, no more enjoyable than when I competed against the friends, duffers all, who were eternally confined to the basement of class "C" along with me. So I continued on in the bottom quarter of the club box ladder and got to know my fellow duffers better. I followed G.K. Chesterton's advice. "If a thing is worth doing, it is worth doing badly." He was referring to painting, but I thought it applied just as well to squash. Anyway, Chesterton would never have played squash. He had about him an air of rotund congibundity, which was incompatible with strenuous sports.

I decided to ignore the doctor's advice and went on playing. I had been told to take vigorous exercise four times a week—get the heart rate up to 150 beats a minute and sustain it for twenty minutes. Well I did that playing squash. So I justified ignoring the cardiologist's medical advice on the grounds that I was following the admonition about the exercise regime. Anyway, it was so much more fun than enduring the deadly and exquisite boredom of working out on stationary bicycles, treadmills, and rowing machines. These were intellectual deserts. You couldn't even read while pumping away on these mechanical dinosaurs.

Then I made a mistake. I told my wife what Dr. Dodek had said. Well, I supposed that I could still continue playing, but she worried every time I packed my squash kit into my little duffel bag and set off for the club. She would bid me goodbye with a patter of comment. "Have a good game." " Don't play too hard." "You don't have to try to win all the time, you know." "Take it easy, and phone me when you're through. I might want something picked up." I knew she did not need me to run errands on the way home. She just wanted to make sure I had made it safely through to the end of the game. What passes for my conscience began to interfere with my desire to go on playing. Should I really go on playing and impose this unnecessary worry on her? Continuing to play was, I knew, a calculated risk.

Two factors are taken into account when calculating a risk. I had read about this in a delightful book entitled *Private Army*, an autobiography written by an officer in the British army. He was technically of Belgian nationality, but his name was Vladimir Peniakoff, of Russian derivation. No one could pronounce his name, so everyone called him Popski. He ran a small platoon of specially trained soldiers who used to creep behind enemy lines in the desert and create havoc with Rommel's communication system and fuel supply. He continued this harassing technique throughout the Italian campaign. One or two of his men were wounded, but his great feat, of which he was justifiably proud, was that he never lost a man. The theory of the calculated risk also surfaced in a judgement of Chief Justice Lamer, in a medical malpractice case that reached the Supreme Court of Canada. A surgeon had knowingly taken a risk and his patient had died. The case turned on the question whether the surgeon was justified in taking the risk.

This is the theory. First you calculate what the odds are that the event, which you are faced with, will occur. Then you calculate what the consequences of the event will be if it occurs. Add a factor for the importance of the objective to be attained and your risk is calculated for you. If the odds of the event occurring are low, say 10 per cent, and the importance of the consequence of its occurrence is small, perhaps a loss of money or time, then as long as the result you are trying to attain is important enough to justify the risk, you go ahead. But if the odds of the event occurring are small, but the consequence is, say, death ... well, you just don't go ahead unless the need to do so is worth the risk of such a disastrous consequence.

Gill's anxiety led me to inexorably calculate the risk of continuing to play squash. What finally forced me to abandon the sport was what Dr. Dodek had told me at the close of his little finger-wagging exercise, and which I had inadvisedly relayed to Gill, who herself took (perhaps) as long as three second to calculate the risk. The good doctor had said, "You know, David, it is a well-known fact that the incidence of death on the field of play is highest in squash and soccer refereeing."

THE UNINTENDED MENDICANT

My shopping list included some wine, and a bottle each of gin and dry vermouth—necessary ingredients for the manufacture of dry Martinis. I was short of cash and the Liquor Distribution Branch had not yet caught on to the advances in retail practices. It still did not take credit cards. Thus I needed to make a diversion to my bank, located conveniently next door to the liquor store. Having succeeded in acquiring the necessary cash from one of those magic machines that deliver money if you insert a bank card and push the appropriate buttons, I emerged to find a man standing beside the liquor store's double doors He was wearing a baseball cap and clutching a paper cup, which he held out in front of him at chest height, an earnest and humble supplicant for charity. He was staring at the roofs of the buildings across the road, a goofy expression on his face. *One of life's mildly demented panhandlers*, I thought. I was minded to slip a dollar into his cup, but I didn't have one handy, and in any event my attention to this minor act of philanthropy was distracted by the thought that I knew the man's face. He was not looking at the passersby. He was just staring across the road as if transfixed by some heavenly vision. Listening to voices, perhaps.

I entered the liquor store and concentrated on the purchases to supplement the family cellar. I sauntered around the store. As I passed the imported scotch shelves, my mind wandered back to the goofy-looking beggar. Where had I seen that face before? By the time I had reached the brandy shelves, it had dawned on me that he was a member of the bar. Beside the shelves that displayed an array of gin, I realized that he bore a remarkable resemblance to the current Attorney General, Geoff Plant.

Of course he wasn't Geoff Plant, or at least, I supposed he wasn't. Why would the Attorney General be loitering outside the local liquor vendor, in the town where he had grown up, begging for money? I had not seen Plant for some time, and though I had met him on couple of occasions, I did not know him well, so I was still in doubt about his identity.

He had been well liked when he was in private practice, and was regarded as a talented counsel. As Attorney General, he ran into a number of unforeseen problems, at least unforeseen by him. He would go down in the history of the legal profession as the only Attorney General ever to have been censured by the assembled members of the Law Society at its annual general meeting—for his perceived lack of funding for legal aid. He had encountered the age-old problem that has beset and occasionally unhorsed, so many cabinet ministers: the need to find funding for an obviously necessary cause and not having enough money to do so—ground between the twin millstones of public need and government restraint. The membership of the bar had different priorities than those that were thrust upon poor Plant. Still and all, that would not explain why he would be standing on the street, petitioning for alms. It couldn't be Plant. I reached this conclusion as I selected four bottles of Finca Los Primos, Malbec from the Argentinian wine section.

Burdened with all my bottles and cursing myself for not seizing a basket on my way in, I approached the cash register and gingerly edged the bottles out of my arms and onto the counter. I paid for my purchases and received seventy-five cents in change. The clerk had filled two stout plastic bags with my half dozen bottles. Feeling vaguely guilty at not having given the beggar some money on my way in, I determined to give him the change clutched in my right hand. The two bags were suspended from my left hand. Hands full, I turned round and opened the door by pushing it with my backside, exiting by shuffling backwards, thus bringing me up beside the beggar, still holding his cup out in a mute plea for funds and staring at the distant rooftops. I lifted up my hand and dropped the three quarters into the cup. There was an impressive splash as a spout of coffee was expelled onto the sidewalk, and much of it onto his shirt-front on its journey downwards. His eyes dropped and met mine. His look was a mixture of surprise and irritation. "Hey, I'm just waiting for my wife."

I did not stay to apologize. I hustled off down the sidewalk, and turned the corner as fast as I could. At the corner, I stole a swift look back to observe the beggar rummaging in the coffee mug with two fingers, trying to retrieve the quarters. I loaded my bags into the car and made off home, leaving the Attorney General richer by seventy-five cents.

THE SOCIETY OF FRIENDS

They are not the dour Puritans that people believe them to be. Quakers are tolerant, gentle, plain folk who espouse the simple life, limiting their possessions to the use of no more than their fair share of the earth's resources. They are way out on the left of the religious spectrum. Roman Catholicism stands its ground, a fortress of righteous infallibility, on the conservative religious right. Anglicans, known in Britain by the more majestic title of Church of England, are currently (if somewhat shakily) inhabiting the centre. The left is host to a collection of non-conformists: Lutherans (spread about northern Europe and Scandinavia); Mormons, Hutterites, Seventh Day Adventists; and then the Presbyterians, Wesleyans, and Baptists, some of whom (in Canada) joined together to form the United Church. George Fox founded the Quakers around 1650 in what is now Cumbria, to be precise, at Swarthmoor Hall, Ulverston, in the Lake District.

The name of the society (the Society of Friends) is an eighteenth-century invention. Before that they were simply known as Quakers, a nickname first used in 1652, when George Fox was prosecuted for blasphemy and Judge Bennett called his sect Quakers, because "We bid them tremble at the word of God."

Not long after the outbreak of war, as the skies above London were rent with anti-aircraft bursts and the rattle of machine-gun fire, my parents sent me to a boarding school near Reading to get me away from the blitz. It was a Quaker school, Leighton Park, run by the Society of Friends. I was about ten years old, and as I recollect, quite impervious to all attempts to educate me.

The Quakers run a totally unstructured religion. Quakers have no clergy and no hierarchy of members, believing that all men and women are born equal—hence the Quakers of days gone by always addressing each other in the singular: 'Thou' and 'thee', rather than the obsequious plural, 'you', which is designed to elevate the one addressed above him that addresses. If you get a letter from a Quaker, it will be addressed to you by name alone: no Mr. or Mrs.. Just plain George Fox. Because they

287

view all men and women as born equal, they do not tolerate what they call "a hireling clergy". Quaker meetings are unstructured, unlike the more conformist religions with their strong sense of theatre. Quaker meetings can be addressed by any member or visitor in attendance, and the discussion often ranges over a wide variety of subjects. Sometimes the meeting will lapse into a meditative silence. At the last meeting I attended, at the meeting house on 70th Avenue in Vancouver, nobody said anything for about eight minutes after it started.

My attendance at this meeting came about in this way. I got to know the Reverend J. Whinfield Robinson when I was acting for one of his parishioners in a divorce case. He was then the vicar of St. Helen's Anglican church in Point Grey. We became friends and he later baptized all our children. Over the years, he sent me a steady stream of clients to look after, most of them parishioners enmeshed in family law problems.

One day he gave me a battered, leather-bound book, saying that he thought I would be interested in keeping it. I suppose he knew that, as a little boy, my parents had sent me to a Quaker boarding school. The book was a collection of the minutes of the annual general meetings of the Society of Friends dating from 1764 to about 1810. The minutes themselves were not very informative and dealt with unexciting and mundane matters, mostly financial. What was interesting was the regular reference to the Quakers' participation in the struggle to abolish the slave trade. Regrettably, the minutes did not go into any detail about this campaign, merely noting, on an annual basis, their involvement, without elaboration.

I kept the book for years. Then some time after my friend's death, I decided that I should not keep it. I ought return it to the Quakers. So one Sunday I donned a suit and tie and journeyed down to the Quaker meeting house, a large old rambling residence, converted to its present use. Clutching the book of minutes, I nervously entered the front door. After all, this would be the first Quaker meeting I had attended in sixty years. The house was institutionally functional and adorned with no frills. I was approached by a lady, who enquired what she could do for me. I told her I had come to the meeting and expressed the hope that they wouldn't mind if I attended. I was, it appeared, welcome to attend.

I walked into the meeting room, a large, completely unadorned hall, with chairs set about an open space. It was gradually filling up and I chose a seat in the back row, so as to be as unobtrusive as possible. I was not sure what I should do about handing over the book. Should I do it during the meeting, or wait till afterwards? I had no idea what was going to happen afterwards. Maybe I should have spoken to the lady who had greeted me and done it then, or at least sought her advice. Well, anyway, there I was—a complete stranger in a meeting of a faith I'd had nothing to do with since I was a little boy. I felt like an interloper, sitting there, my book of minutes my only passport to my attendance. The room was now almost full. In bounced a young woman with two small boys of about ten or twelve. She was bearing an infant in her arms. Her two boys bustled over to the other side of the room. She sat down, unbuttoned her blouse, and began to feed her baby. No one paid any attention.

The congregation was dressed informally. Many wore shorts, as it was a warm summer day. Not one man was wearing a tie. I felt badly over-dressed in my smart grey suit and tie. I remembered that it had been the custom of Quaker women to wear no personal adornment. It was, there-fore, with some surprise that I noticed that most of the women present at the meeting were sporting some jewelry: Earrings, necklaces, and brooches. I surmised that the Quakers, unlike the Catholic church, were moving with the times. Two hundred years ago the Quakers expressed strong disapproval of the theatre. No Quaker ever went to watch a play and certainly never, themselves, went on the stage. To do so would be to pretend that you were someone you were not. I had discovered that this old Quaker philosophy had also moved on with the times. Judi Dench is a Quaker and so is Sir David Lean, the director of (amongst other notable films) *Lawrence of Arabia*, and Paul Eddington, from *Yes Minister* fame. It had been the Quaker custom not to accept titles. To do so was to set oneself up above one's fellows. But now, there was David Lean, a knight of the realm.

The meeting started when a man requested that everyone present intro-duce themselves. My apprehension about what to say increased as each member rose and announced who they were. My turn came. I stood and told the meeting who I was. This information was received in silence and then the man sitting next to me stood to introduce himself. When the last member had spoken, the meeting lapsed into silence.

Of course, I remembered that Quaker meetings were unusual in that nobody functions as chairperson. Quakers at their meetings speak if they have something to say, but usually only if the spirit moves them. Sometimes discussions break out, but never arguments. Quakers are famously non-confrontational.

Hurricane Katrina had, that very week, devastated New Orleans. Somebody rose and spoke about the human tragedy this storm had wrought. A few more rose to speak and the conversation turned to the possibility of offering aid. They did not know, but supposed that there must be some Quakers in Louisiana and within minutes a small committee was struck to canvass the possibility of rendering assistance.

At this point, one of the small boys, seated the opposite side of the room from his mother, rose and started to speak. His mother, still suckling her baby, gestured at him, waving him down. He dutifully sat down, with a look of resigned irritation. A man seated to my left immediately rose. Garbed in rumpled shorts and a t-shirt, he looked as if he had just broken off from tending his garden in order to attend the meeting. He spent five minutes defending the child's right to speak. Although he conceded that children do not normally contribute to the Society's meetings, on this occasion he expressed his feeling strongly that the boy should be permitted to say his piece. There was a murmur of assent. We all turned to hear what the boy wanted to say, but the moment had passed and he remained silent. The gardener resumed his seat and the meeting rambled on.

Various subjects were discussed and there were reports from some members who had been assigned projects. I decided the time had come to offer the Society the minute book. I rose, heart pounding with nervous anxiety. I explained that this was the first Quaker meeting I had attended in over half a century and told them why I was there. I held up the minute book and explained what was in it and how the theme of anti slave trade wove its way through the minutes of all the meetings. My little speech was received in silence. The meeting wound up to be followed by what appeared to be a second stage of the meeting, devoted to business matters and administrative affairs. I realized that I should have waited for this stage of the proceedings to introduce the minutes. My experience of Quaker meetings at school, sixty years ago had not included a business portion, presumably because school boys had no business to conduct.

After the meeting, an informal group thronged around me and I handed over the book of minutes to one of the men. Several expressed their gratitude to me. They thought they should probably send the book to the Quaker headquarters in Toronto. One man diffidently put his hand out and asked, "May I touch it? I don't think I've ever touched anything that is two hundred and fifty years old." We all chattered for a while and then I spied a red, soft-cover book on the table, entitled *Quaker Faith and Practice*. I asked if I might buy it. One of the men picked it up and handed it to me. "You just gave us a book. Now we will give you this book."

I was invited to lunch with them, but I declined as I had left our dogs alone long enough and thought I should get back home. In hindsight I regretted this. It would have been fun to have spent a little more time with these sweet people.

In the seventeenth century, beginning during the Commonwealth, the Quakers (when they became numerous enough to become troublesome) generated the bitter enmity of the non-conformists. The Quakers were the new left, threatening the established religious order, which already occupied the left. Thus they attracted bitter persecution. The Conventicle Acts forbade any group of more than two people to meet for religious purposes, except in a church of one of the established sects. In consequence, many Quakers were imprisoned, some executed, and a famous group was driven (aboard the Mayflower) to establish some of the American colonies.

Most people believe Quakers to be rigid in their beliefs. It is not so. Perhaps their most famous and fundamental principle is that of pacifism. Indeed, it is true that non-violence is central to their philosophy, but during the World War II, not only did the Quakers form the Friends' Ambulance Unit, but many actually joined up and fought. These were known as the Fighting Quakers and were tolerated, even if in sorrow, by their fellow Quakers.

Most Quakers don't drink, but *Quaker Faith and Practice* has this advice: "In view of the harm done by the use of alcohol, tobacco, and other habit forming drugs, consider whether you should limit your use of them or refrain from using them altogether ..." *Quaker Faith and Practice* is not an ordinance or ukase. Its introduction makes it clear that "discipline is not now a popular word. It has overtones of enforcement and correction, but its roots lie in ideas of learning and discipleship. Discipline in our yearly meeting consists, for the most part, of advice and counsel, the encouragement of self questioning, of hearing each other in humility and love."

Integrity is central to Quaker thinking. It is not just that they are honest, which they are, but also (and perhaps more significantly) they require their members to maintain strict integrity in their business transactions, and to resist attempts by others to lower their standards of integrity. You will never get a Quaker to swear an oath, for that would be to imply a double standard. They will affirm instead.

Quakers generally do not spend money beyond their needs. Since their expenditures are modest, many Quaker families have become very wealthy: Notably the Cadburys and the Frys, both makers of chocolate.

The Quakers were famous for their efforts at prison reform and the civilizing of lunatic asylums.

There are those who are wistfully yearning for peace in the world, who maintain that if a significant enough number of governments were headed by women, wars would cease. In view of the record of Elizabeth I, Catherine the Great, and Margaret Thatcher, this premise is of doubtful historical validity. This I do know: if Quakers ran a significant portion of the world's governments, bloodshed would cease and the bulk of the world's poverty would cease with it.

LETTER TO LILY

DAVID ROBERTS Q.C.

4765 Pilot House Road,
West Vancouver, B.C.

Canada. V7W 1J2
Tel- (604) 922 9745
E-mail dproberts@telus.net
N. 49° 20.288′ W. 123° 15.139′

July 1, 2010

My Dearest Lily,

Your father tells me that, when you were born, he and
your mother chose Lily as your name because no one
else in either of their families had ever been called Lily.
Well, surprise, surprise, little did they know that your
great-great-grandmother was called Lily. She was my
grandmother, though the truth is that she was really
my step-grandmother. You see my grandfather, George
Watson, married twice. His first wife was my real grandmother. Her name was Lucy, Lucy Craney. She was an
actress and her stage name was Lucy Manders. She died
of pneumonia on May 14, 1894, when she was only twenty
years old. She had two daughters, my aunt Lucy and my
mother, Grace. My mother was only six months old when
her mother died, so she had no recollection of her.

My grandfather was born on June 6, 1866, and grew up in Sunderland—a seaport at the mouth of the River Wear on the northeast coast of England. His family had owned a shipyard at the mouth of the river for several generations. They not only built ships, which they sold to other people, but also had their own ships, carrying cargo all over the world. This, of course, was in the days of sail, before any radio or GPS systems. So when one of their ships left the home port, they often did not hear from her for as much as two years, until she returned home. Shipping, in those days, was a dangerous trade. My mother's grandfather told her that they used to consider themselves lucky if one of their ships returned home having lost no more than two of the crew. Most of those who died did so falling out of the rigging. With luck they fell into the sea, but it was virtually impossible for a sailing ship to heave to and turn round to rescue a crewman lost overboard.

The Watsons had an old family bible that Anne Fimister, your cousin, now has. It lists, as bibles did in those days, all the members of the family, their birth dates, when they died, when they married, and who their children were. A significant number of the men listed in the bible are shown as having been lost at sea. Then, in the mid-nineteenth century, ships began to be made of steel and powered by steam. The days of sail were doomed. The Watson family had to make a decision. Would they convert their shipyard to make steamships or simply sell off the yard and retire? They decided it would be too much trouble and expense to retool the yard, so they quit the business. They had made enough money that they could all afford to do that. Their decision was hastened by the fact that they had lost three ships to all in one year. One was driven ashore in a gale and wrecked near Deptford and two were destroyed by wreckers. Wreckers operated mainly on the coast of Cornwall. They would create false lights at night to masquerade as lighthouses, luring ships onto the rocks. The wreckers would then descend on the ship and pillage it and sometimes murder its crew, as they wouldn't want any witnesses.

The shipyard was owned by two families, the Watsons and the Hunters. The two families had intermarried; your great-great-great-great-great-grandmother, Margaret

Hunter, married George Watson in 1805. My mother told me that when the question of whether or not to close the yard came up, there was a family quarrel. When the yard was finally closed, one of the Hunters, George Burton Hunter, went off to Newcastle and in 1880 formed a partnership with the widow of a Tyne shipbuilder, Charles Sheridan Swan. The firm was called Swan, Hunter Ltd.. In 1903, it merged with another firm and became known as Swan Hunter & Wigham Richardson. They became the largest shipbuilders in the United Kingdom, and in 1904, built the RMS Mauritania, which held the Blue Ribbon for the fastest crossing of the Atlantic, for many years. They also built, over the years, dozens of Royal Navy ships, including the aircraft carrier, HMS Arc Royal. Sadly, the yard fell upon hard times in the 1990s, with too much competition from Japan and Korea. It fell into bankruptcy.

So when the yard at Wearmouth closed, my grandfather, George Watson, and his brother John, having no shipyard to run, were articled to a firm of solicitors. Uncle John practised as a solicitor all his life. He was with a firm of solicitors in Scarborough, although he ran their branch office at Malton, just up the valley from Scarborough.

My grandfather became a solicitor, but he never practised. He became stage struck in his youth, and to his parents dismay, went onto the stage. He spent a sizable proportion of his early life earning his living as an old-fashioned Victorian music hall comedian. My grandmother Lucy Craney's father was the leader of the band in a travelling circus in which my grandfather sometimes performed. It was called the Manders Circus and was quite well known. Lucy Craney's father was of Irish descent, although I believe he was born in Manchester.

Grandfather inherited quite a large fortune from his parents and grandparents, but he spent most of it on failed promotions of theatrical endeavours. He wanted to be a theatrical impresario, but didn't really have the experience or ability to make a serious success of it. For many years he lived in Twickenham, at a house in Riverside Gardens, just up the road from the Thames. He ended up living in Reading, where he went into partnership with a

Jewish man by the name of Simmons. Together they ran a theatre called the Reading "Palace of Varieties", which was indeed a music hall. Grandfather ran the music hall and Simmons looked after the money. They were always quarrelling, so I conclude that Simmons did a commendable job and prevented my grandfather from embarking upon too many doomed theatrical ventures. Unfortunately this endeavour was set on foot just as the sun was beginning to set on the English music hall scene. So it sputtered along in the twilight of this theatrical genre.

When my grandmother Lucy died, Grandfather found himself with two infant daughters to support. Since he was earning a living as an itinerant comedian, he was quite unable to look after two little girls, quite apart from the fact that men were not expected to function as single parents in those days. He found a widow, Mrs. Whiteley, who lived in Halifax and earned her living by fostering children. So my mother and her sister, Lucy, spent the next ten years growing up in one of the less pleasant industrial revolution towns in Yorkshire. I suppose my mother went to school. She never spoke about it and I know her education was quite rudimentary. She could read and write and do basic arithmetic, but beyond that she seemed to have had little education. After my grandfather and Lily were married, in 1903, Lily insisted that these two little girls be brought down to live with them in Twickenham.

Lily's full name was Lillian Gertrude Lawrence White. She was born and grew up in Nottingham. I never thought to enquire what her father did for a living, but I believe him to have been a shopkeeper. Grandma told me that they lived in a house across the square from Nottingham castle and that there was a secret tunnel that led from their basement to the castle. She became an actress, and took the stage name of "Lily White". I enclose two photos of her, signed by her under her stage name and two more, unsigned. I don't think her career on the stage lasted very long or was very successful. She and my grandfather had three children. George, the youngest, born June 14, 1909, who qualified as a chartered accountant and became the comptroller of the Milk Marketing Board, Dick, born July 11, 1907, who suffered from rheumatic fever as a child and who consequently had a compromised heart, and

Marjorie, born December 4, 1903, who became a librarian and ended up running the Earley branch of the Reading Public Library.

I remember my grandparents when they lived in a house called "Fieldhead" on the Wokingham Road in Reading. Since I was only six when Grandpa died, I have only a vague recollection of him. He used to sit at the end of the dining table, put his hands on each side of his head, wiggle his forefingers at me, and make a noise like a guinea pig. He had an old grandfather clock that had belonged to his grandmother: my great-great-grandmother. She was a Scottish lady from Edinburgh. Her maiden name was MacDonald: Sarah MacDonald. I have a large oil painting of her that hangs on the wall of our playroom. I also have two tapestries she made, both scenes from the life of King Charles I. I suspect that she was a Jacobite; she would, after all, have been born only some sixty years after the last Jacobite rebellion. She was ninety-four when she died, when my mother was eleven. My mother remembered her as a stern old lady and her painting certainly portrays a woman of some considerable character. Her grandfather clock had been made in Sunderland in 1874. My aunt Marjorie kept it in her house for years, but she muffled the strike and it stood silent all the times I visited her. When she died I inherited it and had it shipped to Vancouver. It came in a great wooden coffin-like case and when I broke it open it suddenly started striking. It was an astonishing noise that I had not heard since I was a little boy visiting at Fieldhead: a noise straight out of my early childhood.

Grandma Lily, never really gave up her love of the stage. All the time Grandpa ran the Reading Palace of Varieties, she had a box in the theatre. She used to take my brother to performances on Saturday nights. When Grandpa died, Grandma sold Fieldhead and the theatre, which was converted into a cinema. She bought a house in a small housing development along the driveway of a large estate owned by a diamond merchant by the name of Solly Joels. This was situated in a suburb east of Reading called Earley. During the early part of the war my parents sent me to live with her and I spent a lot of time roaming around Solly Joels' estate. He kept horses and there was a blacksmith next to the stables. I used to go up and watch the smith making horseshoes and a variety of metal implements to be used around the farm. My uncle Dick, who despite his frail health was physically very strong, was employed briefly as a stable hand. Dick had a love of horses and earned his living training and riding them. He spent several years working as a whipper-in at a hunt close by Reading, and for a while earned his living as a jockey.

Lily was a member of a group of amateur actors known as The Earley Players. Dick never went on the stage. George did play some minor parts and hung about on the periphery of the theatrical scene in London. He never married, but I remember that he kept company with a number of actresses. My aunt Marjorie was often on the stage, mostly with the Earley Players. She was a shy, quiet, almost introverted woman, who rarely showed any emotion, but when she came out onto the stage, she became a different character: vivacious, noisy, aggressive, and quite uninhibited. I remember watching her play Puck in A Midsummer Night's Dream. She became a completely different woman to the quiet, mousy aunt I knew—flinging herself about the stage and speaking in a voice that could be easily heard in the last row of the dress circle. She never married. I think she was too shy to do so. Oddly, of the five of my grandfather's children, only my mother married and had children.

I remember my Grandmother Lily well, from when I lived with her in her house in Earley Park, for quite a long period at the beginning of the war. This was to get me out of London, which was then being bombed by the Germans on a daily basis. My Aunt Marjorie lived with Grandma and worked at the Reading library and so the three of us lived together, visited by Uncle George when he came home on leave from the army, and by Uncle Dick who then worked on a farm. I was eight years old when I went to live with Grandma, sometime in late 1939, and I stayed with her until I went to boarding school. Earley Park, where Grandma had her house, was a wonderful place for a small boy to play. It boasted acres of rolling fields and a big wood where my friends and I built tree houses. Down the road, just a few minutes by bicycle, was Woodley Aerodrome, where the Miles Aircraft Company used to build aircraft—the "Miles Master" and the "Miles Magister", both of which were used as training aircraft. My friends and I would often bicycle down to the airfield, stand outside with our faces pressed to the high, wire fence that denied access to unauthorized people like us, and watch the aircraft land and take off. It was there that I first saw the famous "Harvard" trainer, which like the Master and the Magister, was a two seater, usually painted yellow, and with a very noisy engine that sounded like a badly calibrated lawn mower. It was at Woodley aerodrome, in 1931 (the year that I was born) that the famous British air ace, Douglas Bader, crashed and lost both his legs. Alas, now the airfield where the Wellington bombers used to take off for their nightly sorties over Germany, only some of them returning, is now given over to a housing development—the great grass airstrips buried under a graceless array of little brick houses.

Grandma was a sweet lady and I grew very fond of her. I never knew her to go back on the stage while I lived with her, though she always kept in touch with her old stage friends and the members of the Earley Players were frequent guests in her house. Indeed her house was often full of stage people: charming, insincere philanderers, all. Grandma had a habit, long a custom of aging actresses, of always sitting with her back to the light—an old trick to veil in shade the stealthy ravages that time wrought on her face. She kept several oil paintings of sailing ships, and old merchantmen that had belonged to the Watson shipyard. There was also one huge portrait of an actor recumbent on the grass. She insisted, without any evidence to support the claim, that it was a portrait of David Garrick, the famous English actor, playing Hamlet.

I enclose (for you to keep) five photographs of Grandma Lily. One is signed by her. The second shows her dressed for a part in a play. The third is a picture of her with her son, my uncle Dick. I think it must have been taken about 1919. This was the grandmother I remember. There are two other photos, both taken by north-country photographers.

So, Lily, now you know about your namesake, Lily Watson, or Lily White as she called herself when she was earning her living on the stage.

All my love, little girl,
Your grandfather, Gorfa

ABOUT THE AUTHOR

David Roberts is a retired lawyer. Called to the Bar of England and Wales in 1953 and to the Bar of British Columbia in 1954, for forty nine years he practised law in Vancouver, B. C. He ran a general litigation practice with emphasis on commercial, medical related work, securities, and municipal law. For twenty nine years he was the editor of *The Advocate*, a publication of the Vancouver Bar Association, which is circulated to every lawyer in the province. He retired in 2002, but still continues to function as an arbitrator and as a member of several administrative tribunals. He keeps bees in his back garden. Bees, he says, unlike dogs, need no training. They are not as arrogant as cats and much more interesting than guinea pigs. They also make honey, weather permitting.

He has lived in the same house in Caulfeild, West Vancouver, with his wife Gillian, (and his bees) for fifty two years. It was in this house that they brought up three boys and a girl: The children to whom these letters were written.

www.davidproberts.ca

Printed in Canada